The Rāgs of North Indian Music

THE RĀGS OF NORTH INDIAN MUSIC

Their Structure and Evolution

by

N. A. JAIRAZBHOY

WESLEYAN UNIVERSITY PRESS

Middletown, Connecticut

First American Edition

ISBN: 0–8195–4027–7

Library of Congress catalog card number: 77–120260
Manufactured in Great Britain and published there
by Faber and Faber, Limited

Acknowledgements

It gives me great pleasure to acknowledge my indebtedness to the many associates and students who have helped in the preparation of this work. In particular I should like to mention A. A. Dick, O. Wright, R. Clausen, J. Montagu and K. Woodward for their valuable advice and thought-provoking comments. I also wish to express my thanks to G. Gibberd for his help in designing the model of the system of scales discussed in the Appendix and to Miss M. Bennett for her assistance with the notation of Vilayat Khan's record.

I feel greatly honoured that one of India's leading musicians, *Ustād* Vilayat Khan, should have consented to play the musical examples for this work. Limited as he was to under two minutes for each *rāg*, he has nevertheless managed to illustrate the melodic movement as well as to capture the essence of the *rāg*, and the result in each case is a work of art. I should like to express my extreme gratitude to *Ustād* Vilayat Khan for his contribution to this work.

In seeing this book through the press, I am deeply indebted to M. Kingsbury of Faber Music for his patient and critical editorial assistance which included many valuable suggestions for making this book more readable.

Much credit is due to the late Dr. A. A. Bake, my mentor for many years, and to my wife for her forbearance and encouragement as well as technical assistance.

N.A.J.
University of Windsor,
Windsor, Ontario,
Canada, 1970

Contents

Preface

There is a remarkable uniformity in the performance of classical music in North India, an area comprising various geographical regions, which, in this context, includes Pakistan and extends southward into the Deccan. There are, of course, differences in detail—in the interpretation of various *rāgs*, in style of performance and in the types and texts of compositions—but on the whole these are only minor differences. The overall uniformity is especially remarkable in view of the fact that these regions contain a heterogeneous population—both racially and culturally—who speak a variety of languages and differ widely in their religious beliefs. North Indian classical music cuts across the usual barriers imposed by differences of language and religion, much as does classical music in the West. Nevertheless, many classical songs have religious texts, both Hindu and Muslim. But religious content is not an essential requisite of the music, for some songs are concerned with mundane subjects and some are even composed of meaningless syllables. Just as in Western classical music where great religious works written specifically for the Roman Catholic Church can be appreciated as works of art by those of all religious beliefs, so too in Indian music religious themes often serve as vehicles for artistic expression.

Classical music is not the music of the masses but is largely confined to the urban areas of North India. It is performed either in concert halls or in private homes. Its *raison d'être* lies in its purely musical content and it is basically on melody and rhythm that its quality is assessed. While a study of the cultural background of the people is essential for a social and historical perspective of this music, its appreciation depends largely on comprehension of the musical idiom, and it is to this end that the present work is dedicated. It had its origin in a series of lectures given at the School of Oriental and African Studies, London, to university students who had no previous knowledge of the subject. At an equivalent age level in India, students would have had several years of musical study at High Schools in both theory and practice, and this would have been supplemented by many hours of listening to both radio broadcasts and recitals. Some of the Western students had not even heard North Indian classical music until they attended the lectures at the School. Thus it was necessary to adopt a completely different approach to the subject from that which is usual in Indian universities. To the Western students Indian music was only incidental to their main course of study and therefore the amount of time which they could devote to it was severely limited. In view of this, it was necessary to concentrate on broad principles and outlines rather than on the details which are the main concern in Indian music colleges.

Preface

The critical attitude of the Western student provided a stimulus for the formulation of many of the ideas expressed in this work. With his training in and experience of Western music he has contributed new ideas and interpretations; and by his reluctance to accept traditional Indian explanations, frequently lacking coherence, he has also provoked further enquiry into many topics. The question 'why' has been uppermost in his mind. 'Why does Indian music have its present form? Why are only certain scales used in Indian music?' To these and other similar questions the traditional reply—'because it was performed in this way by my teacher'—has been unsatisfactory. To a large extent this work has been motivated by such questions and attempts to provide some of the answers. In this respect, it is an exploration into certain aspects of Indian music which have not hitherto received sufficient attention. It is hoped that the reader will be stimulated to further enquiry.

Note on Transliteration and Pronunciation

Since this book is concerned primarily with present-day Indian music, terms are generally given in their modern Hindi forms in preference to the classical Sanskrit forms. Exception is made in the following instances: (1) the Sanskrit form is used when referring to Sanskrit treatises, their authors and the musical theory described by them; (2) the common English spelling is used when referring to well-known place names and personalities, for example, *Delhi* rather than the Hindi *Dillī* or the Urdu *Dehlī*—this follows the procedure adopted by Vincent Smith in the *Oxford History of India* (Oxford 1958); (3) Muslim names, other than those in common use in English, are transliterated according to the system used in the *Bulletin of the School of Oriental and African Studies.*

The Devnāgrī (Devanāgarī) script is syllabic and all consonants carry the inherent vowel *a* unless otherwise indicated. The principal difference between modern Hindi and the classical Sanskrit forms is the omission in Hindi of this inherent *a* when in final position (e.g. *rāga* in Sanskrit and *rāg* in Hindi) and frequently in medial position (e.g. *Māravā* in Sanskrit and *Mārvā* in Hindi).

Vowels		*Transliteration*	*Approximate guide to pronunciation* (based on Received Standard English pronunciation)
short	अ	a	as in *shut*
	इ	i	,, ,, *bit*
	उ	u	,, ,, *put*
	ऋ	ṛi	a Sanskrit vowel, in Hindi treated as a consonant *r* + vowel *i* and pronounced as in *rip* (with rolled *r*)
long	आ	ā	as in *bath*
	ई	ī	,, ,, *seed*
	ऊ	ū	,, ,, *boot*
	ए	e	,, ,, *gate*
	ऐ	ai	in Hindi approximately as in *bear* (in Sanskrit as in *isle*)
	ओ	o	as in *boat*
	औ	au	Hindi as in *saw* (Sanskrit as in *cow*)
Consonants (without inherent *a*)			In English the difference between aspirate and non-aspirate forms is not generally recognised whereas in Hindi and Sanskrit the majority of the consonants have both forms.

unaspirated			The English examples in this group are accompanied by a certain measure of aspiration which should be eliminated for a more accurate representation of the unaspirated Indian consonants.
	क	k	approximately as in *baker*
	क़	q	derived from Arabic, it is a 'k' sound produced as far back as possible, i.e. uvular as against the velar *k*. It has no aspirated form. In Hindi, often replaced by *k*.
	ग	g	as in *get*
	च	c	,, ,, *chat*
	ज	j	,, ,, *jab*
	ट	ṭ[1]	,, ,, *toe* but with tongue curled back
	ड	ḍ	,, ,, *do* ,, ,, ,, ,, ,,
	ड़	ṛ	not found in Sanskrit. An 'r' sound produced by drawing the tongue back and flapping it forward
	त	t	as in *toe* but with tongue against the teeth.
	द	d	,, ,, *do* ,, ,, ,, ,, ,, ,,
	प	p	,, ,, *pot*
	ब	b	,, ,, *bat*
aspirated			These can be approximated by exaggerating the aspiration in the examples given above. They can also be illustrated by the fusion of certain words as below.
	ख	kh	as in *ba/ck hand*
	घ	gh	,, ,, *sla/g heap*
	छ	ch	,, ,, *mu/ch hope*
	झ	jh	,, ,, *bri/dge hand*
	ठ	ṭh	,, ,, *car/t horse* with tongue curled back
	ढ	ḍh	,, ,, *roa/d house* ,, ,, ,, ,,
	ढ़	ṛh	not found in Sanskrit. The aspirated form of *ṛ*
	थ	th	as in *coa/t hanger* but with tongue against teeth.
	ध	dh	,, ,, *roa/d house* but with tongue against teeth.
	फ	ph	,, ,, *lea/p high*
	भ	bh	,, ,, *ru/b hard*
	ह	h	,, ,, *perhaps*, a voiced *h*

[1] *ṭ* and *ḍ*, their corresponding aspirates, *ṭh* and *ḍh*, and the corresponding nasal *ṇ*, are retroflex or cerebral sounds produced with the tongue curled back and pressed against the hard palate. The English *t* and *d* are mid-way between these and the Indian dental *t* and *d*. The Indian *ṭh* and *th* should never be pronounced as in English *thick*, *this*; nor should the Indian *ph* be pronounced as in English *physic*.

Nasals			
	ङ	ṅ	as in *sing*
	ञ	ñ	,, ,, *ni* in *onion*
	ण	ṇ	,, ,, *running* but with tongue curled back for the *n*
	न	n	,, ,, *now*
	म	m	,, ,, *man*
Semi-vowels			Traditionally classified as a group, but in Hindi the *r* and *l* are treated as consonants.
	य	y	as in *yet*
	र	r	the *r* is rolled as in the Scottish pronunciation of *road*
	ल	l	as in *light*
	व	v	generally mid-way between the English *v* and *w* and less emphatic than in *never*
Fricatives	श	ś	as in *show*
	ष	ṣ	in Hindi generally pronounced as above (in Sanskrit with tongue curled back)
	स	s	as in *sit*
	ख़	k͟h	of Persian and Arabic origin, pronounced as in the Scottish *loch* (approximately). In common Hindi replaced by *kh*.
	ग़	g͟h	also of Persian and Arabic origin and is the voiced equivalent of *kh*. In Hindi often replaced by *gh*.
	ज़	z	as in *zoo*. Persian–Arabic origin. In common Hindi often replaced by *j*.
	फ़	f	as in *father*. Persian–Arabic origin. In Hindi often replaced by *ph*.
Others	अः	ḥ	voiceless *h*, occurring in Sanskrit and Sanskrit loan-words in Hindi
	अं	ṃ	a nasal, which may represent one of the nasal consonants, in which case it is transliterated by the appropriate consonant. Where it occurs before a sibilant or a semi-vowel it is transliterated as indicated (ṃ).
	अँ	ã	nasalisation of a vowel

For a fuller discussion of pronunciation see T. Grahame Bailey, *Teach Yourself Urdu*, English Universities Press Ltd., London 1956.

Introduction to the Historical Background

Modern North Indian classical music has its roots in ancient Indian music, but appears to have acquired its present form after the 14th or 15th century A.D. Indian musical theory is expounded in considerable detail in the *Nāṭyaśāstra*, probably the earliest extant treatise on the dramatic arts, among which music is included. This work, attributed to the sage Bharata, has been dated variously from the 3rd century B.C. to the 5th century A.D. Some of the technical terms in present-day musical theory and practice derive from this ancient source. Nevertheless, internal evidence shows that the musical system of ancient India as described in the *Nāṭyaśāstra* differed considerably from that of today.

The ancient melodic system was based on modes (*jāti*), each with its characteristic features, which were constructed on heptatonic series of notes (*mūrcchanā*), beginning on the successive degrees of two parent scales, *Ṣaḍjagrāma* and *Madhyamagrāma*. These scales were composed of intervals of three different sizes, comparable in some respects to the major wholetone, minor wholetone and semitone of Just Intonation, which were expressed very approximately in terms of their highest common factor—about a quartertone—called *śruti*.[1] The musical intervals in the two parent scales are described as being of four, three and two *śruti*s, and since there were in both parent scales three of the large intervals and two each of the medium and small intervals, the octave comprised a total of twenty-two *śruti*s. An interval of one *śruti* was not considered musically satisfactory. The only difference between the two parent scales was in the location of one single note which was one *śruti* flatter in the second parent scale. In this period the *śruti* was a functional element since it was the only distinguishing feature between the two parent scales.

Rāg, which is the present basis of melody in Indian music, was not yet a technical term in the *Nāṭyaśāstra*. It was apparently evolved during the centuries following for it is first discussed in detail in Mataṅga's *Bṛihaddeśī* (*c.* 9th century A.D.) and later expanded in Śārṅgadeva's *Saṅgītaratnākara* (first half of the 13th century A.D.). This latter work is particularly interesting as it was written at the court of the Yādava dynasty in the Deccan shortly before the Muslim conquest of this area and is, to a large extent, free from Islamic influence. New conventions had evidently already entered Indian music and *rāga*s had proliferated, for Śārṅgadeva mentions 264 of them.[2] It is difficult to assess positively, however, whether the ancient music

[1] Many scholars have given precise values for these *śruti*s. Fox Strangways in *Music of Hindostan*, Oxford 1914, pp. 115–17, concludes that *śruti*s are of three different sizes: 22, 70 and 90 cents.

[2] *Saṅgītaratnākara*, 'Adyar Library Series', II (2), 19. However, many of these are described as 'ancient' and were probably not current in Śārṅgadeva's time.

based on the *jātis* and the two parent scales was also in existence at this time, for the *Saṅgītaratnākara*, like many other Indian musical treatises, does not always distinguish clearly between current practice and antiquated theory.

The conquering Muslims encountered in India a musical system which was highly developed and probably quite similar to their own. Their reaction to it was clearly favourable.[1] The poet Amīr Khusraw, who was expert in both Indian and Persian music at the court of 'Ala' al-Dīn Khiljī, Sultān of Delhi (1296–1316), is unsparing in his praise of Indian music,[2] and his attitude is one which probably prevailed in the Islamic world, for both al-Djāḥiẓ[3] in the 9th century A.D. and al-Mas'ūdī[4] in the 10th had commented favourably on it.

Music flourished in Islamic India in spite of the puritan faction, supported by the Muslim legal schools, which believed that music was unlawful in Islam.[5] However, the gathering momentum of the Sūfī movement with its unorthodox doctrines based on the practices of ascetic and mystic groups, who found in music a means to the realisation of God, more than compensated for the restrictions imposed by orthodox Islam.

From Amīr Khusraw's time until well into the Mughal period, foreign music, particularly from Iran, was commonly heard at the Indian courts together with Indian music. Under these circumstances it is not surprising that Indian music was subjected to new influences. Amīr Khusraw, in spite of his dedication to traditional Indian music, was a great innovator and is credited with the introduction of a number of Persian and Arabic elements into Indian music: new vocal forms as well as new *rāgs*, *tāls*, and musical instruments including the *sitār* and *tablā* which are so prominent today. Of the vocal forms two are particularly important: *Qaul*, which is said to be the origin of *Qawwālī*, a form of Muslim religious song, and *Tarānā* (or *Tarāna*), a song composed of meaningless syllables, both of which are still common today.[6]

During the reign of Sultān Muḥammad b. Tughluq (1325–1351), music was apparently encouraged on a grand scale, although he was a ruler with strong religious convictions. The traveller, Ibn Baṭūṭa, reports that the Sultān kept 1,200 musicians in his service and had, in addition, 1,000 slave musicians.[7] Similarly, Ibrāhīm Shāh

[1] Music apparently flourished in the Deccan under the Yādava kings to such an extent that, after the Muslim conquest led by Malik Kafur (*c.* 1310), all the musicians and their Hindu preceptors were taken with the royal armies and settled in the North. V. N. Bhātkhaṇḍe, *A Short Historical Survey of the Music of Upper India*, Bombay 1934, p. 11.

[2] 'Indian music, the fire that burns heart and soul, is superior to the music of any other country. Foreigners, even after a stay of 30 or 40 years in India, cannot play a single Indian tune correctly.' M. W. Mirza, *Life and Works of Amir Khusraw*, Calcutta 1935, p. 184.

[3] M. Z. Siddiqi, *Studies in Arabic and Persian Medical Literature*, Calcutta 1959, p. 32.

[4] A. Sprenger, *El Mas'ūdī's historical encyclopaedia*, '*Meadows of Gold . . .*', London 1841, p. 186.

[5] H. G. Farmer, *A History of Arabian Music*, London 1929, p. 20, discusses music in Islam. See also M. L. Roychoudhury, 'Music in Islam', *Journal of Asiatic Society, Letters*, Vol. XXIII, No. 2, 1957.

[6] *Khyāl*, which is the most prominent type of song in classical music today, is also sometimes said to have been invented by Amīr Khusraw, but the evidence for this is inconclusive. Similarly, M. W. Mirza, *ibid.*, p. 239, draws attention to the fact that there is no mention of the *sitār* in Amīr Khusraw's own writings, nor for that matter in any Indian treatises until much later.

[7] Mahdi Hussain, *Rehla of Ibn Baṭūṭa*, Baroda 1953, pp. 50–1.

Sharqī of Jaunpur (1401–1440) and Sultān Zain-ul-'Ābidīn of Kashmir (1416–1467) were both renowned for their patronage of the arts. A musical treatise (in Sanskrit), *Saṅgītaśiromaṇi*, was dedicated to Ibrāhīm Shāh in 1428[1] and Zain-ul-'Ābidīn is said to have been responsible for the composition of a treatise named *Mamak* (?) which is, unfortunately, not extant.[2]

In the following years music received further impetus from rulers, some of whom were excellent musicians themselves. One of these was the Hindu Rājā, Mān Siṅgh Toṃwar of Gwalior (1486–1516). His principal contribution was the rejuvenation of the traditional form of song, *Dhrupad* (Sanskrit *Dhruvapada*), by his compositions in Hindi,[3] some of which are still said to exist today. Mān Siṅgh was also responsible for the formulation of a progressive treatise in Hindi entitled *Mān Kautūhal*, a work which was compiled by the leading musicians of his court and incorporated many of the innovations that had been introduced into Indian music since Amīr Khusraw's time.

A contemporary of Mān Siṅgh, Husayn Shāh Sharqī (1458–1528), initially Sultān of Jaunpur, was also an excellent performer and an innovator, in importance perhaps second only to Khusraw. He is credited with the introduction into North Indian music of a new form of song, *Khyāl* (*khayāl*), which gave greater scope for improvisation and technical virtuosity than did the traditional and austere *Dhrupad*. The rivalry between the advocates of these two forms of song and their respective styles of performance continued until the beginning of the 19th century when *Khyāl* finally gained supremacy.[4]

Sultān Sikandar Lodī of Delhi (1489–1517) was a bigot and in most respects a strict follower of Quranic law. Yet he was himself a poet of considerable merit and keenly interested in music. Under his patronage probably the first treatise on Indian music in Persian, the *Lahjat-i Sikandar Shāhī*, was written. This was a traditional work based on existing Sanskrit treatises.[5]

Before the efforts of Mān Siṅgh and Sikandar Lodī, musical treatises had always been written in Sanskrit, a scholarly language which was beyond the comprehension of most musicians, Hindu as well as Muslim. There was now a growing interest in musical theory and especially in the systems of aesthetics with which it was associated —the relationship of sound with sentiment or emotion (*rasa*), colour, the Hindu deities, etc., as well as the visual representation of *rāg*s. This interest was particularly notable during the reign of Ibrāhīm 'Ādil Shāh II of Bijapur in the Deccan (1580–1626), who by his patronage and enthusiasm for the arts attracted poets, musicians,

[1] Abdul Halim, *Essays on History of Indo-Pak Music*, Dacca 1962, p. 15.

[2] *Ibid.*, p. 18.

[3] N. Augustus Willard, *Music of India*, Calcutta 1962, p. 67. Writing in the first half of the 19th century, Captain Willard states that this kind of composition has its origin from the time of Rājā Mān Siṅgh, who is considered as the 'father' of *Dhrupad* singers.

[4] Captain Willard says that in his time *Dhrupad* was not generally understood or relished and its use seemed about to be superseded by 'lighter compositions' (*ibid.*, p. 81).

[5] The *Lahjat-i Sikandar Shāhī* is discussed in some detail by Dr. Nazir Ahmad in *Islamic Culture*, Vol. 28, 1954, pp. 410 ff.

artists and architects to his court. He was himself a renowned poet and musician and the *Kitāb-i Nauras* (Sanskrit *nava rasa*—the nine emotions) contains a collection of his poems intended to be sung in different *rāgs*.[1] His reign is characterised by his liberal views and his earnest attempts to integrate the opposing elements in Islamic and Hindu philosophy.

The patronage of music reached its peak under the Mughal Emperors, Akbar (1555–1605), Jahangir (1605–1627) and Shahjahan (1628–1658). Much of Akbar's reign was devoted to the expansion and the consolidation of the Mughal Empire. Nevertheless, he maintained a magnificent court at which literature, philosophy and the arts occupied a prominent place. Music was presented on a lavish scale,[2] and Akbar himself is said to have been a prolific composer.[3]

The most famous musician of this period was undoubtedly Mīyā̃ Tānsen, around whom so many legends have grown that it is now difficult to separate fact from fiction. He was unquestionably a great musician as well as a composer. Several *rāgs* still bear his name, *Mīyā̃ Malhār* for example, and many of his songs are still sung today. Another prominent musician at Akbar's court was Bāz Bahādur, the last Muslim ruler of the state of Malwa, whose tragic affair with Rūpmatī, a singer and dancing girl, has also become legendary.[4] In the later part of his life, after he had lost his empire, he became one of the leading musicians in Akbar's retinue.

The *Dhrupad* style of singing was pre-eminent in Akbar's time and the majority of vocalists came from Gwalior, presumably following the tradition initiated by Rājā Mān Siṅgh, and it is in this city that Tānsen is buried. Many of the instrumentalists, however, were foreigners who came from as far as Mashhad and Tabriz in Iran and from Herat in modern Afghanistan.[5]

Jahangir's court was perhaps even more opulent and ostentatious than Akbar's had been. As he too was a great patron of the arts (being himself skilled at painting),[6] music continued to flourish. One of the principal musicians of his court was Bilās Khan, the son of Tānsen, whose compositions are occasionally heard today.

Shahjahan's reign marks the culmination of the Mughal dynasty. The wealth of his extensive empire, coupled with the conditions of comparative peace, permitted him to maintain a magnificent court and to devote a great deal of attention to the arts. While this does not appear to have been a period notable for innovation, the art of

[1] This work has appeared in print with introduction and notes by Nazir Ahmad, published by Bharatiya Kala Kendra, New Delhi 1956. It is interesting that the *rāgs* are referred to as *maqāms*, a fact which suggests the similarity between the Indian and Arabic or Persian systems even at this time.

[2] According to Abu'l-Fazl 'Allāmī, *Ā'īn-i-Akbarī*, tr. H. Blochmann, Calcutta 1873, i, pp. 50–1, for instance, the orchestra which played at the gateway of the Royal palace (*naqqārakẖāna*) had more than sixty members.

[3] *Akbarnāma*, Beveridge, i, p. 50, quoted by O. C. Gangoly, *Rāgas and Rāginīs*, Bombay 1958, p. 54.

[4] This legend is the subject of a Persian manuscript by Aḥmad-ul-Umri, written in 1599, which has been translated by L. M. Crump under the title of *The Lady of the Lotus*, London 1926.

[5] Abu'l-Fazl 'Allāmī, *op. cit.*, i, pp. 611–13.

[6] Vincent A. Smith, *The Oxford History of India*, Oxford 1958, p. 373.

music is said to have reached a polish and grace unprecedented in the past.[1] The leading musician of the period was Lāl Khan, pupil and son-in-law of Bilās Khan who, presumably, continued the tradition of Mīyā̃ Tānsen. He was a matchless *Dhrupad* singer, and was frequently presented with large gifts by Shahjahan. Although foreign musicians were still imported, their numbers had decreased since Akbar's time.[2]

The 16th and 17th centuries are of great importance for the musical literature of India. Written in 1550, the *Svaramelakalānidhi* of Rāmāmātya—a minister of Rāma Rājā, prince of Vijayanagar[3]—focuses attention on the fact that the music of South India, which had experienced relatively little Islamic influence, was evolving in its own way and was beginning to acquire an independent character. This is corroborated by the *Rāgavibodha* of Somanātha (1609), although there is some evidence of his contact with North India—for example, the occurrence of Muslim *rāg* names in his work. One of the most important treatises on the South Indian system was the *Caturdaṇḍīprakāśikā* of Veṅkaṭamakhī written in 1660, in which the classification of *rāga*s in terms of 72 basic scales (*mela*) was first advocated. This system still prevails in South India.

Several important North Indian treatises were also composed during this period. Of these the *Rāgataraṅgiṇī* by Locana Kavī (of uncertain date),[4] *Sadrāgacandrodaya* and other works of Puṇḍarika Viṭṭhala (end of 16th century), *Hṛidayakautaka* and *Hṛidayaprakāśa* by Hṛidaya Nārāyaṇa (*c.* 1660), and *Saṅgītapārijāta* by Ahobala (*c.* 1665) have considerable bearing on the history of present-day classical music.[5]

These works, with the exception of the *Saṅgītapārijāta*, also follow the classification of *rāga*s in terms of basic scales (*mela*), and for this reason can be more clearly comprehended than the ancient system based on *mūrcchanā* (which is followed in the *Saṅgītaratnākara*), where the tonic or ground-note of the mode is not explicitly stated. Thus there is some confusion as to whether the base note of the *mūrcchanā*, the important note (*aṁśa*)[6] or the final note of the mode (*nyāsa*) should be considered as the tonic.

[1] Abdul Halim, *op. cit.*, p. 38, quoting Faqirullah (Faqīr Allāh), *Rāg Darpan.* Muslim University Ms. f., 16a, dated 1661–1665.

[2] *Ibid.*, p. 43.

[3] O. C. Gangoly, *op. cit.*, p. 51. Rāmāmātya is said to be a descendant of Kallinātha who wrote a commentary on the *Saṅgītaratnākara* in the 15th century.

[4] The date of this work is discussed by O. C. Gangoly, *op. cit.*, p. 41, f.n. 3. The argument is as follows: The colophon in the work itself gives the date of 1082 of the *Śaka* era, i.e. 1160 A.D. The occurrence in this work of Indo-Persian *rāg*s, some of which are said to have been invented by Amīr Khusraw, indicates that this date is too early. Further, there is a reference in the work to a poet, Vidyāpati, which could refer to the well-known poet who lived 1395–1440. The evidence suggests that the earliest date of this work could be the second half of the 15th century. Bhātkhaṇḍe, *A Comparative Study of some of the Leading Music Systems of the 15th, 16th, 17th and 18th centuries*, p. 22, states that Hṛidaya Nārāyaṇa has borrowed a whole section from the *Rāgataraṅgiṇī*, and as the date of Hṛidaya Nārāyaṇa's works is in little doubt the middle 17th century would appear to be the latest possible date for the *Rāgataraṅgiṇī*.

[5] The *Saṅgītadarpaṇa* by Dāmodara Miśra is another well-known work of this period written in 1625 A.D. Bhātkhaṇḍe, *A Short Historical Survey of the Music of Upper India*, Bombay 1934, p. 26, describes it as being as unintelligible and mysterious as the *Saṅgītaratnākara*.

[6] See p. 44.

By the second half of the 17th century we can be sure that the ancient musical system as conveyed in the *Nāṭyaśāstra* was no longer in existence, and that the prevailing system was very similar to that which pertains at the present time. The treatises begin with the traditional description of the scale in terms of twenty-two *śrutis*. The *śrutis* are, however, no longer functional as one of the two ancient parent scales, the *Madhyamagrāma*, is no longer in use.[1] In spite of the mention of twenty-two *śrutis*, the octave seems to have been composed of twelve basic semitones.[2] In the *Sadrāgacandrodaya*, for instance, the octave is said to contain fourteen notes, but in his description of the fretting of the *vīṇā* (stick zither) Puṇḍarika locates only twelve frets, because, he says, the frets for the other two notes would be too close to their adjacent frets on the fingerboard. He adds that if these two frets should be needed in any *rāga*, the adjacent higher frets would be quite acceptable, as the difference of one *śruti* will not make much of a difference in the general effect of the *rāga*.[3]

A large number of musical treatises were concerned primarily with the iconography of *rāgas* and were devoted to establishing familial relationships between *rāgas* on some extra-musical basis. In this very brief survey, we are necessarily obliged to forego any mention of these.[4]

Shahjahan's reign was followed by that of Aurangzeb (1658–1707). The latter was fond of music and skilled in its theory, but he chose a life of asceticism in keeping with the tenets of Islam, relinquished all pleasure and withdrew his patronage of the arts. Musicians were obliged to leave the Mughal court and seek their livelihood at the lesser provincial courts. It was only with the later Mughals, Bahadur Shah (1707–1712) and Muhammad Shah (1719–1748), that music regained some of its former glory. Although the reign of Muhammad Shah was beset with troubles and the Mughal Empire was rapidly declining, he was keenly interested in music and was an accomplished singer and composer. Largely as a result of Muhammad Shah's own endeavours and the compositions of his two leading musicians, Sadāraṅg and Adāraṅg, *Khyāl* finally came to the fore, and a large proportion of the modern repertoire stems from this source.

This was not a fruitful period for musical literature. Bhāva Bhaṭṭa wrote three works at the end of the 17th century, but these are said to be largely in imitation of *Saṅgītaratnākara*.[5] In the second half of the 17th century Faqīr Allāh wrote two works in Persian, *Rāg Darpan* and *Mān Kautūhal*, the latter being to a large extent a translation of the 16th-century Hindi treatise, *Mān Kautūhal*, by Rājā Mān Siṅgh.[6]

[1] Bhātkhaṇḍe, *A Short Historical Survey*, p. 25.

[2] Locana uses only twelve notes in describing his *rāgas* (see Bhātkhaṇḍe, *A Short Historical Survey*, p. 9). Similarly, Ahobala only uses twelve notes in describing his *rāgas* although he gives the names of nineteen altered (*vikrit*) notes (*ibid.*, p. 27).

[3] Bhātkhaṇḍe, *A Comparative Study*, pp. 47–8. If Puṇḍarika had indicated the lower adjacent frets as a substitute, it could have been argued that the desired notes could have been achieved by the technique of deflecting the playing string in order to raise its pitch, a technique which is commonly used today.

[4] Many of these are discussed in O. C. Gangoly, *op. cit.*

[5] Bhātkhaṇḍe, *A Comparative Study*, p. 69.

[6] Halim, *op. cit.*, p. 20.

In 1724 the *Saṅgītapārijāta* was translated into Persian by Pandit Dīnānāth.[1] These translations were very necessary, for, while the Muslims took readily to Indian music, the treatises and the words of the traditional songs were in Sanskrit and the Indian vernacular languages, and were generally quite meaningless to Muslim musicians. In addition, they were frequently based on Hindu religious and mythological subjects. These must all have proved formidable barriers to the Muslims. While many songs were composed in Persian, it is very likely that Muslim musicians were required to sing traditional Indian songs, particularly at the courts of the more broad-minded rulers such as Akbar and Ibrāhīm 'Ādil Shāh II. It is equally probable too that Hindu musicians were sometimes required to sing Muslim compositions in Persian, some of which were based on religious Islamic themes. In either case the words can have been of little significance to the musicians,[2] and in practice the voice came to be used more and more as a musical instrument, with words serving primarily to lend colour and timbre to the music.

In the second half of the 18th century India was divided into several conflicting factions, the most important of which were the Marathas, Mughals, Afghans and a coalition headed by the Nizam of Hyderabad. It was just at this time too that the British began to assert themselves in Indian politics. Musicians were dispersed to the various courts and palaces of noblemen throughout the country, their fortunes, as always, depending on the affluence of their patrons.

There was little sign of British interest in Indian music, except for a treatise written by the Oriental scholar, Sir William Jones, entitled *On the Musical Modes of the Hindus*, which appeared in 1799. Two important treatises were written at the beginning of the 19th century: the Hindi *Saṅgīt-sār* (*c.* 1800), compiled as a result of a conference of leading musicians in the court of the Jaipur Maharājā, Pratāp Siṃh Dev; and the Persian *Naghmāt-i-Āsafī* (1813), written by Muḥammad Rezā, a nobleman of Patna. The latter has received considerable attention because it is said to be the first 'reliable' authority in which *Bilāval ṭhāṭ* is referred to as the natural (*śuddh*) scale.[3] The fact remains that until about the 19th century the natural scale described in North Indian texts was based on the ancient *Ṣaḍjagrāma*, comparable to the D mode (the ecclesiastic Dorian). Today *Bilāval ṭhāṭ*, comparable to the Western major scale or the C mode (the ecclesiastic Ionian), is generally accepted as the natural scale.[4]

[1] Bhātkhaṇḍe, *A Comparative Study*, p. 31.

[2] Some of Ibrāhīm 'Ādil Shāh's songs in the *Kitāb-i-Nauras*, composed in the Dakhani language, are dedicated to the Hindu deities (mainly Sarasvatī and Ganeś), others to Muslim saints (Sayyad Muḥammad Husayn-i-Gesū Darāz). Musicians of his court, whether Hindu or Muslim, would presumably have been expected to sing all of them.

[3] Bhātkhaṇḍe, *A Short Historical Survey*, p. 35. However, G. H. Ranade, *Hindustani Music*, Poona, 1951, p. 12, draws attention to the fact that, in his *Hindustānī Saṅgīt Paddhatī*, III, p. 136, Bhātkhaṇḍe has written that Rezā has nowhere referred to his notes as *śuddh*.

[4] It is tempting to think that this might be a result of Western influence, but this seems unlikely in view of the widespread acceptance in India of *Bilāval ṭhāṭ* as the natural scale. It should be noted that very few traditional musicians have any familiarity with Western music, and most of them find it completely alien.

In 1834 Captain N. Augustus Willard, an army officer attached to a small princely state, wrote *A Treatise on the Music of Hindusthan*, in which he drew attention to the considerable gap that had grown between musical theory and practice over the centuries.[1] In the second half of the 19th century musical theory was rejuvenated in Bengal. The publication of K. Goswami's *Saṅgīta Sārā* in 1868 was followed by various publications by S. M. Tagore[2] and a particularly important work by K. Banarjī, *Gīta Sūtra Sāra* (1855), written in Bengali. Banarjī made a serious attempt to integrate musical theory and practice and his work is remarkable for its critical assessment of musical theory. In 1914 Fox Strangways wrote *Music of Hindostan*, another commendable attempt to relate the numerous aspects of Indian music. The work shows an extraordinary perception and grasp of the subject. Fox Strangways's comments on contemporary Indian music are particularly praiseworthy and his analogies with Western music are often enlightening. But his discussions of ancient Indian music must be viewed with caution as they contain some very basic misinterpretations.[3]

The beginning of the 20th century was, however, dominated by the works of Pandit V. N. Bhātkhaṇḍe. His first important work, *Śrīmal-lakṣyasaṅgītam*, was written in Sanskrit and published in 1910 under the pseudonym of Catura Paṇḍita. Although Bhātkhaṇḍe quotes from many prominent Sanskrit sources, it is quite clear that his main intent is to reconcile musical theory with existing practice. This work was followed shortly by the first of four volumes of a magnum opus in Marathi entitled *Hindusthānī Saṅgīt Paddhatī* (hereafter abbreviated to *H.S.P.*) which was finally completed in 1932 and later translated into Hindi.[4] Bhātkhaṇḍe here expands many of the ideas expressed in *Śrīmal-lakṣyasaṅgītam* and introduces many new concepts to explain the musical practice of his day. He traces the historical development of *rāg*s through Sanskrit treatises and attempts to analyse and present a standard form for each, while acknowledging divergent traditions. Bhātkhaṇḍe's second major work, *Kramik Pustak Mālikā*, in six volumes (hereafter abbreviated to *K.P.M.*) was published between 1920 and 1937 and was also later translated into Hindi.[5] This work is primarily devoted to the notation of more than two thousand traditional songs in different *rāg*s and *tāl*s which Bhātkhaṇḍe was able to collect from musicians belonging to different *gharānā*s (family traditions) throughout North India.[6] *K.P.M.*

[1] The works of both Augustus Willard and Sir William Jones have recently appeared in a second edition as *Music of India*, Calcutta 1962.

[2] The article 'Hindu Music' has been reprinted from the *Hindoo Patriot*, 1874, in *Hindu Music from Various Authors*, Varanasi 1965, compiled by S. M. Tagore.

[3] For instance, the ancient *Ṣaḍjagrāma* is assumed to begin on the Ni note which he equates with the Western note C: *Music of Hindostan*, Oxford 1914 (reprinted 1966), p. 109. This would mean that the *Ṣaḍjagrāma* was similar to the C mode or the Western major scale. In fact, it has since been firmly established that it is equivalent to the D mode.

[4] Published by Saṅgīt Kāryālay, Hathras 1956–7. All the references to *H.S.P.* in this work refer to this translation.

[5] Published by Saṅgīt Kāryālay, Hathras 1954–9. All the references to *K.P.M.* in this work refer to this translation.

[6] The following list of contributors and their provenance is given by L. N. Garg, the writer of the preface of *K.P.M.*, Vol. IV. The list is, however, incomplete and includes only those musicians who gave permission for their names to appear in print. For instance, *Ustād* Bundu Khan, a famous

also contains quotations from Sanskrit and Hindi sources on each of the *rāgs* (numbering about 180) and brief verbal descriptions of them. In addition, Bhātkhaṇḍe gives his own interpretation of the musical characteristics of these *rāgs*: the ascending and descending lines (*āroh* and *avroh*), a typical or 'catch' phrase (*pakaṛ*) by which each can be recognised (Vols. V and VI employ a slightly different method), and at the end of each volume as many as twenty or twenty-five series of phrases (*svarvistār*—extension of notes), compiled to illustrate the melodic contours of each *rāg*.

Muḥammad Nawāb 'Alī Khan, a pupil of Bhātkhaṇḍe, followed his preceptor in that he too based his musical treatise, *Ma'ārif-ul naghmāt*, written in Urdu, on songs which he had collected from practising musicians. In recent times there have been many musical texts written in the Indian vernaculars which for the most part borrow heavily from Bhātkhaṇḍe's works. A considerable number of publications on Indian music have also appeared in English and other European languages, the standard of scholarship often leaving much to be desired. A. A. Bake's publications, although they have not found expression in a major work, are one of the noteworthy exceptions.[1] Herbert Popley's *The Music of India* (Calcutta 1950) is generally reliable and is a useful guide to both North and South Indian music. A particularly

---

sāraṅgī player of Indore who spent the last years of his life in Pakistan, is also said to have contributed to Bhātkhaṇḍe's collections (L. N. Garg, *Hamāre Saṅgīt Ratna*, Hathras 1957, p. 479).

1. H. H. Ḥāmid 'Alī Ṣāḥib Bahādur	Ruler of Rampur and follower of Tānsen's descendants.
2. Ṣaḥibzāda Sa'ādat 'Ali Khan Ṣāḥib Bahādur	Rampur—follower of Tānsen's descendants.
3. Khan Ṣāḥib Muḥammad 'Alī Bāsat Khan	Rampur—descendant of Tānsen.
4. Khan Ṣāḥib Muḥammad Vazīr Khan and Amīr Khan	Rampur—descendants of Tānsen, and teachers of His Highness.
5. Khan Ṣāḥib Muḥammad 'Alī Khan	Jaipur—Manaraṅg (son of Sadāraṅg) *gharānā*.
6. Khan Ṣāḥib 'Āshiq 'Alī Khan	Jaipur—Manaraṅg *gharānā*.
7. Khan Ṣāḥib Aḥmad 'Alī Khan	Jaipur—Manaraṅg *gharānā*.
8. Khan Ṣāḥib Haidar Khan	Dhar—pupil of Bahrām K͟hān.
9. Khan Ṣāḥib Faiyāz Khan	Baroda—Raṅgīle *gharānā*.
10. Khan Ṣāḥib Amīr Khan Gulāb Sāgar	Baroda—instrumentalist.
11. Śrī Rāojī Buvā Belbāgkar	Bombay—follower of 'Abdullah Khan, *dhrupad* singer.
12. Śrī Eknāth Paṇḍit	Gwalior—follower of Nathan Pīrbak͟hsh's descendants and of *k͟hyāl* singer, Śaṅkar Paṇḍit.
13. Śrī Viṣṇubuvā Vāman Deśpāṇḍe	Gwalior—descendant of Vāmanbuvā, a *dhrupad* singer.
14. Śrī Rājābhaiyā Pūchvāle	Gwalior—pupil of Śaṅkar Paṇḍit.
15. Śrī Kr̥iṣṇarāo Gopāl Dāte	Gwalior
16. Śrī Kr̥iṣṇabuvā Gokhle	Miraj—follower of Amīn Khan's descendants.
17. Śrī Kr̥iṣṇa Śāstrī Śukl	Ujjain (Gwalior).
18. Śrī Gaṇpatibuvā Bhilvaḍīkar	Satara.

[1] 'The Music of India', in *Ancient and Oriental Music* (*New Oxford History of Music*, Vol 1), London 1957, and 'Indische Musik' in *Die Musik in Geschichte und Gegenwart* (*Allgemeine Enzyklopädie der Musik*, Bd. 6), Kassel 1957.

valuable critical work, discussing the comments and theories put forward by Willard, Bhātkhaṇḍe and K. Banarjī, is H. L. Roy's *Problems of Hindustani Music* (Calcutta 1937). Roy highlights the inadequacies of some of the present-day terminology and gives suggestions for the reconstruction of musical theory. G. H. Ranade's *Hindusthani Music: An outline of its Physics and Aesthetics* (Poona 1951) is particularly useful for its analysis of the acoustics of the drone. A number of other writers have been concerned primarily with precise intonation in Indian music. Their work is based on the acoustic properties of individual intervals as determined by mathematical ratios, without reference to the varying musical context in which those intervals occur. In addition they attempt to explain modern Indian practice in terms of ancient musical theory. This 'school' was initiated by K. B. Deval, *The Hindu Musical Scale and the Twenty-Two Shrutees* (Sangli 1910), and E. Clements, *Introduction to the Study of Indian Music* (London 1913), and has recently been followed by A. Danielou, *Northern Indian Music* (London 1949, 1954).

On the other hand, there have been several valuable works on the history of Indian music. Foremost among these are, once again, the writings of Bhātkhaṇḍe. His two monographs in English—*A Short Historical Survey of the Music of Upper India* (Bombay 1934), originally a speech delivered at the First All-India Music Conference at Baroda in 1916, and *A Comparative Study of some of the leading Music Systems of the* 15*th*, 16*th*, 17*th and* 18*th Centuries* (Bombay, n.d.)—present in concise form some of the historical material which extends throughout his other writings. O. C. Gangoly's *Rāgas and Rāginīs* (Bombay 1935, reprinted 1948) is another scholarly work which deserves to be mentioned. As a source of reference it is of considerable value, but it does not go into details of musical theory. The works of Swami Prajnanananda, *Historical Development of Indian Music* (Calcutta 1960) and *A History of Indian Music*, Vol. 1 (Calcutta 1963), also contain valuable material. Most of the historical research has been based on Sanskrit sources. Perhaps the only useful work based on Islamic sources is a collection, *Essays on History of Indo-Pak Music* (Dacca 1962) by Abdul Halim. Much work still remains to be done in this field.

In this brief resumé of the musical literature of the present century many works have not been mentioned.[1] Considering the body of material on Indian music, it is surprising that so very little is concerned with the analysis of present-day Indian music.

This century has seen fundamental changes in the preservation and presentation of North Indian classical music. The traditional system of patronage has been gradually disappearing and musicians now earn their livelihood mainly by public recitals, radio broadcasts, gramophone records, and teaching in schools and music colleges, and only incidentally by private recitals and individual tuition. New devices have already been evolved to cope with the formal atmosphere in the concert hall where rapport with the listener is not so easily achieved. Many musicians have been

[1] Some of these have been discussed by Harold S. Powers in 'Indian Music and the English Language: A Review Essay', *Ethnomusicology*, ix, January 1965.

experimenting with microphone techniques and, since, as a result, they are now less concerned with producing a large volume of sound, there has been greater emphasis on tone production. This is once again a period of exploration and change, and it will certainly influence the form of Indian music in years to come. At the present time, however, there is no reason to believe that the basic fundamentals of Indian music are in any danger of distortion in the foreseeable future.

I

An Outline of Present-Day North Indian Classical Music

Present-day classical music is directly descended from the court tradition of earlier centuries and some of the prominent musicians of today can still trace their ancestry back to the court musicians of the Mughal period.[1] Under the patronage system musicians were continually vying for the favours of the court and this gave rise to a highly competitive atmosphere in which virtuosity, invention and showmanship played a vital part. These characteristics still apply today. The musician aims to impress as well as entertain, but above all to convey an aesthetic experience. He is not rendering a traditional piece in a stereotyped manner, but refashioning his musical material afresh in each performance. Although a traditional song or melody often serves him as a basis, it is usually very short and in performance is elaborated and varied, and repeated statements of it are interspersed with improvisations. Thus the length of the performance is, to a large extent, determined by the inventiveness of the musician.

There are four main aspects of Indian music to be considered:

1. *Main melody line.* The Indian musical scheme is essentially monodic—it has a single melody line with an accompaniment.[2] The voice is usually thought to be the most effective carrier of the melody line, not because it is also capable of conveying verbal content, but because of its flexibility and expressive properties. However, any instrument can be used for this purpose, some naturally being more suitable than others. The following are the most prominent melody instruments: the *sitār*, a long-necked plucked lute with frets; the *surbahār*, a larger version of the *sitār*; the *sarod*, another plucked lute with a shorter neck and without frets; the *sāraṅgī*, a bowed lute; the *bā̃srī*, a side-blown bamboo flute; and the *shahnā'ī* (*shenai*), a double-reed wind instrument similar to the oboe, but without keys. Many other instruments are also used; some, like the violin and the clarinet, have been borrowed from the West.

[1] For instance, *Ustād* Vilayat Khan whose background is mentioned in Appendix B on p. 186.

[2] Duets (*jugalbandī*), in which there are two carriers of the melody line—two voices or two instruments, who generally perform alternately—are becoming increasingly popular.

2. *Drone.* The melody line is generally played against a fixed, unchanging drone which is based on the tonic, its octave and its fifth or fourth.[1] This is usually played on a *tambūrā* (*tānpūrā*), a long-necked lute with four or five strings which has no frets and consequently sounds only the open-string notes. The drone may also be produced on a hand-pumped harmonium (*sur-peṭī*). The *shahnā'ī* is often accompanied by other drone *shahnā'ī*s.

3. *Accompanying melody line.* A vocalist is accompanied by a secondary melody line, usually played on a *sāraṅgī* or a harmonium, which echoes the phrases produced by the singer. The *sāraṅgī* is usually played by an accompanist, while the harmonium is often played by the singer himself. When the vocalist pauses, the accompanying instrument assumes momentarily the role of the main melody carrier.

4. *Percussive line.* This is usually produced on the *tablā*, a pair of small kettledrums struck with the hands. Occasionally, a two-ended barrel-shaped drum, *pakhvāj* (*pakhāvaj*) or *mṟidaṅg*, may be used instead. The *shahnā'ī* is generally accompanied by another type of kettledrum, the *khurḍak* or *ḍukaṛ*, also played in pairs. The percussive instrument serves primarily as a time-keeper, but is also used for rhythmic variations and improvisations.

Many musical instruments fulfil more than one function. The *sitār*, for example, not only carries the melody line, but also has special strings (*cikārī*) for supplying its own drone, and in addition has sympathetic strings (*tarab*) which provide an echo, in some ways like the effect produced by an accompanying instrument.

Indian classical music has two fundamental elements: *rāg*, the melodic framework, and *tāl*, the time measure.

RĀG

The term *rāg* has no counterpart in Western musical theory. The concept of *rāg* is based on the idea that certain characteristic patterns of notes evoke a heightened state of emotion.[2] These patterns of notes are a fusion of scalar and melodic elements, and each *rāg* can be described in terms of its ascending and descending lines (which may involve 'turns') as well as its characteristic melodic figures in which certain intervals are emphasised and attention is focused on particular notes. More than two hundred *rāg*s are extant and each is a melodic basis for composition and improvisation. Most of the *rāg*s have been in existence for several centuries and have evolved to their present form as a result of successive interpretations by generations of musicians.

A performance of a *rāg* usually begins with an *ālāp*, a kind of improvised prelude in free time in which the melodic characteristics of the *rāg* being performed are clearly established and developed. It is rendered on a melody instrument or by the voice, and is usually accompanied by a drone. The vocal *ālāp* may also be accompanied by a secondary melody instrument. The instrumental *ālāp* tradition is very

[1] At the present time variant drone tunings are also used (see p. 187).

[2] The word *rāg* is derived from the Sanskrit root *rañj* or *raj* = to colour or tinge (with emotion).

prominent today and the *ālāp* generally consists of a number of sections, some of which, like *joṛ* and *jhālā*, are played against a pulse or beat but without fixed metre. At the conclusion of the *ālāp* a composed piece set in a particular *tāl* is introduced.

TĀL

The term *tāl*, perhaps best translated as 'time measure', is conceived as a cycle. It has two principal aspects: (1) quantitative, meaning the duration of a cycle measured in terms of time units or beats (*mātrā*), which are generally held to be in three tempi (*lay*)—slow (*vilambit*), medium (*madhy*) and fast (*drut*); and (2) qualitative, meaning the distribution of stresses or accents within the cycle. These stresses occur at different levels of intensity: the principal stress at the beginning of the cycle (*sam*); secondary stresses within the cycle (*tālī*); and then there is a negation of stress (*khālī*) which always occurs at points where a secondary stress may be expected but is consciously avoided.[1] The following illustrations show the quantitative and qualitative patterns of three prominent North Indian *tāl*s. Following Bhātkhaṇḍe's system, X represents the *sam*, the numbers 2, 3 and 4 the *tālī*s and 0 the *khālī*s:

Ex. 1.

(a) *Tīntāl* (*Tritāl*)

Time units	1	2	3	4	5	6	7	8	9	10	11	12	13	14	15	16
Stresses	X				2				0				3			

(b) *Ektāl*

Time units	1	2	3	4	5	6	7	8	9	10	11	12
Stresses	X		0		2		0		3		4	

(c) *Jhaptāl*

Time units	1	2	3	4	5	6	7	8	9	10
Stresses	X		2			0		3		

The metrical framework of each *tāl* is represented by a basic drum pattern, *ṭhekā*, which is a fixed sequence of drum-syllables produced on a pair of *tablā*.[2] These sounds are produced by striking different parts of the two skins on the drum heads and are symbolised by mnemonic syllables such as *dhā*, *dhin*, *nā*, *tin*, *ke*, *ghe*, etc.[3] A common *ṭhekā* of *Ektāl*, for example, is:

Ex. 2. Ektāl

1	2	3	4	5	6	7	8	9	10	11	12
dhin	dhin	dhāge	tirakiṭa	tū	nā	kat	tā	dhāge	tirakiṭa	dhin	nā
X		0		2		0		3		4	

[1] Most of the common North Indian *tāl*s have an even number of time units, the prominent exceptions being *Rūpak* and *Tīvrā* which have seven units. The *khālī* frequently occurs midway between two 'positive' stresses creating something of the effect of an 'up' beat against the 'down' beat of the *sam* and the *tālī*s. When keeping time the *khālī* is usually indicated by a wave of the hand, while the *sam* and the *tālī*s are marked by claps.

[2] Certain *tāl*s are played primarily on the *pakhvāj*, which has its own drum syllables. The basic pattern of a *tāl* is then called *thapiyā*.

[3] A description of drumming techniques is found in A. H. Fox Strangways, *The Music of Hindostan*, p. 225 ff., and in W. Kaufmann, *Musical Notations of the Orient*, Bloomington 1967, pp. 218–63.

It is in the composed piece that *rāg* and *tāl* meet on common ground. In instrumental music this piece or tune is called *gat* and in vocal music, set to words, it is called *cīz* (*cīj*). The *gat* or *cīz* is not only in a particular *rāg* but also has a fixed relationship with the metre of a particular *tāl*. In instrumental music, especially that on plucked stringed instruments such as the *sitār* and *sarod*, the *gat* is constructed on percussive patterns obtained when the instrument is plucked. The following pattern, called *Majīd* (*Masīt*) *K̲h̲ānī gat*, is a very common example:[1]

Ex. 3. Majīd K̲h̲ānī gat

Time units	12	13	14	15	16	1	2	3	4	5	6	7	8	9	10	11
Percussive pattern	♪♪	♩	♪♪	♩	♩	♩	♩	♩	♪♪	♩	♪♪	♩	♩	♩	♩	♩
Stresses		3				X				2				0		

While the melody of the *gat* is based on a *rāg*, the percussive pattern is a feature not of *rāg*, but of *tāl*. It is the counterpart on a melody instrument of the *ṭhekā* on the drums. In practice these patterns are not rigidly maintained and are commonly embellished, but the relationship with the basic pattern is nevertheless preserved.

In vocal music the song (*cīz*) serves the same purpose as the *gat*, providing a fixed relationship between *rāg* and *tāl*. There are at present several different types of songs—*khyāl* (*k̲h̲yāl*), *ṭhumrī*, *tarānā*, *dhrupad*, etc.—each with their individual forms and styles of performance. They are sometimes also associated with particular *rāg*s and *tāl*s. The text of the *cīz* is generally traditional, particular themes tending to be associated with specific types of songs. The words are not generally noted for their poetic content and are relatively unimportant in classical music. The voice is used rather like a special instrument, capable of varying its timbre through the enunciation of different syllables.

The composed piece in both instrumental and vocal music generally has two sections, *sthāyī* (*astāī*) and *antrā*. The former is the main part of the composition and is said to be usually limited to the lower and middle registers, while the *antrā* extends from the middle to the upper registers.[2] The vocal composition may sometimes have additional sections (*sañcārī*, *ābhog* and *bhog*), and in its full form may have a number of verses and extend over ten or more cycles of the *tāl*. However, since the main function of the composition is to provide a frame of reference for the *tāl*, only the first verse extending over one cycle is really essential,[3] the others being used by the musician as and when needed, either to introduce variety or to draw attention to a different part or aspect of the *rāg*.

[1] It is composed of two equal parts, from 12–3 and 4–11. The melody, beginning on beat 12, leads to a climax at 1 and tapers away to 3. The second part of the melody builds to a false climax at 9 and tapers away to 11, the first part resuming at 12.

[2] *H.S.P.* I, p. 41.

[3] In the *baṛā khyāl*, sung in very slow tempo (e.g. ♩ = 12), even this much is not usually used, for the full cycle of the *tāl* may last more than a minute and the song is too long to repeat in its traditional form. Here the relationship with the *tāl* is established only one or two time units (*mātrās*) before the *sam*, the remainder of the cycle being devoted to improvisation. In the short fragment of the composition which leads to the *sam* (called *mukhṛā*), only the last few syllables of the full text may be used.

The composed piece is not the primary focus of attention in North Indian classical music. This role is occupied by the melodic and rhythmic extemporisations which the musicians introduce during the course of their performance. The composition serves as a springboard for these and a frame of reference to which the musicians periodically return. Thus the form is similar to that of the Rondo, the composition alternating with the improvisations.[1] It must be stressed that the melodic improvisations are not variations on the composition itself, but elaborations of the different features of the *rāg* phrased against the metre of the *tāl*. Similarly, the rhythmic extemporisations are not variations of the basic pattern of the *tāl* but are phrases played against the metre of the *tāl* and regularly go across its stress patterns. The improvisations of the melody instrument (or voice) and those of the drums are generally undertaken successively, the metre of the *tāl* being maintained by the non-improvisator who plays his basic pattern softly in the background. Occasionally, both may improvise at the same time, but this would probably occur late in the performance when the basic patterns have already been heard several times and the listener is, to some extent, able to supply the underlying patterns for himself.

Traditionally it is the melody instrumentalist or the vocalist who is the leader of the ensemble in North Indian classical music.[2] It is he who determines the extent to which the drummer may improvise, if at all. In recent times the drummer has been getting an increasing share of the improvisation, though there are some musicians who still prefer their drummers to be merely accompanists and do not permit them much licence.

The improvised variations may begin at any point of the *tāl*, they may continue for any part of one cycle or several cycles and the return to the composition may be accomplished at any point, provided that the original relationship between the metre of the *tāl* and the composition is maintained. In practice many variations begin either on the *sam* or shortly after, and are very frequently concluded either at the *sam* or just before the beginning of the composition (e.g. in Ex. 3 just before time unit 12).

Whilst the form of North Indian classical music resembles that of the Rondo, the successive cycles generally increase in intensity, thereby creating the effect of an upward spiral. This is accomplished by the development of melodic ideas,[3] the increasing complexity of both melodic and rhythmic variations, and the accelerating tempo which frequently culminates in a powerful climax.

[1] The degree of creativity in these extempore passages is not easily assessed, for in playing the same *rāg* and *tāl* again and again, musicians acquire musical habits and evolve favourite phrases which may recur from time to time. It is, however, when the musician is performing beyond his normal capacity that the music becomes 'alive'.

[2] The roles are reversed in what is referred to as a '*tablā* solo' where a melody instrument and drone may accompany the drums. Here the melody instrument serves as time-keeper, repeating a short tune (*lahrā*, similar to *gat*) against which the *tablā* player improvises. In the normal instrumental performances of a *rāg* it is quite usual for the melody instrument to assume the role of time-keeper at appropriate moments, to give an opportunity for the drummer to improvise.

[3] As, for instance, in the gradual expansion of the range of the *rāg*. A more detailed discussion of the development of melodic ideas can be found in N. A. Jairazbhoy, 'Svaraprastāra in North Indian Classical Music', *Bulletin of the School of Oriental and African Studies*, Vol. XXIV, part 2, 1961, pp. 307–25.

II

Basic Elements of Theory

A *rāg* does not exist in any precise form in the sense that a symphony can be said to exist in score, but is a complex of latent melodic possibilities. Although this seems to suggest an amorphous quality, each *rāg* is an independent musical entity with an ethos of its own, which becomes manifest through recognisable melodic patterns. In the course of time a corpus of technical terms has been evolved by theorists and musicians in order to convey some idea of the nature of *rāg*s. Since these technical terms are used primarily to supplement musical practice they are not always precise enough for purposes of analytical study. Therefore, in the following pages, as we consider the salient features of *rāg*s, it will be necessary to discuss not only the pertinent technical terms but also to extend the discussion to related musical principles.

NOTES

SVAR

In North Indian musical theory seven notes (*svar*) are recognised. In their Hindi form, the names of these notes are *Ṣaḍj* (or *Khaḍj*), *Riṣabh*, *Gāndhār* (or *Gandhār*), *Madhyam*, *Pañcam*, *Dhaivat* and *Niṣād* (or *Nikhād*); or in the commonly used abbreviated form, Sa, Re (or Ri), Ga, Ma, Pa, Dha and Ni. It is these abbreviations that are used throughout this work, with the occasional addition, for the convenience of the Western reader, of the note's scale degree in brackets. The Indian nomenclature is comparable to that of Western tonic-solfa: there is no absolute or fixed pitch attached to the notes, and the ground-note (the note which serves as the point of reference of the scale) is called Sa, irrespective of its pitch. Once the pitch of the ground-note has been established, however, it remains unchanged throughout the performance of a *rāg* as there is no modulation in Indian music.

ACAL

CAL

Of these seven notes, Sa and Pa (I and V) are 'immovable notes' (*acal svar*)—they have no flat or sharp positions and Pa is always a perfect fifth above the Sa. The remaining five notes are 'movable notes' (*cal svar*). These each have two possible positions, a semitone apart. One of these is

ŚUDDH called *śuddh* (pure) which is comparable to the 'natural' of the West. In the *śuddh* scale, *Bilāval,* composed of Sa, Pa and the five movable notes in their *śuddh* position, the distribution of tones and semitones corresponds to that in the Western major scale.[1]

When the movable notes are not in the *śuddh* position, they are called VIKṚIT *vikṛit*—altered. In the case of Re, Ga, Dha and Ni (II, III, VI and VII) they are a semitone lower than their *śuddh* counterparts and are called KOMAL *komal*—soft, tender. The altered Ma (IV), however, is a semitone above TĪVR the *śuddh* position, and is called *tīvr*—strong, intense.

The terms *komal* and *tīvr* are not exactly comparable to their Western counterparts, flat and sharp, as they apply only to specific *vikṛit* notes, whereas in the West every note has a flat and a sharp form. The Sa and Pa, being immovable, cannot have either *komal* or *tīvr* forms; nor can a *komal* note be referred to as the *tīvr* of the note below, which in the Western use of flat and sharp is common practice. (The semitone above C may be called either C♯ or D♭, depending on the circumstances, but in Indian music Re *komal* is not referred to as Sa *tīvr*.) Notwithstanding this difference, in this work we are using the symbol ♭ to indicate *komal* and ♯ to indicate *tīvr*, and, where necessary to avoid confusion, ♮ to indicate *śuddh*.

The full series of intervals in the gamut are set out below:

Śuddh svar	Sa	Re	Ga	Ma	Pa	Dha	Ni	(Sa)
Vikṛit svar		Re♭	Ga♭		Ma♯	Dha♭	Ni♭	

These are represented in Western staff notation as follows, the Sa being arbitrarily equated with the C but not implying its absolute pitch:

Ex. 4.

This system of nomenclature has wide acceptance in India, and is generally used by Bhātkhaṇḍe (though he uses different symbols to represent *komal* and *tīvr*).[2]

[1] In its present-day application the *śuddh* concept does not entail the idea of parent scale from which other scales are derived, but serves only as a standard for comparison.

[2] Another system of nomenclature is also sometimes used in India, and is referred to by Bhātkhaṇḍe (*K.P.M.* II, p. 12) as being used primarily by vocalists. In this tradition, the higher position of the movable notes is referred to as *tīvr* and the lower position as *komal.* Here the term *tīvr* should be translated as the upper of two alternative notes, not as sharp, and *komal* as the lower rather than as flat. A considerable amount of confusion is caused by the co-existence of these two systems. Of the many examples which could be quoted, those from record sleeves are the most obvious. For instance, on H.M.V. ALP 2312, the *rāg Jaijaivantī* is described as having all seven sharp notes in ascent. This is completely misleading and may even suggest to the Western reader that the ground-note can be made sharp in certain *rāg*s. The writer has evidently equated the *śuddh* of Bhātkhaṇḍe's system with *tīvr* of the other. This is only justified in application to Re, Ga, Dha and Ni. In fact, the ascending line of *rāg Jaijaivantī* has 'natural' intervals.

REGISTERS

STHĀN · SAPTAK · MADHY · TĀR · MANDR · ATI-MANDR · ATITĀR

North Indian classical music is not, of course, limited to one octave, and the same names apply to the notes in the other octave registers above and below. There are three registers (*sthān*—position; or *saptak*—aggregate of seven) generally recognised, each extending from Sa to the Ni above: middle (*madhy*); high (*tār*) which is here indicated by a dot above the note name, e.g. Ṡa (İ); and low (*mandr*) which is indicated by a dot below the note name, e.g. Ṇi (ṾII). Although musical theory usually acknowledges only these three registers which are based on the natural limitations in the range of the voice and most Indian instruments, the very low register (*atimandr*), indicated by two dots below the note name, is sometimes used by players of stringed instruments, especially the *sitār* and the *surbahār*. The very high register (*atitār*) is rarely heard.

INTONATION

While the present-day North Indian gamut is comparable to the twelve-semitone octave of the West, some discussion on the subject of intonation is necessary. In the classical music of North India there is no need for equal temperament, since the factors which lead to this—changing harmonies and the system of keys—do not apply. Moreover, the technique of tempering notes by the use of beats is generally unknown, and since it is uncommon to find a number of melody instruments playing together, no objective standard of tuning is in general use. The only Indian instrument with fixed intonation is the harmonium which is often used for accompanying singers, but even here the precise tuning varies with each instrument. In general, intonation is governed by the individual musician's feeling for intervals. Except for the simple consonances of the ground-note, octave, fifth and fourth, these only approximate to a twelve semitone standard. Electronic analysis has confirmed that there is variation in intonation from one musician to another, as well as for a single musician during the course of a performance.[1]

Apart from this unconscious variation in intonation, there are musical traditions in North India which consciously recognise that in a few particular *rāg*s one or two notes are flatter or sharper than that which they conceive of as the standard in the *rāg*s as a whole. Bhātkhaṇḍe refers to these traditions on a number of occasions; for instance, when discussing the *rāg Āsāvrī* he says, 'Some say that the Dha (VI) of *Āsāvrī* is flatter than

[1] For further discussion on intonation see N. A. Jairazbhoy and A. W. Stone, 'Intonation in present-day North Indian classical music', *Bulletin of the School of Oriental and African Studies*, Vol. XXVI, Part 1, 1963, pp. 119–32.

that of the *rāg Bhairvī*'. However, he does not appear to give much credence to this and prefers not to go further into the matter.[1]

ĀNDOLAN GAMAK ŚRUTI

There is, however, one special case where subtle distinctions in intonation are particularly noticeable. This occurs when a note is subjected to a slow shake or an exaggerated vibrato (*āndolan* or *gamak*), either as a decoration or as a functional feature in certain *rāgs*.[2] It is in this context that certain musicians use the term *śruti* to indicate the subtle intervals produced as a result of this oscillation in pitch. They do, however, maintain that these microtonal deviations from the 'standard' intonation may only be used in oscillation and may not be sustained as a steady note.[3]

In the introductory chapter we have already suggested that the *śruti*, which was the basis of distinction between the two parent scales in ancient India, had certainly lost its original significance by the 17th century. In modern times certain musicologists and musicians still attempt to apply the old twenty-two *śruti* system to present-day music, while others go so far as to assert that the present-day gamut can only be explained in terms of forty-nine or even sixty-six different intervals. The fact remains that *śruti*s are no longer functional, that is they are not a primary basis of distinction between *rāg*s.

Bhātkhaṇḍe attempted in his early works to relate the twelve semitones to the ancient *śruti*s as follows: [4]

Śuddhsvar	Sa				Re			Ga		Ma				Pa				Dha			Ni	
Śruti	1	2	3	4	5	6	7	8	9	10	11	12	13	14	15	16	17	18	19	20	21	22
Vikṛitsvar			Re♭				Ga♭					Ma♯				Dha♭				Ni♭		

The twelve-semitone system, however, is clearly at odds with the twenty-two *śruti* system since some of the semitones are composed of one *śruti* and others of two *śruti*s.[5] In his later writings Bhātkhaṇḍe contradicts this earlier opinion when he says, 'To distinguish between two *rāg*s on the basis of the difference of only one *śruti* would not be acceptable to any present-day vocalist or instrumentalist'.[6] If this statement is applied to the

[1] *H.S.P.* IV, p. 428. He continues, 'But I can see no reason why we should get involved in these minute intervals. In current practice, the [following] rule always obtains: "*svarasaṃgatyadhīnāni svarasthānāni nityaśaḥ*" [The position of notes depends upon the notes they are combined with].' Elsewhere, *H.S.P.* IV, p. 584, he is more explicit: 'When a note is connected with lower notes, then it is noticed to be lower [in pitch], and when with higher notes then it is seen to be raised. This difference is noticed only by people with acute perception. That is why wise people do not like to exert themselves unduly with the trouble of trying to ascertain the minute intervals.' We shall be discussing this question of intonation in Chapter VIII.

[2] An example of this can be heard in the *rāg Darbārī* on the accompanying record.

[3] This view has been stated by Baṛe Ghulām 'Alī Khan. For further discussion see Chapter VIII.

[4] *K.P.M.* II, pp. 10–11.

[5] It is sometimes stated that the octave contains twenty-four *śruti*s, presumably so that each semitone can have two *śruti*s.

[6] *K.P.M.* VI, p. 21. This remark is reminiscent of that made by Puṇḍarika Viṭṭhala more than 350 years ago which has been referred to earlier (see p. 21).

above scheme representing the semitones in terms of *śruti*s, it would mean that musicians could not distinguish between *rāg*s having a minor third (Ga♭) and a major third (Ga♮) or a minor seventh (Ni♭) and a major seventh (Ni♮), for the difference between these is only one *śruti.* Obviously this is not so. Bhātkhaṇḍe goes on to say that there is no absolute measure of *śruti* available to him and that he recognises that the position (intonation) of a note in any one *rāg* fluctuates with the changing context in which it occurs.[1]

The gamut is a conceptual standard and, though it is derived from musical practice, it cannot take into account all the minute deviations from the norm, many of which are quite unconscious. Thus we are obliged to accept the twelve semitone standard, while making allowances for minor variations, conscious as well as unconscious.

ALTERNATIVE NOTES

The *śuddh* and *vikr̲it* varieties of each of the five movable notes are alternatives and do not normally occur as consecutive steps in a melodic sequence. Thus, in principle, the complete musical series will consist of the two immovable notes, Sa and Pa, and one of each pair of alternatives, Re♮ or Re♭, Ga♮ or Ga♭, Ma♮ or Ma♯, Dha♮ or Dha♭, and Ni♮ or Ni♭. In general, Indian music can be described as 'diatonic' in the sense that the successive steps of a scale are different degrees, rather than as 'chromatic' where the steps could include both alternatives of any note.[2] But many *rāg*s are quite complex and have both forms of one or more movable notes. These usually occur each in their own particular melodic context from which the other is excluded. It sometimes happens that a skilful musician will merge the two contexts so that the two forms of a note may be heard in succession. This generally requires some preparation of ground, as in the

1 *K.P.M., ibid.* This was written during the latter part of Bhātkhaṇḍe's life by which time he had obviously modified his earlier views on *śrutis*.

2 In this work the terms diatonic and chromatic are used in this rather specialised sense. Here diatonic does not refer necessarily to scales whose steps are only wholetones and semitones. When applied to a heptatonic scale, chromatic indicates the use of both alternatives of a note as scalar steps and implies the corresponding omission of one of the other degrees, usually that just preceding or just following the alternatives. Thus in the following illustration scale A would be diatonic, in spite of its augmented-second intervals, while scale B would be chromatic because both alternatives of Ga are used and Re, the second note, is omitted. The fact that scale B has an interval of a minor third—virtually the same as augmented second—has no bearing on the subject.

A

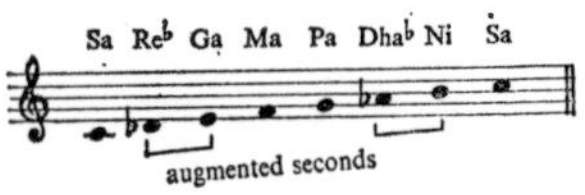

B

following example illustrating the successive use of both forms of Ni (VII):[1]

Ex. 5.

There is, however, a major exception to the scheme of alternative notes as outlined above. This is provided particularly by the *Lalit* group of *rāg*s in which both forms of the fourth, Ma♮ and Ma♯, commonly occur as consecutive steps. These will be discussed in greater detail in a later chapter. We may note here that it is primarily the two Ma's which sometimes provide exceptions to the rule that the *śuddh* and *vikr̲it* positions of a note are alternatives.

SCALE SPECIES

While many *rāg*s have both forms of one or more of the five movable notes, there are some from which one or two notes are omitted entirely—the Sa alone by definition cannot be omitted. Such *rāg*s are described as transilient. In North Indian theory *rāg*s are sometimes classified according to the number of notes they contain, the classes thus obtained being known as *jāti*s (species): *rāg*s with all of the seven notes are called *sampūrṇ* (complete), those with six, *ṣāḍav* (or *khāḍav*) and those with five, *auḍav*. These terms are equivalent to the Western hepta-, hexa- and pentatonic. It should be noted that alternatives do not count here as separate notes: in a heptatonic *rāg* any or all alternatives may be used as accidentals; similarly, in a pentatonic *rāg* any alternatives of the five notes of the *rāg* may be used as accidentals. The *rāg Vr̲indāvnī* (*Br̲indābnī*) *Sāraṅg*, for instance, is classified as pentatonic although both alternatives of Ni (VII) are used:[2]

JĀTI
SAMPŪRṆ
ṢĀḌAV
AUḌAV

Ex. 6. rāg Vr̲indāvnī Sāraṅg

[1] This is often an oversimplification of what actually occurs in practice. The circumstances are complicated by the fact that musicians have been preparing the ground for this sort of movement in certain *rāg*s perhaps for several generations. Consequently, there are instances when the preparation of the ground is taken as read. Some musicians avoid this apparent chromaticism entirely, but probably for the majority this is something which can be done in a few specific instances, and then only with nicety.

[2] *K.P.M.* III, p. 496. Bhātkhaṇḍe does not explain the exact significance of commas in his notations of *rāg*s. The commas are not used in his notations of *cīz* where the duration values are regulated by the *tāl*. In the *ālāp*-type of phrases of the *svarvistār*, the *āroh–avroh* and *pakaṛ*, which are

ṬHĀṬ The most important system of classifying *rāg*s is, however, in terms of heptatonic scales, *ṭhāṭ* (*thāṭ*), which are discussed in some detail in the next chapter.

MELODIC MOVEMENT

PAKAṚ **SVAR-VISTĀR**

It is not enough to define a *rāg* in terms of mode or scale alone, as a number of *rāg*s have the same notes, yet each maintains its own musical identity. When we examine different performances of the same *rāg* we find that, allowing for divergence of tradition and the possibility of experimentation, not only are the same notes consistently used, but also particular figurations or patterns of notes occur frequently. The most characteristic pattern of notes in a *rāg* is described as *pakaṛ*, a 'catch' phrase by which the *rāg* can be easily recognised. This is inevitably a subjective concept as *rāg*s are not generally limited to just one pattern and the 'catch' phrase of a *rāg* varies, to some extent at least, with the interpretation of the musician. A more complete delineation of a *rāg* is obtained in the *svarvistār*—a series of phrases devised to show the various note-patterns which are permissible in, and characteristic of, the *rāg*. These, too, are subject to varying interpretations.

VARṆ **STHĀYĪ** **ĀROH** **AVROH** **SAÑCĀRĪ**

These patterns of notes can be described in terms of their melodic movement, *varṇ*. Sanskrit treatises have recognised four types: *sthāyī*—steady, unchangeable; *āroh* (*ārohī*)—ascending; *avroh* (*avrohī*)—descending; and *sañcārī*—wandering, i.e. a mixture of ascent and descent. Only the terms *āroh* and *avroh* are now commonly used in the description of *rāg*s and refer to the most characteristic ascending and descending lines of a *rāg*, whether step by step or including irregular movements (*sañcārī varṇ*) if these are essential functional features of the *rāg*. For instance, in the *rāg* *Des* (*Deś*) the common *āroh* (ascent) is a step by step pentatonic movement

---

not regulated by *tāl*, a comma could indicate either a pause or the lengthening of the preceding note. The former seems highly improbable in view of the frequent occurrence of the comma which, if interpreted as a pause, would disjoint the melodic line, as can be seen in the following typical example (*K.P.M.* III, p. 23):

rāg Bhūpālī

Thus it would seem more reasonable to interpret it as extending the time value of the preceding note. There are no specific breathing indications except, by implication, at the end of variations in the *svarvistār* which are marked by bar lines, and we presume that breath may be taken as required.

In this work the notes preceding the comma have been given double the time value of the other notes; however, there is no evidence that Bhātkhaṇḍe intended such precise values and our notation system has been adopted for the convenience of the reader.

—which can be described as directional transilience—while the common *avroh* (descent) is heptatonic and has two irregular turns at *x* and *y*:

Ex. 7. rāg Des

These turns, which are characteristic features of certain *rāgs*, are

VAKR designated by the term *vakr* (crooked or oblique), and the note from which this oblique movement begins, i.e. Pa and Re in the example above,

VAKRSVAR is called *vakrsvar*[1] (oblique note).

On the basis of the given *āroh* and *avroh*, the *rāg Des* could be described as having a pentatonic ascent in which the Ga (III) and Dha (VI) are omitted, and a heptatonic descent in which Pa (V) and Re (II) are *vakrsvar* and Ni♭ (VII♭) replaces Ni♮ (VII♮). The terms *āroh* and *avroh* do not always refer to the typical ascending and descending lines in a *rāg*, but are sometimes used to indicate specific upward or downward movement. The dual implications of these terms occasionally create confusion. For instance, in describing the *rāg Kāmod*, Bhātkhaṇḍe states that the Ma♯ (IV♯) is used only in the *āroh*, and yet when he gives the typical *āroh* and *avroh* of the *rāg*, the Ma♯ occurs in both the lines:[2]

Ex. 8. rāg Kāmod

There is a further complication in the description of this *rāg*, for although the Ga (III) is omitted in the typical *āroh* line, it occurs in the ascending phrase Ga Ma♮ Pa (III IV♮ V) which is in the typical *avroh* line, and Bhātkhaṇḍe describes this *rāg* as being heptatonic in both *āroh* and *avroh*. It thus becomes necessary to distinguish clearly between the use of the terms to indicate the typical ascending and descending lines (which

[1] According to Bhātkhaṇḍe, only Re is *vakr* in the *rāg Des* (*K.P.M.* III, p. 521). However, in the *svarvistār* of this *rāg* (pp. 760–1) the Pa is frequently *vakr*, as in the example above.

[2] *K.P.M.* IV, p. 92.

may involve oblique movement), and the use of the terms to indicate the function of each individual note appearing in an ascending or descending context within a *rāg*. It is the latter which we must now discuss in greater detail.

There are two aspects to a note which belongs in a simple ascending movement: that it is approached from a lower note, and that the note following is higher. When these two conditions are fulfilled, it can be said that the note is clearly an ascending note. However, in certain *rāgs* it is permissible to approach a note from below, but the following note may not be a higher one. Here only one condition is fulfilled and it is a matter of interpretation whether this note should be considered as ascending or not. In fact, in both Indian musical theory and practice, it would not be considered an ascending note, as it leads downwards. This is commonly taken for granted in the system, and a note prohibited in ascent may generally be approached from below but must be followed by a lower note. The descending line in *rāg Des* provides a good illustration of this, where, although the Dha (VI) and Ga (III) are prohibited in ascent (except in certain phrases to be discussed later), the descending line has turns leading upwards to these notes (see *x* and *y*, Ex. 7). On the other hand, if a note may not be approached from below, but the following note is a higher one, that note is commonly thought to be in an ascending line; for instance, in the *rāg Kāmod* the Ma♯ (IV♯) can only be approached from above and is always followed by a higher note (see Ex. 8, *w*). These three possibilities are shown in the following examples, where L stands for a lower note, H for a higher note, and the note under consideration is represented by N:

Ex. 9.

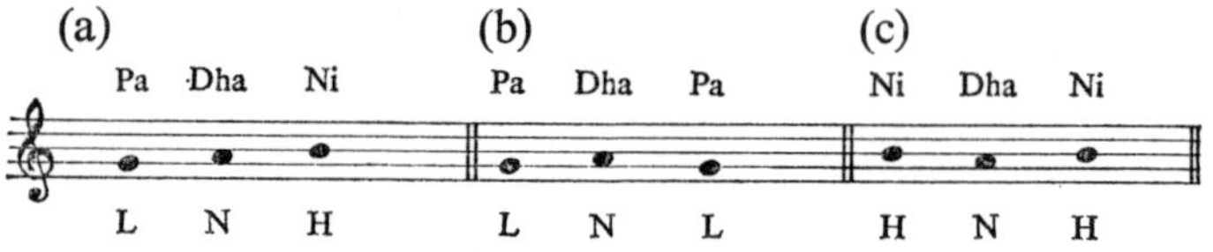

(a) N is clearly a direct ascending note.
(b) N is not an ascending note.
(c) N is an incomplete ascending note, and since it can only be approached by a turn from above (as in Ex. 8, *w*) it can also be referred to as an oblique (*vakr*) ascending note.

These same three possibilities also occur in relation to descent:

Ex. 10.

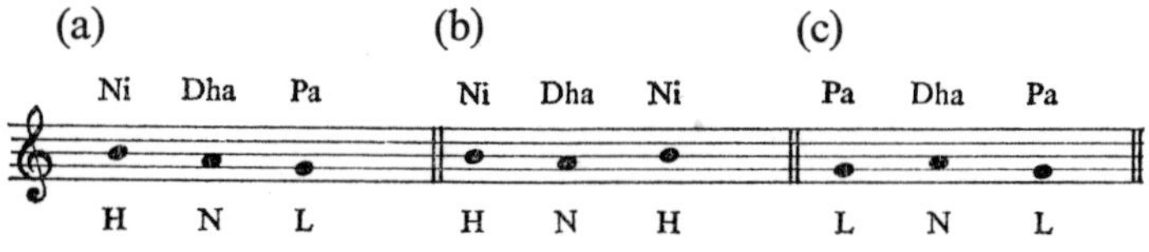

(a) N is a direct descending note.
(b) N is not a descending note (cf. Ex. 9c).
(c) N is an oblique descending note (cf. Ex. 9b).

There still remains one further distinction to be made. In some *rāg*s a note which is generally omitted in the ascending line may nevertheless occur as an ascending note in certain characteristic figures: for instance, in the *rāg Kāmod* (Ex. 8), where the Ga (III) is normally omitted in the ascending line but may be used as an ascending note in a melodic figure usually found in the descending line:

Ex. 11. rāg Kāmod

Here the use of the Ga as an ascending note limits the possibilities which may follow. In step by step movement the Dha (VI) may not be exceeded and the phrase is only felt to be completed by the cadential fragment *v*. A determining feature of this movement is that it does not extend into the next octave but turns back on itself. Thus Ga in *Kāmod* is an oblique ascending note (as it can only be approached from above) which occurs only in a discontinuous ascending figure, and can be described as a discontinuous, oblique ascending note. The Ma♮ (IV♮) in this *rāg* is not usually used in ascent, but occurs as a discontinuous, direct ascending note in the above example.

Similarly, in the *rāg Des*, both Ga (III) and Dha (VI), while omitted in the continuous, direct ascending line (see Ex. 4), may be used as discontinuous direct ascending notes, the former in melodic figures beginning and ending on the Re (II), the latter on the Pa (V):

Ex. 12. rāg Des

Bhātkhaṇḍe describes *Des* as heptatonic in both ascent and descent, with the qualification that the Ga and Dha are generally omitted in ascent,[1] but in fact, the continuous ascent of *Des* is pentatonic, the Ga and Dha being used only occasionally as discontinuous direct ascending notes.

[1] *K.P.M.* III, pp. 250–1. These discontinuous direct ascending notes can be heard in the *rāg Des* on the accompanying record.

IMPORTANT NOTES

In every *rāg* two notes, in theory, are given greater importance than the others. These notes are called *vādī*—sonant, and *saṃvādī*—consonant. According to Bhātkhaṇḍe the prime character of a *rāg* appears in the *vādī*.[1] The *vādī* is that note which is sounded clearly again and again, a note which is superabundant in a *rāg*.[2] The *saṃvādī* is described as being a note used less than the *vādī* but more than the other notes in the *rāg*. The *saṃvādī* should not be near the *vādī* as it will tend to detract from the importance of the *vādī*. Ideally it should be a perfect fifth away or, if that note is not present in the *rāg*, it should be one of the adjacent notes, the fourth or the sixth, preferably the former.[3] These definitions of *vādī* and *saṃvādī* appear to relate primarily to frequency of occurrence, but statistics applied to Bhātkhaṇḍe's own notations reveal irreconcilable inconsistencies.[4] Obviously much depends on the interpretation of the key phrase 'sounded clearly again and again', which Bhātkhaṇḍe does not clarify. He seems aware of the inadequacy of his definition and quotes a divergent view from the *Gīta Sūtra Sāra* by K. Banarjī (Bannerjee) in which the author questions the validity of these terms.[5]

VĀDĪ

SAṂVĀDĪ

Much of this difficulty seems to arise from the fact that *rāg*s have different facets which are successively developed in the course of a performance. In this connection Bhātkhaṇḍe equates *vādī* with *viśrānti svar* (or *maqām sthān*), terminal or resting notes, when he states that singers choose different notes on which to end their melodic phrases, momentarily presenting each of these notes as *vādī*, finally returning to the prescribed *vādī* without detriment to the *rāg*.[6] Thus in a particular *rāg* there are several important notes which may be emphasised either by frequency of occurrence or by their use as terminal notes. In theory the *vādī* is chosen because it is the most important note in the characteristic phrase (*pakaṛ*) of that *rāg*. There are, however, further qualifications. In all *rāg*s, the Sa (I) is a vitally important note, both as a frame of reference and as a melodic terminal. Yet the Sa is not a good candidate for the position of *vādī* because it is a feature common to all *rāg*s and gives no indication of the

VIŚRĀNTI SVAR

[1] *H.S.P.* I, p. 20.

[2] *K.P.M.* II, p. 14 and *K.P.M.* VI, p. 23.

[3] *H.S.P.* I, p. 22.

[4] In the *svarvistār* of *rāg Yaman*, as set out in *K.P.M.* II, pp. 487–8, there are 62 Sa, 83 Re, 70 Ga, 54 Ma, 74 Pa, 47 Dha and 45 Ni. On a statistical basis, Re should be *vādī* and Pa *saṃvādī*. Bhātkhaṇḍe, however, gives Ga as *vādī* and Ni as *saṃvādī*. In the other *rāg*s examined there is also a similar deviation between the most often used notes and Bhātkhaṇḍe's given *vādī* and *saṃvādī*. This is discussed further by A. N. Sanyal, *Ragas and Raginis*, Calcutta 1959, p. 20.

[5] *H.S.P.* I, pp. 79, 80. Banarjī gives an example of the *rāg Yaman* in which some say Pa is *vādī*, others Ga or even Re and Ni, suggesting that, in the hands of an expert, there may be even greater latitude. The important notes of this *rāg* are discussed in Appendix B on p. 205.

[6] *K.P.M.* V, p. 49.

character of a particular one. The same applies, although to a lesser extent, to the Pa (V). Further, Bhātkhaṇḍe's choice of *vādī* is often influenced by his

TIME THEORY

time theory which is an attempt to relate the musical characteristics of a *rāg* to its hour of performance.[1] In this connection, he divides the octave into

PŪRVĀṄG
UTTRĀṄG

two parts, *pūrvāṅg*, first portion, the lower tetrachord Sa to Ma (I to IV) or the pentachord Sa to Pa (I to V); and *uttrāṅg*, second portion, the upper tetrachord Pa to Ṡa (V to İ), or the pentachord from Ma to Ṡa (IV to İ). According to his theory, in the *rāgs* performed between noon and midnight the *pūrvāṅg* is emphasised, i.e. the *vādī* is in the lower tetrachord; while in the *rāgs* performed between midnight and noon the *uttrāṅg* is prominent, i.e. the *vādī* is in the upper tetrachord.

This theory tends to influence the choice of *vādī* in Bhātkhaṇḍe's system. For instance, in the *rāg Tilak Kāmod* the Ni (VII) is very prominent and is considered the *vādī* by a number of musicians. Bhātkhaṇḍe fully recognises the importance of this note in *Tilak Kāmod* when he says that the quality of the Ni in this *rāg* is so spectacular that nearly everyone recognises it from the (particular) way this note is used.[2] *Tilak Kāmod* is, however, sung at night and according to Bhātkhaṇḍe's theory should have its *vādī* in the lower tetrachord. In *K.P.M.* Bhātkhaṇḍe gives the *vādī* as Re (II) and the *saṃvādī* as Pa (V),[3] but in the *H.S.P.* he says that, according to experts, the Re is weak in descent[4] and gives the *vādī* as Sa (I).[5]

From the foregoing discussion it is apparent that the concept of *vādī* and *saṃvādī* is not quite consistent with present-day musical practice. The terms have been used in the musical treatises since the *Nāṭyaśāstra* where *vādī*—sonant, *saṃvādī*—consonant, *vivādī*—dissonant and *anuvādī*—assonant (i.e. neutral) represent a general theory of consonance which is now either forgotten or has at least lost its earlier significance as Fox Strangways has pointed out.[6] The terms, however, have persisted to the present time. The original concept appears to have been quite reasonable. Only perfect fourths and fifths were recognised as consonant, while the semitone and/or perhaps the major seventh was recognised as dissonant. The other intervals were considered assonant. These terms were thus

[1] Bhātkhaṇḍe's time theory has been described in *Rāgas and Rāginīs*, by O. C. Gangoly, Bombay, reprinted 1948, pp. 90–2. The time theory of *rāgs* is a controversial subject and there are several different attitudes which may briefly be expressed here. There are some who will not tolerate a *rāg* at any but the prescribed time. Bhātkhaṇḍe is not so dogmatic, but states that a particular *rāg* sounds especially beautiful at a particular time. Some musicians look at this matter in an entirely different light; they feel that if a particular *rāg* is performed well it will create an atmosphere of a particular time of day or night. Finally, there are those who believe that the time theory has no application to present-day practice and Banarjī, quoted in *H.S.P.* I, p. 75, says that the tradition of performing *rāgs* at particular times of the day and night is 'purely imaginary'.

[2] *H.S.P.* I, p. 243.

[3] *K.P.M.* III, p. 297.

[4] *H.S.P.* I, p. 250.

[5] *H.S.P.* I, p. 243.

[6] Fox Strangways, *The Music of Hindostan*, p. 114.

intended to express the phenomena of consonance and dissonance as conceived in that period. Obviously consonance and dissonance were particularly significant in relation to the important notes in a mode (*jāti*).

AṂŚA These important notes were designated by the term *aṃśa*. Bharata, the author of *Nāṭyaśāstra*, says, 'That note which is the *aṃśa*, that note is *vādī*',[1] indicating that the *aṃśa* is the sonant note whose consonance and dissonance are particularly important, not that *vādī* is a synonym of *aṃśa*. But later writers have equated the two terms, and so *vādī* has come to mean important note and the term *aṃśa* has now become redundant.

This has led to some confusion. Whereas in Bharata's time modes frequently had several important notes (*aṃśa*s), and indeed there was one, *Ṣaḍjamadhyamā*, in which all the seven notes were considered important, the present-day *rāg*s can have designated only one *vādī* and one secondary important note, *saṃvādī*. The ancient *saṃvādī*s comprised the consonant fourth and fifth, while the present *saṃvādī* refers to the second most important note in a *rāg*, which, to preserve the importance of the *vādī*, is removed from it by generally a fifth or fourth, not necessarily perfect intervals,[2] or perhaps by a sixth.[3]

VIVĀDĪ ANUVĀDĪ The terms *vivādī* (dissonant) and *anuvādī* (assonant) are also occasionally used at the present time, especially by theoreticians. *Vivādī* as 'disputing' is particularly meaningless in the present context in which the minor second and the major seventh have a very prominent place in the system. Bhātkhaṇḍe explains *vivādī* as that note which, when used in a *rāg*, would damage it, and refers to it as *varjitsvar*—omitted note. He concedes that the *vivādī* may, however, be used by expert singers and players without detriment to the *rāg*.[4] Here again the precise meaning of the term remains unclear. Are all the omitted notes called *vivādī*, or just those notes which may occasionally be used by experts, but are not essential to the *rāg*? In discussing the *rāg Kāmod*,[5] he says that sometimes Ni♭ (VII♭) may be used in descent as a *vivādī* note, indicating that it is the latter meaning

VARJIT-SVAR

[1] *Nāṭyaśāstra*, 'Kāshi Sanskrit Series' (No. 60), prose following śl. 20, chapter 28.

[2] *K.P.M.* III, p. 612. In *rāg Pīlū*, for example, the *vādī* is given as Ga♭ and the *saṃvādī* as Ni♮—an augmented fifth. The same applies to the *rāg Mārvā* where *vādī* and *saṃvādī* are given as Re♭ and Dha♮. Some musicologists are disturbed by the fact that these two do not form a perfect interval and give Dha♮ and Ga♮ as its *vādī* and *saṃvādī*. V. N. Paṭvardhan in *Rāg Vijñān*, Vol. II, p. 1, discussing *rāg Mārvā*, says, 'Re♭ is prominent in its lower tetrachord (*pūrvāṅg*), Dha in its upper tetrachord (*uttrāṅg*). . . . Sometimes one also pauses on Ga, because Ga makes a consonant (*saṃvādī*) relationship with Dha. But if this is done often it gives the appearance of the *rāg Pūriyā*. . . . It is customary to give Re♭ and Dha as *vādī* and *saṃvādī* of *Mārvā*, but seen from the point of view of the *śāstra*s (treatises) it is not possible for Re♭ and Dha♮ to be *saṃvādī* (i.e. consonant) to each other. For this reason, in our opinion it is proper to accept Dha as *vādī* and Ga as *saṃvādī*.' These comments reflect the confusion which prevails among musicologists regarding the interpretation of these terms. A further discussion of the *rāg Mārvā* will be found in Appendix B on p. 202.

[3] Some musicians also accept the third as *saṃvādī*.

[4] *K.P.M.* II, p. 14.

[5] *K.P.M.* IV, p. 92.

that he has in mind. When this *vivādī* or accidental is used with sensitivity, it is considered particularly beautiful—a far cry from its original meaning of dissonant. The term *anuvādī* still refers to the notes in a *rāg* other than *vādī*, *saṃvādī* and *vivādī*, though these may, in the present period, include the perfect fourth or fifth of the *vādī*.

To summarise, Bhātkhaṇḍe's choice of *vādī* for a *rāg* is influenced by three factors:

1. It should be an important note in the characteristic phrase of the *rāg*.
2. It should belong to the correct part of the octave in relation to his time theory.
3. Sa (I), and to a lesser degree Pa (V), are less meaningful as *vādī* than the other notes because they give little indication of the character of the *rāg* and so become *vādī* only when there is no other reasonable possibility to fit his time theory. It will be seen that much depends on the validity of the time theory. This is difficult to assess, but the fact that the theory is widely accepted in India suggests that it is reconcilable, at least to some extent, with the time of day at which *rāg*s are traditionally performed.[1] We shall have more to say about the time theory in the chapter following.

SUMMARY

This discussion of technical terms can be concluded with a summary of the principal features by which a *rāg* may be distinguished from others:

1. Basic notes used (*ṭhāṭ*).
2. Transilience (*sampūrṇ*, *ṣāḍav*, *auḍav*).
3. Emphasised notes (*vādī*, *saṃvādī*).
4. Ascending and descending lines (*āroh*, *avroh*):
    (a) alternative notes used as accidentals (*vivādī*?);
    (b) directional transilience;
    (c) oblique movement (*vakr*).
5. Register of emphasis (*sthān–mandr*, *madhy*, *tār*).
6. Shakes (*āndolan*) and intonation (*śruti*).

These factors will be discussed in the following pages.

[1] There are, of course, differing traditions regarding the time at which *rāg*s should be performed and no time theory can satisfy all of these.

III

Ṭhāṭ

In North Indian classical music *rāgs* are generally classified into groups according to scale. These scales are called *ṭhāṭ* (*thāṭ*, *ṭhāṭh*—framework) or sometimes *mel* (*mela*). In Bhātkhaṇḍe's system the term *ṭhāṭ* applies only to those scales which fulfil certain conditions:[1]

1. A *ṭhāṭ* must have seven notes.
2. The notes must be in sequence Sa Re Ga Ma Pa Dha and Ni (whether *śuddh* or *vikṟit* position—both versions of a single note being forbidden).
3. A *ṭhāṭ* does not have separate ascending and descending lines (as do *rāgs*).
4. A *ṭhāṭ* does not have any emotional quality (in contrast with *rāgs* which, by definition, have the power to convey emotions).
5. *Ṭhāṭs* are named after prominent *rāgs* in order to make them easy to remember and recognise, whether or not these *rāgs* are heptatonic.

In summary it can be said that, of all possible musical scales, only heptatonic, diatonic[2] scales are called *ṭhāṭ*.

In accordance with these conditions, thirty-two scales are possible: one with all natural notes, five with one altered note, ten with two altered notes, ten with three altered notes, five with four altered notes and one with all five altered notes. With a few exceptions to be discussed later, these thirty-two scales could provide the framework for the classification of the *rāgs* used at the present time.

Each of these thirty-two scales is related to five others which differ from it in only one note. Thus the *śuddh* or 'natural' scale (*Bilāval ṭhāṭ*) is related to the five other scales which have only one altered note. Each of these, in turn, is connected with five scales, one of which is *Bilāval*, while the remaining four each have an additional altered note. Similar relationships extend throughout the system, and for convenience the thirty-two scales (as well as three other important scales to be considered later in these pages) are set out in full on p. 47. Their sequence is discussed and their relationships further defined in Appendix A, The System of 32 *Ṭhāṭs*, on p. 181.

[1] *K.P.M.* II, p. 12.
[2] The terms diatonic and chromatic are defined on p. 36, f.n.2.

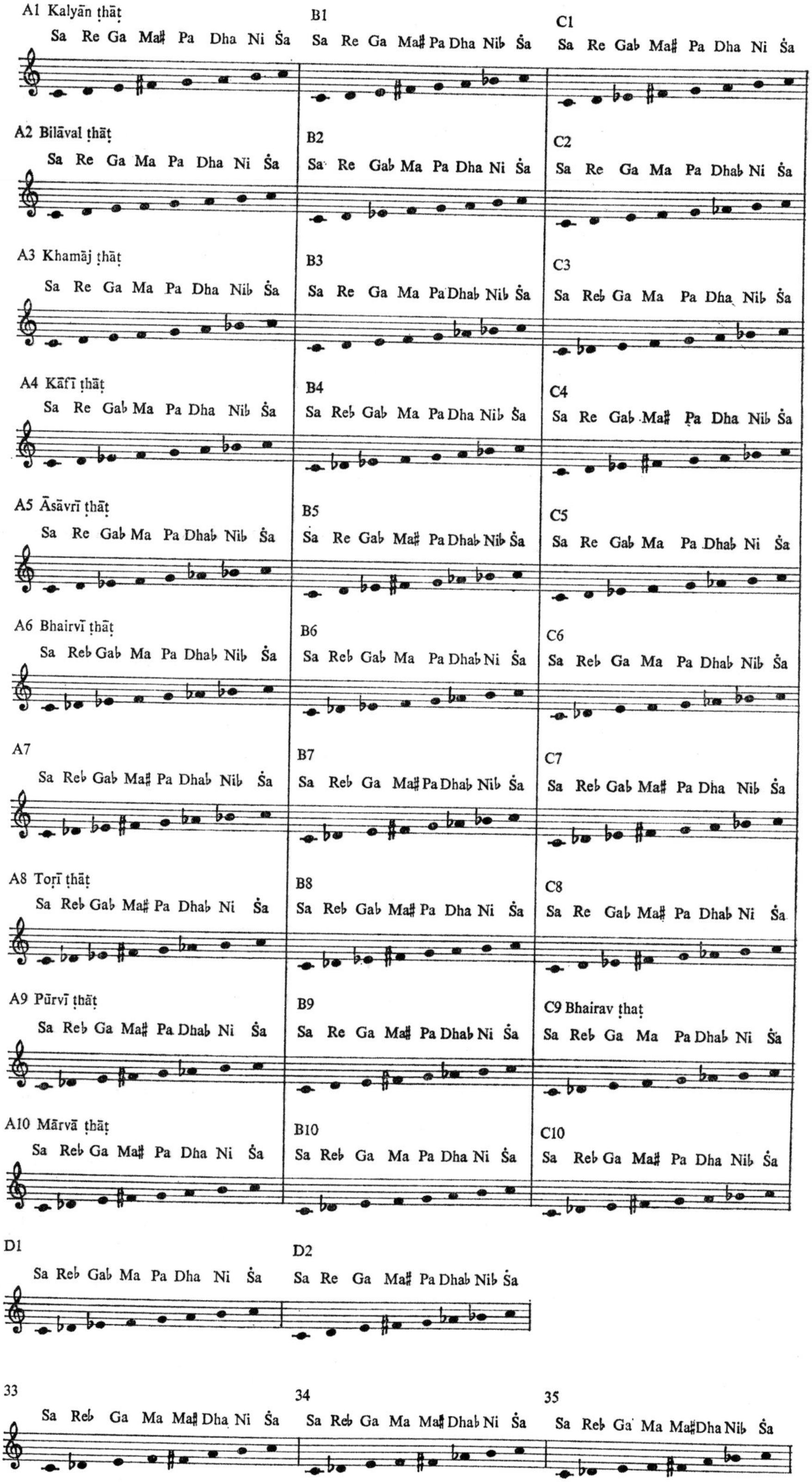
A1 Kalyān ṭhāṭ
Sa Re Ga Ma♯ Pa Dha Ni Ṡa
B1
Sa Re Ga Ma♯ Pa Dha Ni♭ Ṡa
C1
Sa Re Ga♭ Ma♯ Pa Dha Ni Ṡa
A2 Bilāval ṭhāṭ
Sa Re Ga Ma Pa Dha Ni Ṡa
B2
Sa Re Ga♭ Ma Pa Dha Ni Ṡa
C2
Sa Re Ga Ma Pa Dha♭ Ni Ṡa
A3 Khamāj ṭhāṭ
Sa Re Ga Ma Pa Dha Ni♭ Ṡa
B3
Sa Re Ga Ma Pa Dha♭ Ni♭ Ṡa
C3
Sa Re♭ Ga Ma Pa Dha Ni♭ Ṡa
A4 Kāfī ṭhāṭ
Sa Re Ga♭ Ma Pa Dha Ni♭ Ṡa
B4
Sa Re♭ Ga♭ Ma Pa Dha Ni♭ Ṡa
C4
Sa Re Ga♭ Ma♯ Pa Dha Ni♭ Ṡa
A5 Āsāvrī ṭhāṭ
Sa Re Ga♭ Ma Pa Dha♭ Ni♭ Ṡa
B5
Sa Re Ga♭ Ma♯ Pa Dha♭ Ni♭ Ṡa
C5
Sa Re Ga♭ Ma Pa Dha♭ Ni Ṡa
A6 Bhairvī ṭhāṭ
Sa Re♭ Ga♭ Ma Pa Dha♭ Ni♭ Ṡa
B6
Sa Re♭ Ga♭ Ma Pa Dha♭ Ni Ṡa
C6
Sa Re♭ Ga Ma Pa Dha♭ Ni♭ Ṡa
A7
Sa Re♭ Ga♭ Ma♯ Pa Dha♭ Ni♭ Ṡa
B7
Sa Re♭ Ga Ma♯ Pa Dha♭ Ni♭ Ṡa
C7
Sa Re♭ Ga♭ Ma♯ Pa Dha Ni♭ Ṡa
A8 Toṛī ṭhāṭ
Sa Re♭ Ga♭ Ma♯ Pa Dha♭ Ni Ṡa
B8
Sa Re♭ Ga♭ Ma♯ Pa Dha Ni Ṡa
C8
Sa Re Ga♭ Ma♯ Pa Dha♭ Ni Ṡa
A9 Pūrvī ṭhāṭ
Sa Re♭ Ga Ma♯ Pa Dha♭ Ni Ṡa
B9
Sa Re Ga Ma♯ Pa Dha♭ Ni Ṡa
C9 Bhairav ṭhaṭ
Sa Re♭ Ga Ma Pa Dha♭ Ni Ṡa
A10 Mārvā ṭhāṭ
Sa Re♭ Ga Ma♯ Pa Dha Ni Ṡa
B10
Sa Re♭ Ga Ma Pa Dha Ni Ṡa
C10
Sa Re♭ Ga Ma♯ Pa Dha Ni♭ Ṡa
D1
Sa Re♭ Ga♭ Ma Pa Dha Ni Ṡa
D2
Sa Re Ga Ma♯ Pa Dha♭ Ni♭ Ṡa
33
Sa Re♭ Ga Ma Ma♯ Dha Ni Ṡa
34
Sa Re♭ Ga Ma Ma♯ Dha♭ Ni Ṡa
35
Sa Re♭ Ga Ma Ma♯ Dha Ni♭ Ṡa

These scales are implicit in Bhātkhaṇḍe's definition of *ṭhāṭ*, yet they are not all mentioned by him.[1] Having defined *ṭhāṭ*, he states that nearly all the *rāg*s used in North Indian classical music can be distributed among the following ten *ṭhāṭ*s:

1. *Kalyāṇ* (No. A1)
2. *Bilāval* (No. A2)
3. *Khamāj* (No. A3)
4. *Bhairav* (No. C9)
5. *Pūrvī* (No. A9)
6. *Mārvā* (No. A10)
7. *Kāfī* (No. A4)
8. *Āsāvrī* (No. A5)
9. *Bhairvī* (No. A6)
10. *Toṛī* (No. A8)

Bhātkhaṇḍe does acknowledge the existence of *rāg*s in scales other than the above, but, as these are relatively few, he ascribes them to one or other of the above ten *ṭhāṭ*s as follows:

rāg Lalit (No. 33) ascribed to *Mārvā ṭhāṭ* (No. A10)
rāg Basant (*Vasant*) *Mukhārī* (No. C6) ascribed to *Bhairvī ṭhāṭ* (No. A6)
rāg Ānand Bhairav (No. B10) ascribed to *Bhairav ṭhāṭ* (No. C9)
rāg Ahīr Bhairav (No. C3) ascribed to *Bhairav ṭhāṭ* (No. C9)

At the present time there are several other *rāg*s not mentioned by Bhātkhaṇḍe, whose scales do not readily fit into the ten *ṭhāṭ* system. Some of these are given below:

rāg Madhukānt (No. C4)
rāg Madhuvantī (No. C1)
rāg Naṭ Bhairav (No. C2)
rāg Cārukeśī (No. B3)
rāg Simhendra Madhyamā (No. C8)
rāg Ahīr Lalit (No. 35)
rāg Lalit (No. 34)
(common version today)
rāg Kīrvāṇī (No. C5)
rāg Paṭdīp[2] (No. B2)

About twenty of the thirty-two scales are actually in use today and the number appears to be increasing. Some, like *Cārukeśī*, *Simhendra Madhyamā* and *Kīrvāṇī*, have recently been borrowed from the South Indian classical system which has many more scale possibilities than the North Indian system since it admits chromaticisms foreign to the North. The South Indian system acknowledges seventy-two scales (*melakartā*) which include the thirty-two we have been discussing. The remainder involve the use of the augmented second and sixth (which in North Indian terms may be expressed as Re♯ and Dha♯) and the diminished minor third and seventh (Ga♭♭ and Ni♭♭). The South Indian system of seventy-two scales was first introduced, largely as a theoretical exercise, by Veṅkaṭamakhī in the *Caturdaṇḍīprakāśikā* (1660), only nineteen of them being currently found in practice.[3] Subsequently, songs[4] have

[1] H. L. Roy, in *Problems of Hindustani Music*, p. 118, states that he wrote of these thirty-two scales to Bhātkhaṇḍe in 1932 who agreed that these scales would be adequate for the needs of present-day North Indian music. However, Bhātkhaṇḍe's system of ten *ṭhāṭ*s had been well established by this time and one can understand his reluctance to introduce a new system.

[2] Bhātkhaṇḍe does refer to this *rāg* as *Pradīpkī* or *Paṭdīpkī* and ascribes it to *Kāfī ṭhāṭ* (No. A4), since in his version there is also a Ni♭ (VII♭). At the present time it is commonly heard with only Ni♮ (VII♮).

[3] *Caturdaṇḍīprakāśikā*, The Music Academy, Madras, 1934, p. 52.

[4] The instrumental tradition in South India is based largely on vocal compositions.

actually been composed in all seventy-two, with the result that a greater variety of scales is used in South Indian music than in the North. We may expect enterprising and progressive North Indian musicians to continue to adopt some of the South Indian scales, particularly those which are diatonic. It is thus valuable to extend the North Indian system beyond Bhātkhaṇḍe's ten *ṭhāṭ*s and to accept the thirty-two diatonic scales as the basis for the classification of *rāg*s in North India.[1]

In addition to these thirty-two scales there are three *rāg*s in which there is apparently a form of chromaticism. In these, the two versions of *Lalit* and *Ahīr Lalit*,[2] both the natural and the sharpened fourth (Ma♮ and Ma♯) are used in succession. This is a particularly North Indian development since they are not included in the seventy-two South Indian scales. There are indications that this is not really 'chromaticism' and that the Ma♯ is, in effect, a diminished fifth which would perhaps have been called Pa♭ were it not that Pa is considered an immovable note. This view can be justified to some extent by a consideration of alternative notes. If the Ma♯ is indeed an augmented fourth we should be able to find some evidence among the *rāg*s to show that it temporarily replaces the natural fourth (Ma♮). Similarly if it is an alternative for the fifth (Pa) and temporarily replaces it, it would be quite legitimate to consider it a diminished fifth (Pa♭). There are many *rāg*s in which the Ma♯ is in fact an augmented fourth and temporarily replaces the natural fourth. The *rāg Rāmkalī* of *Bhairav ṭhāṭ* (No. C9) is one such example. Bhātkhaṇḍe gives its ascending and descending lines as follows:[3]

Ex. 13. rāg Rāmkalī

Initially the natural fourth is followed by the fifth (at *x*) but later (in the phrase *y*) the fifth is preceded by the *augmented fourth*. The two fourths, however, do not occur together in sequence. It is evident that the augmented fourth temporarily replaces the scalar natural fourth of *Bhairav ṭhāṭ* in the phrase *y* which is constructed around the Pa, just as Ni♭ temporarily replaces the scalar Ni♮ in this same phrase.

In certain other *rāg*s, however, the Ma♯ is really a diminished fifth and is an alternative for the Pa. In the *rāg Bhairvī*, for instance, the first two phrases (a and b) in the following example are permissible and are often played,[4] but the third phrase (c) is not generally acceptable:

[1] This is particularly significant in view of the fact that certain well-known musicians, among whom *Paṇḍit* Ravi Shankar is one, find the ten *ṭhāṭ* system quite inadequate and prefer to use the South Indian seventy-two *melakartā* system as a theoretical basis, in spite of the fact that it includes a number of 'chromatic' scales.

[2] A *rāg* said to have been invented by *Paṇḍit* Ravi Shankar.

[3] *K.P.M.* IV, p. 312.

[4] These phrases can be heard on the record of *Bhairvī* played by *Ustād* Ali Akbar Khan, H.M.V. ALPC 2.

Ex. 14. rāg Bhairvī

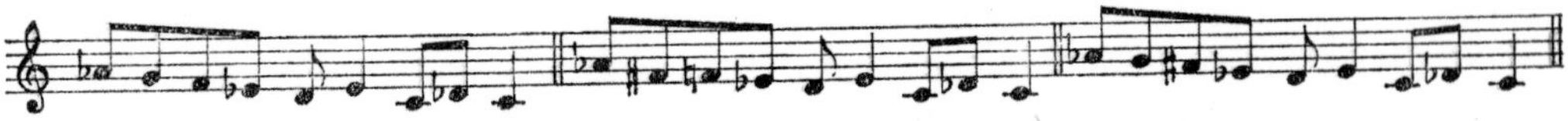

It is interesting that musicians do not appear to distinguish between the Ma♯ as an augmented fourth and the Ma♯ as a diminished fifth, thereby reinforcing the argument for a twelve semitone system.[1] Because this distinction is not made, it is not always possible to determine whether, in a particular instance, it is an alternative for the natural fourth or the natural fifth, especially as there are *rāg*s in which the Ma♯ appears to function in both ways at different moments. In the *rāg Lalit Pañcam*, for example, which Bhātkhaṇḍe gives in *Bhairav ṭhāṭ* (No. C9), both the following two phrases appear:[2]

Ex. 15. rāg Lalit Pañcam

In the former the Ma♯ (IV♯) presumably replaces the natural fourth of the *ṭhāṭ*, while in the latter it replaces the fifth.

The fact that in the two versions of the *rāg Lalit* and in *Ahīr Lalit* as well the Ma♮ and the Ma♯ may be used in succession (the natural fifth is absent in these *rāgs*) suggests quite clearly that the Ma♯ is, in fact, a diminished fifth:[3]

Ex. 16. rāg Lalit (Bhātkhaṇḍe's tradition)

Bhātkhaṇḍe classifies *Lalit* as a hexatonic (*ṣāḍav*) *rāg*, in which the fifth is omitted, implying that the Ma♯ replaces the Ma♮. There is some justification for this as there is

[1] In Just Intonation the augmented fourth and diminished fifth are, respectively, 590 cents and 610 cents. In Pythagorean Intonation they are 612 cents and 588 cents. It is in the Tempered twelve semitone system that these two are the same at 600 cents (Willi Apel, *The Harvard Dictionary of Music*, London 1960, p. 362).

[2] *K.P.M.* V, p. 362 and p. 509, var. 6. The function of the Ma♯ is extremely complex in this *rāg* and Bhātkhaṇḍe also gives phrases in which a succession of semitones is used, e.g. (V, p. 509, var. 10):

[3] *K.P.M.* IV, p. 490.

a clearly noticeable tendency to omit the natural fourth in the flow of movement; yet it is used as a resolution since the secondary drone is generally tuned to this note:

Ex. 17. *rāg Lalit*

This, however, does not necessarily indicate that the Ma♮ is omitted to avoid chromaticism. In the same *rāg* the ground-note Sa (which has no chromatic counterpart) is also omitted in the flow of movement, while it, too, occurs at the end of a phrase as a resolution:[1]

Ex. 18. *rāg Lalit*

It would seem reasonable to consider the Ma♯ in these *rāgs* as a diminished fifth rather than an augmented fourth. The *rāgs* could then be described as heptatonic and diatonic, in spite of the occurrence of the two Ma's in succession. The scales of these three *rāgs* cannot be accommodated in the thirty-two *ṭhāṭ* scheme, but would require another complete system of thirty-two scales having a diminished fifth. In view of the limited number of such scales in use this hardly appears to be justifiable at the present time. Admittedly, chromatic passages, some of which may be inspired by Western music, are increasingly heard in North Indian music. As yet they are used only for special effects and have not altered the structure of the music, but there is a possibility that continued experimentation in this direction may eventually lead to the introduction of chromatic scales.

Before we examine the validity of Bhātkhaṇḍe's system of ten *ṭhāṭs* in relation to present-day North Indian classical music, we must discuss the inadequacies of this kind of heptatonic *ṭhāṭ* system as a basis for classifying *rāgs*.

A prime difficulty occurs in the classification of hexatonic and pentatonic *rāgs* which could fit equally well in more than one heptatonic *ṭhāṭ*. The pentatonic *rāg* *Bhūpālī*, for example, could be classified in any of four *ṭhāṭs*: *Kalyāṇ* (No. A1),

Ex. 19. *rāg Bhūpālī*

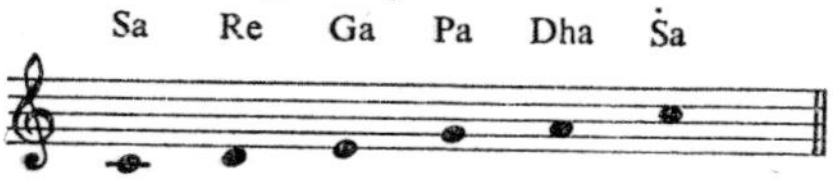

[1] *K.P.M.* IV, p. 821.

Bilāval (No. A2), *Khamāj* (No. A3) and the *ṭhāṭ* with Ma♯ (IV♯) and Ni♭ (VII♭) (No. B1) which is not used in classical music at present. These *ṭhāṭ*s differ from each other only in the use of the alternatives of the Ma and Ni, the very notes omitted in the *rāg Bhūpālī*. Bhātkhaṇḍe classifies this *rāg* in *Kalyāṇ ṭhāṭ*, implying that the omitted notes are, in fact, the sharpened fourth and the natural seventh. This is, of course, impossible to confirm on purely objective grounds. One reason he gives for this classification is that *Bhūpālī* is also called *Bhūp Kalyāṇ* by some musicians.[1] However, there seems less justification for his classification of the pentatonic *rāg Mālśrī* in this same *ṭhāṭ*, and a strong case can be made for its inclusion in *Pūrvī ṭhāṭ* (No. A9) as the *rāgs Śrī* and *Jetśrī*, which are connected at least in name, both belong to this *ṭhāṭ*. Musically too *Mālśrī* resembles the heptatonic *Jetśrī* which is pentatonic in ascent, omitting Re♭ (II♭) and Dha♭ (VI♭), the very notes omitted in *Mālśrī*. In ascent *Jetśrī* and *Mālśrī* are identical in scale:

Ex. 20. *rāgs Mālśrī* and *Jetśrī* (ascent)

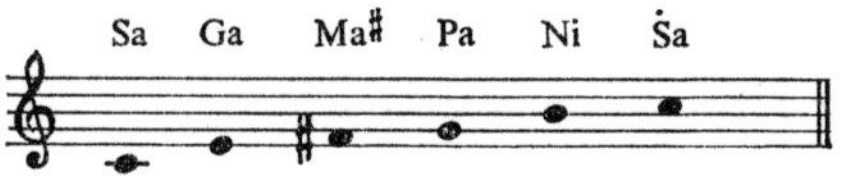

It might be thought reasonable to consider that the resemblance both in name and in melodic features is not entirely fortuitous.[2] But this argument is not conclusive since there are instances of *rāgs* which, though related in name, do not have the same scale.

A second difficulty lies in determining the basic scale of a *rāg* in which more than one of the alternative notes are used. In the *rāg Des*, for example, Ni♮ is used in the ascending line and Ni♭ in the descending:[3]

Ex. 21. *rāg Des*

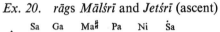

This *rāg* could be classified either in *Bilāval ṭhāṭ* (No. A2) with the Ni♭ as an accidental, or in *Khamāj ṭhāṭ* (No. A3) with the Ni♮ as an accidental. Bhātkhaṇḍe chooses the latter course, thereby giving importance to the descending line. This is a reasonable criterion of classification since cadential phrases, which are of considerable importance in *rāgs*, are generally descending. However, he does not apply it consistently. Many of the *rāgs* which he ascribes to *Kalyāṇ ṭhāṭ* (No. A1), for instance the

[1] *H.S.P.* I, p. 86.

[2] In the chapter on Transilient Scales (p. 122) we suggest, however, that *Mālśrī* is the pentatonic derivative of *Mārvā ṭhāṭ*.

[3] *K.P.M.* III, p. 251.

*rāg*s *Kedār* (*Kedārā*) and *Hamīr*, have Ma♮ (IV♮) in both ascending and descending lines, while the Ma♯ (IV♯) occurs only as an oblique ascending note. The classification of *Kedār* in *Kalyāṇ ṭhāṭ* becomes quite incomprehensible as Bhātkhaṇḍe gives the Ma♮ as the *vādī* in this *rāg*. It seems quite unreasonable to consider the most important and the 'most often used note' of a *rāg* as an accidental, i.e. as not being part of the basic scale of the *rāg*.

There are genuine difficulties in the classification of certain *rāg*s in which several alternative notes may be used. The *rāg Pīlū*, for example, in which all the alternatives are permitted, is classified by Bhātkhaṇḍe in *Kāfī ṭhāṭ* (No. A4), while Grosset gave its scale as the *ṭhāṭ* with Ga♭ and Dha♭ (No. C5).[1]

From the foregoing discussion it will be apparent that there is an element of subjectivity in the classification of *rāg*s according to scale. The *rāg*s *Kedār* and *Hamīr* referred to above might easily be classified in *Bilāval ṭhāṭ* (No. A2) with the Ma♯ as an accidental. In this particular instance, as in many others, the choice lies between two scales, both of which are among the ten *ṭhāṭ*s of Bhātkhaṇḍe's system. There seems little doubt that his ten *ṭhāṭ*s are very prominent in North Indian classical music today. In each of them there are a number of *rāg*s, varying from seven in *Toṛī* (No. A8) to as many as forty-two in *Kāfī* (No. A4) according to Bhātkhaṇḍe's system of classification. In contrast there is at most only one *rāg* in each of the other scales listed on p. 48.

Where there are many *rāg*s in one *ṭhāṭ*, each of these is, of necessity, clearly delineated by its characteristic melodic patterns. Were this not so, *rāg*s would merge one into another and lose their identity. When there is only a single *rāg* in a particular *ṭhāṭ*—such *rāg*s are described as 'isolate'—the melodic possibilities are not so closely defined since the *rāg* can always be distinguished from others on the basis of scale. Two musicians may evolve quite different melodic characteristics in these 'isolate' *rāg*s. For instance, in the *rāg Naṭ Bhairav* (No. C2), *Paṇḍit* Ravi Shankar tends to use successive minor thirds (Dha♭ to Ni is really an augmented second) thus omitting the Sa, Ga and Pa (I, III and V)[2] (Ex. 22a), while *Ustād* Ali Akbar Khan often omits the Ga and Ni (III and VII)[3] (Ex. 22b):

Ex. 22. rāg Naṭ Bhairav

This difference is found even though both musicians belong to the same tradition

[1] J. Grosset in A. Lavignac, *Encyclopédie de la Musique*, Paris 1921, première partie, p. 326.
[2] H.M.V. disc, 78 r.p.m. No. N 94756.
[3] H.M.V. disc, 45 r.p.m. No. 7 EPE 1219.

(*gharānā*) and have been taught by the same teacher, *Ustād* Allauddin Khan. Nevertheless, both versions are recognisable as *Naṭ Bhairav*, principally because there is no other *rāg* with this scale. Here we may see the beginning of a process which could eventually result in two differentiated melodic patterns crystallising from the one scale. If both versions are propagated, they may some day be differentiated in name. It is not unreasonable to suppose that it was a similar process which has led to the differentiation of *rāg*s based on the same scale. From this we could say that a large number of *rāg*s in any scale is an indication of the antiquity of that scale, since the process of crystallisation of *rāg*s and their widespread acceptance must be reckoned in terms of generations. The very large number of *rāg*s in *Kāfī ṭhāṭ* is a case in point, for this scale is the modern counterpart of the ancient Indian *Ṣaḍjagrāma*. While time is an essential factor, the rate of this process of crystallisation is also influenced by the popularity of the scale, and this factor is particularly significant today in view of the ease of communication. *Bhairav ṭhāṭ* (No. C9) did not belong to the ancient Indian modal system, and yet Bhātkhaṇḍe gives as many as eighteen *rāg*s in this *ṭhāṭ*.

On the other hand, the 'isolate' *rāg*s clearly suggest their relatively recent introduction into North Indian music, although there is the slight possibility that an old *rāg*, which has not been generally accepted, is preserved relatively unchanged in a family of musicians. If, in the course of time, these *rāg*s are accepted and performed frequently, we may expect that individual melodic features will crystallise into several separate *rāg*s and that they will no longer be 'isolate'.

Bhātkhaṇḍe's ten *ṭhāṭ* system does not allow for these 'isolate' *rāg*s, most of which may be thought of as modern experiments. Experimentation has certainly been going on in India for several hundred years and some of the *rāg*s which are mentioned in texts over this period are no longer heard in North India. Bhātkhaṇḍe's ten *ṭhāṭ*s give an indication of the principal scales used in present-day North Indian classical music —scales which have withstood the test of time. It is not unreasonable to presume that these ten scales have greater musical justification within the Indian system than do the others of the thirty-two.

Bhātkhaṇḍe has organised the ten *ṭhāṭ*s in a classificatory order, to some extent in imitation of the South Indian *melakartā* system.[1] The first three *ṭhāṭ*s, *Kalyāṇ*, *Bilāval* and *Khamāj*, have Re♮ and Ga♮ (II♮ and III♮); the next three, *Bhairav*, *Pūrvī* and *Mārvā*, have Re♭ and Ga♮ (II♭ and III♮); the next two, *Kāfī* and *Āsāvrī*, have Re♮ and Ga♭ (II♮ and III♭); while the last two, *Bhairvī* and *Toṛī*, have Re♭ and Ga♭ (II♭ and III♭). Although this kind of arrangement is convenient, it tends to obscure the relationship between the *ṭhāṭ*s. For example, *Khamāj ṭhāṭ* (No. A3) is followed by the very dissimilar *Bhairav ṭhāṭ* (No. C9).

Six of the ten *ṭhāṭ*s, *Kalyāṇ*, *Bilāval*, *Khamāj*, *Kāfī*, *Āsāvrī* and *Bhairvī*, are musically related as they are serial progressions of each other; in other words, beginning with

[1] The South Indian *melakartā* system is described in the introduction to the *Mela-rāga-mālikā* of Mahā-vaidya-nātha Śivan, Adyar 1937.

any one of these scales, the others can be derived by treating each successive degree as the ground-note for the new scale. In Western musicology these progressions, known as modes, are sometimes referred to by the names of their ground-note, taking the 'natural' scale beginning on the note C as the standard.[1] Thus the D mode refers to that succession of intervals obtained by playing, for instance, the white notes of a piano from D to d. These serial modes with their modern Indian counterparts are shown below.

'C' mode
Bilāval ṭhāṭ

'D' mode
Kāfī ṭhāṭ

'E' mode
Bhairvī ṭhāṭ

'F' mode
Kalyāṇ ṭhāṭ

'G' mode
Khamāj ṭhāṭ

'A' mode
Āsāvrī ṭhāṭ

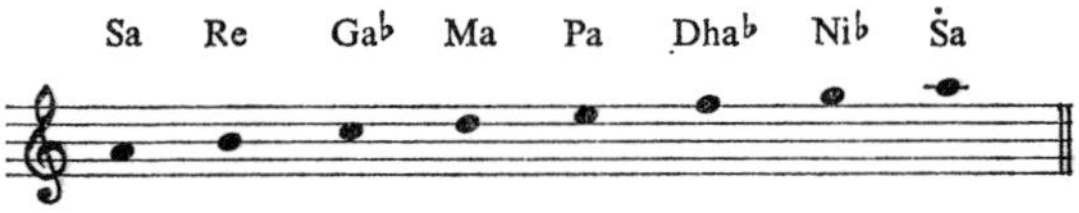

'B' mode

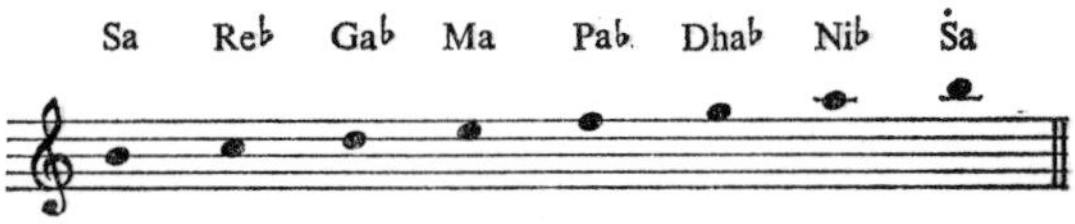

A similar system of nomenclature was in use in ancient Indian musical theory where the seven *śuddh jātis* (pure or natural modes) were named after the notes of the scale: *Ṣāḍjī* after *Ṣaḍja* (Sa), *Ārṣabhī* after *Riṣabha* (Ri), *Gāndhārī* after *Gāndhāra* (Ga), *Madhyamā* after *Madhyama* (Ma), *Pañcamī* after *Pañcama* (Pa), *Dhaivatī* after

[1] In this context the Western notes have no implications of precise pitch.

Dhaivata (Dha) and *Naiṣādī* after *Niṣāda* (Ni). These seven serial modes[1] were comparable to six of the modern Indian *ṭhāṭ*s as well as to the seven ancient Greek diatonic modes and the mediaeval Ecclesiastical modes. These are all shown, with C as the ground-note, in the table below.

Ground-note	Scale transposed to C	Ancient Greek name (Ptolemy)	Ecclesiastical name (Glarean)	Ancient Indian name (Nāṭyaśāstra)	Modern Indian name
C Sa		Lydian	Ionian	Naiṣādī	Bilāval
D Re		Phrygian	Dorian	Ṣāḍjī	Kāfī
E Ga	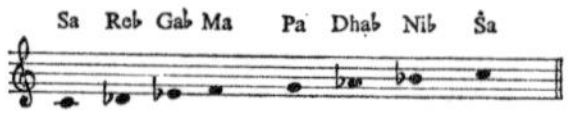	Dorian	Phrygian	Ārṣabhī	Bhairvī
F Ma		Hypolydian	Lydian	Gāndhārī	Kalyāṇ
G Pa		Hypophrygian	Mixolydian	Madhyamā	Khamāj
A Dha	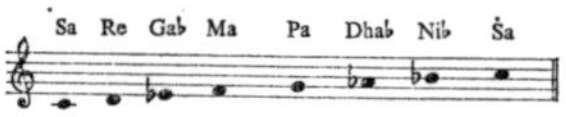	Hypodorian	Aeolian	Pañcamī	Āsāvrī
B Ni	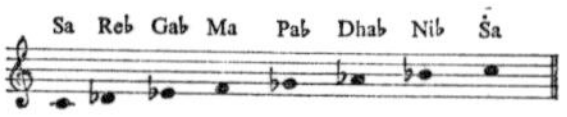	Mixolydian	Locrian	Dhaivatī	—

The similarity between the modern *ṭhāṭ*s and six of the ancient Indian *jāti*s clearly suggests an unbroken continuity of tradition. However, the serial relationship of these six *ṭhāṭ*s is not commonly appreciated in India at the present time.

The relationship between these six *ṭhāṭ*s can also be expressed in a different way. In each there is only one imperfect interval, a tritone, which as its name implies, consists of three wholetones making an augmented fourth, with its complementary interval, a diminished fifth. Elsewhere the fourths and fifths are perfect. The position of the tritone differs in each of these serial *ṭhāṭ*s. If we correct the tritone in any of them, lowering the upper note by a semitone (or raising the bottom note by a semitone), this shifts the tritone a fourth higher (or lower) and produces another of these

[1] Strictly speaking, these were not serial modes as they were derived from two parent scales, *Ṣaḍjagrāma* and *Madhyamagrāma*, which differed microtonally in their tuning of one note, the Pa.

ṭhāṭs. When this process is continued it results in the following succession (the tritones are indicated by square brackets):

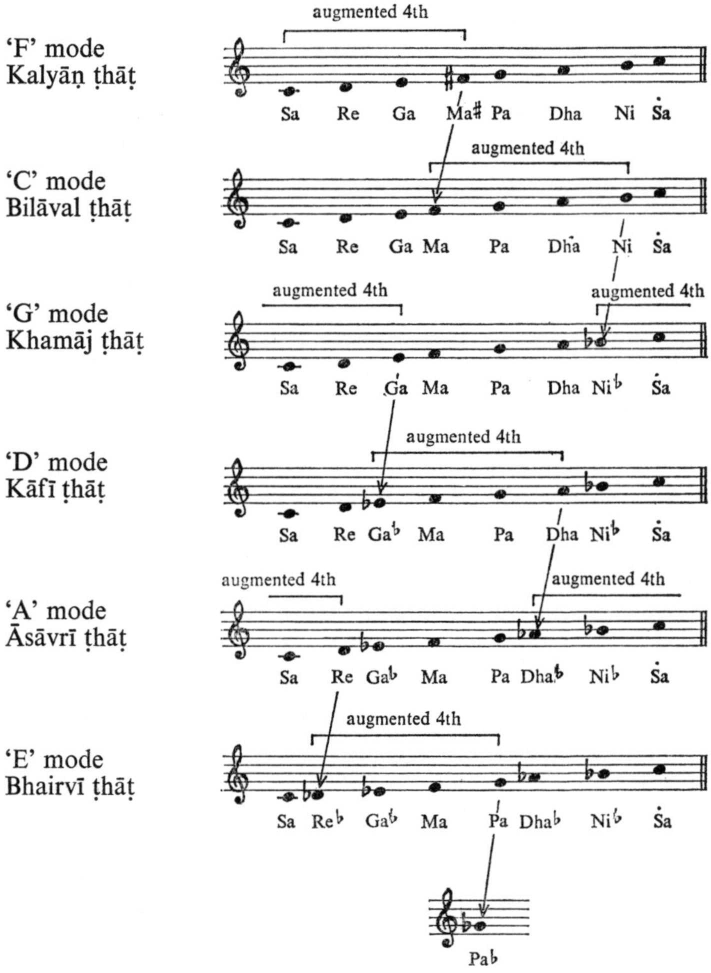

If this series were continued, the next scale would be the seventh mode which, as we have stated earlier, has a diminished fifth (Pa♭) in direct relationship with the tonic (Sa). As this scale would violate a fundamental premise of modern North Indian musical theory, the series cannot be continued any further in this direction. If we retrace our steps, raising the bottom note by a semitone, the next step after *Kalyāṇ* would be a scale in which the tonic would have to be raised (Sa♯). This too is prohibited in the system. Thus, strictly speaking, this series of modes, as applied to North Indian music, should end at *Bhairvī* and *Kalyāṇ*.

Bearing in mind, however, that the enharmonic difference between the augmented fourth, Ma♯, and the diminished fifth, Pa♭, does not appear to be recognised, we could continue the series beyond *Bhairvī*, replacing the Pa♭ by the enharmonic Ma♯. Similarly, we could continue the series beyond *Kalyāṇ*, replacing the Sa♯ by its enharmonic Re♭. In Chapter V this enharmonic change is discussed further and we have attempted to show how this could have occurred in musical practice.

As a result of this enharmonic change the tritone irregularity of the six serial *ṭhāṭs* now becomes a diminished fourth (with its complement the augmented fifth). This can now be corrected by raising the upper note a semitone (or lowering the bottom note an equal amount). It will be seen that the two extensions beyond *Bhairvī* and *Kalyāṇ* meet:

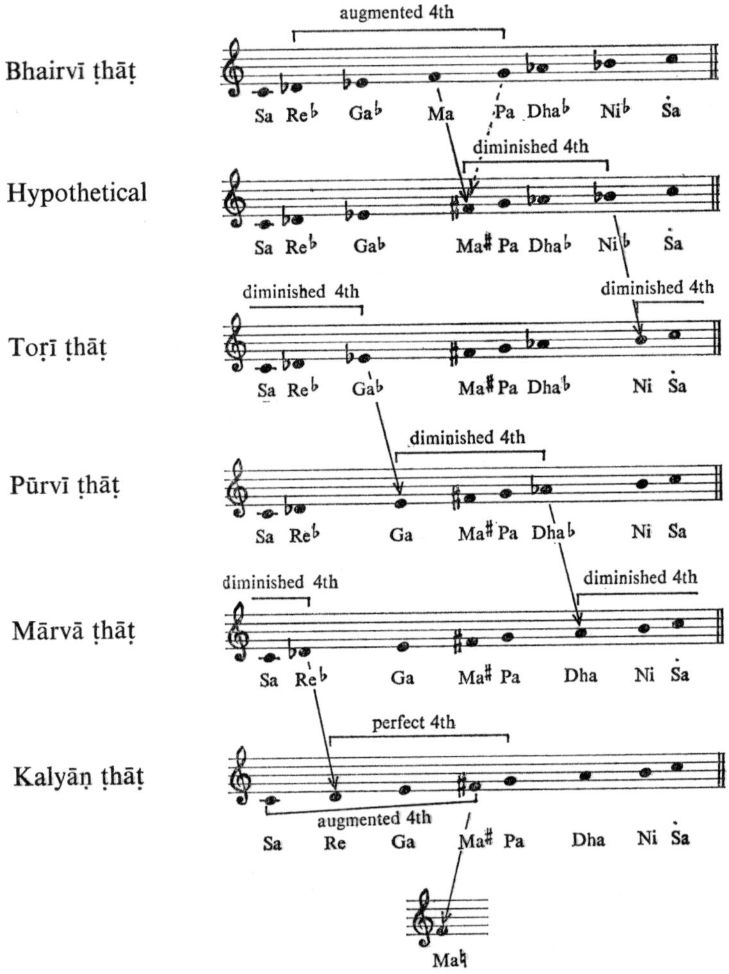

We can therefore present these ten *ṭhāṭs* as a circle.[1] Nine of the ten are, in fact,

[1] This Circle of *Ṭhāṭs* is identical with the outer circle of the thirty-two *ṭhāṭs* shown in Appendix A on p. 181, which was especially designed to show the most consonant scales.

Bhātkhaṇḍe's *ṭhāṭ*s; the other, No. A7, is not used in North Indian music at the present time. A tentative explanation for this will be offered in a later chapter.

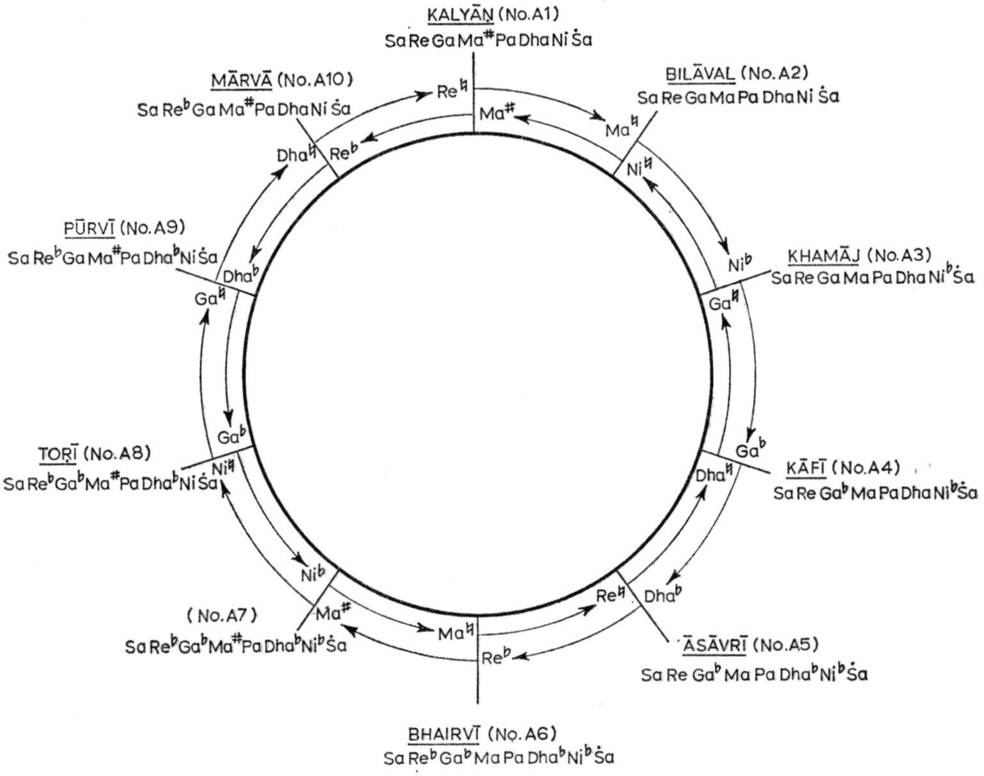

Circle of *Ṭhāṭ*s

In this diagram we have indicated the note that changes from one scale to another. The succession of changing notes in a clockwise direction form a circle of fourths (or in an anticlockwise direction a circle of fifths) similar to that in the Western Circle of Keys. The true succession of fourths is a spiral in which the twelfth successive fourth is a Pythagorean comma (24 cents) flatter than the fifth octave of the initial note, while the twelfth successive fifth is a comma sharper than its seventh octave.

In the Western Circle of Keys this spiral is broken at one of three possible points and completed as a circle by an enharmonic compromise. This theoretically implies an adjustment of a comma, but in the Western tempered twelve semitone system does not involve any actual change. In the Indian Circle the enharmonic change takes place at a particular point to avoid the Pa♭ (V♭), or, in the reverse direction, to avoid the Sa♯ (I♯). In the Indian system, however, as the Sa and Pa never change, there are only ten changes, and there is a discontinuity in the Circle. This appears in the Circle of *Ṭhāṭ*s in which the sequence of fourths (or fifths) is broken, Re♮ (II♮) being followed by Ma♮ (IV♮). The reason for this is simply that Pa (V) and Sa (I), being immovable notes, cannot be included in the circle of changing notes. If they were inserted in the Circle between Re (II) and Ma (IV)—Re Pa Sa Ma (II, V, I, IV)—this discontinuity would be eliminated.

For ease of comparison, we give below the true spiral of fourths, the Western Circle of Keys, and the Indian circle of fourths as they occur in the Circle of *Ṭhāṭs*, in both Western and Indian notation.

Western notation

True spiral of fourths:	C	F	B♭	E♭	A♭	D♭	G♭	C♭	F♭	B♭♭	E♭♭	A♭♭	D♭♭
Circle of Keys:	C	F	B♭	E♭	A♭	D♭	G♭	C♭					
						C♯	F♯	B	E	A	D	G	C
Circle of *Ṭhāṭs*:	(C)	F	B♭	E♭	A♭	D♭							
							F♯	B	E	A	D	(G)	(C)

Indian notation

True spiral of fourths:	Sa	Ma	Ni♭	Ga♭	Dha♭	Re♭	Pa♭	Sa♭	Ma♭	Ni♭♭	Ga♭♭	Dha♭♭	Re♭♭
Circle of Keys:	Sa	Ma	Ni♭	Ga♭	Dha♭	Re♭	Pa♭	Sa♭					
						Sa♯	Ma♯	Ni	Ga	Dha	Re	Pa	Sa
Circle of *Ṭhāṭs*:	(Sa)	Ma	Ni♭	Ga♭	Dha♭	Re♭							
							Ma♯	Ni	Ga	Dha	Re	(Pa)	(Sa)

The fact that *Mārvā*, *Pūrvī* and *Toṛī ṭhāṭs* (Nos. A10, A9 and A8) are prominent in North Indian classical music appears to be clear proof that this circle is not mere theory but has substantial basis in practice. From the theoretical standpoint this Circle of *Ṭhāṭs* has several satisfying features. Above all, it shows that nine of the ten *ṭhāṭs* in common use can be connected in a logical scheme consistent with the theory and practice of North Indian Classical music. In the Circle, opposite poles always represent scales in which the opposite alternative notes are used, i.e. opposite *Bilāval* (No. A2), the natural scale, lies scale No. A7 in which all the altered notes are used; opposite *Kāfī* (No. A4), in which Ga♭ and Ni♭ are used, lies *Pūrvī* (No. A9) in which the other three altered notes, Re♭ Ma♯ and Dha♭ are used, while the Ga and Ni are natural. At the north pole of the diagram lies *Kalyāṇ* (No. A1) in which each of the alternative notes is in its higher position, while at the south pole lies *Bhairvī* (No. A6) in which they are all in their lower positions. It is thus easy to see which of these *ṭhāṭs* are related and the nature of their relationships.

The cyclic nature of the North Indian scales has been recognised by Fox Strangways.[1] This appears to have arisen from his intuition rather than from any logical process, a fact which says much for his understanding of North Indian classical *rāgs*. His circle differs from ours in two ways: it includes *Bhairav ṭhāṭ* and it does not include scale No. A7. Having established the succession of the six principal serial *ṭhāṭs* (Nos. A1–6) just as we have done, he acknowledges that the B mode is not applicable in present-day music because it requires a flattened fifth (Pa♭). He then

[1] Fox Strangways, *op. cit.*, pp. 169–70.

proceeds to *Bhairav* (No. C9) through the intermediate scale (No. B6) which he calls *Bilaskhānī Toḍī*. From this he proceeds to *Toḍī* (No. A8) through *Gaurī* (No. A9). From *Toḍī* he returns to this same scale, calling it *Basant*, then going on to *Mārvā* (No. A10) and back to the serial modes through *Kalyāṇ* (No. A1) as follows:

Fox Strangways's *rāg*s — Bhātkhaṇḍe's *ṭhāṭ*s

Bhairvī

Bhairvī (No. A6)

Bilaskhānī Toḍī

— (No. B6)

Bhairav

Bhairav (No. C9)

Gaurī

Pūrvī (No. A9)

Toḍī

Toṛī (No. A8)

Basant

Pūrvī (No. A9)

Pūriyā Kaliān

Mārvā (No. A10)

Kaliān
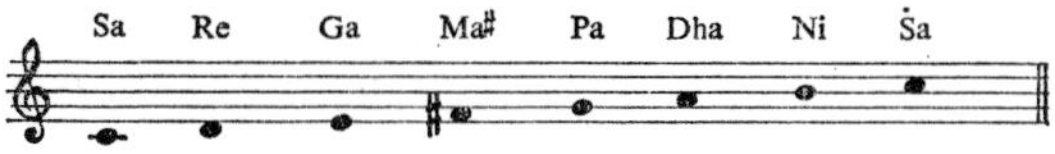

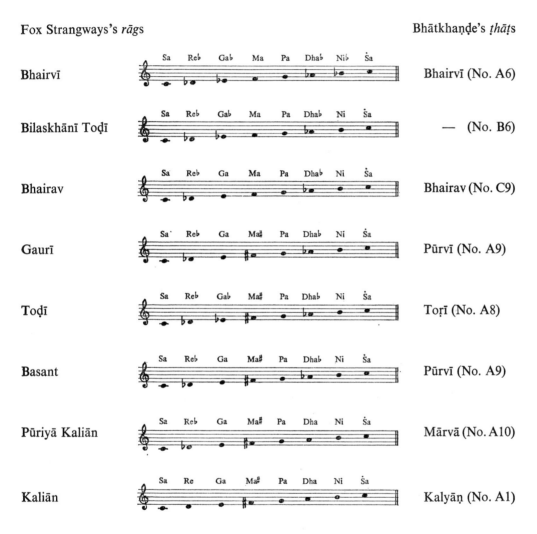

Kalyāṇ (No. A1)

It will be noticed that Fox Strangways has been obliged to repeat *Pūrvī ṭhāṭ* in order to complete his cycle. In the following chapter we shall be discussing *Bhairav ṭhāṭ* and its relationship with the circle of *ṭhāṭ*s.

The only cyclic concept in Bhātkhaṇḍe's works is connected with his theory that the time of performance of a *rāg* is related to its musical characteristics, particularly to its scale and its *vādī*. In this theory the cyclic concept is implicit as the succession of *rāg*s is resumed afresh at the beginning of each new day and it is in this connection that Bhātkhaṇḍe refers to a circle of *rāgs*.[1] According to his time theory the *rāgs* are divided into three groups:[2]

1. Those which have Re♮ (II♮), Dha♮ (VI♮) and Ga♮ (III♮); i.e., *rāgs* belonging to *Kalyāṇ*, *Bilāval* and *Khamāj ṭhāṭs*.
2. Those which have Re♭ (II♭), Ga♮ (III♮) and Ni♮ (VII♮); i.e., those belonging to *Bhairav*, *Pūrvī* and *Mārvā ṭhāṭs*.
3. Those which have Ga♭ (III♭) and Ni♭ (VII♭); i.e. those belonging to *Kāfī*, *Āsāvrī* and *Bhairvī ṭhāṭs*.

Strictly speaking this scheme does not include *Toṛī ṭhāṭ* which has Ga♭ (III♭) and Ni♮ (VII♮), but Bhātkhaṇḍe includes it in the third group on the grounds that some *rāgs* of the Toṛī family have Ga♭ (III♭) and Ni♭ (VII♭).[3]

For the purpose of his time theory Bhātkhaṇḍe divides the day into two twelve-hour periods, from midnight to midday and from midday to midnight. Each of these is further divided into three sections: the period from four to seven which is called *sandhiprakāś* and is the period of sunrise and sunset; the period immediately preceding, from approximately ten to four; and the period immediately following, from seven to approximately ten.[4] He then associates the *rāg* groups with the three sections of the twelve-hour periods. The *rāgs* of group 1, i.e. those with Re♮, Dha♮ and Ga♮, are ascribed to the period after sunrise and sunset, from seven to ten either morning or evening. The *rāgs* of group 2, i.e. those with Re♭, Ga♮ and Ni♮, are the *sandhiprakāś rāgs* to be performed at either sunrise or sunset. The *rāgs* of group 3, i.e. those with Ga♭ and Ni♭ but including *Toṛī*, are ascribed to the period before sunrise and sunset, from approximately ten to four. The feature which finally determines whether a particular *rāg* is to be performed in the morning (from midnight to midday) or the evening is the *vādī* of that *rāg*, as we have mentioned earlier. If the *vādī* is in the lower tetrachord (*pūrvāṅg*) it will be an evening *rāg*, if in the upper (*uttrāṅg*) it will be a morning *rāg*. If, however, the *vādī* is Sa (I), Ma (IV) or Pa (V) the *rāg* may be performed in either period.[5]

The cyclic succession of *ṭhāṭs* therefore repeats after twelve hours, while the cyclic succession of *rāgs* only repeats after twenty-four hours or two *ṭhāṭ* cycles. Bhātkhaṇḍe refers only to a circle of *rāgs* but does not carry the matter any further. If, however, we arrange the various *ṭhāṭs* in the circle implied by Bhātkhaṇḍe according to the time

[1] *H.S.P.* IV, p. 22.
[2] *Ibid.*, p. 7.
[3] *Ibid.*, Preface, p. 7.
[4] Bhātkhaṇḍe avoids mentioning the precise duration of these periods. The figures given above are taken from H. A. Popley, *The Music of India*, Calcutta 1950, p. 63. O. C. Gangoly, *op. cit.*, p. 90, quoting a paper read by Bhātkhaṇḍe at the Fourth All-India Music Conference at Lucknow (1925), gives the period after sunrise and sunset as extending from seven to twelve and the period before, from twelve to four. It seems reasonable to presume that Bhātkhaṇḍe intended a certain latitude in the precise duration of these periods.
[5] A further modification to the time theory is provided by the Ma♯ which, according to Bhātkhaṇḍe, is also indicative of the time of performance and occurs generally in night *rāgs* (*K.P.M.* V, p. 31). However, there are some day-time *rāgs* such as *Multānī* and *Toṛī* which have Ma♯.

of performance of the groups, the resulting circle is similar to that suggested by Fox Strangways and differs from our Circle of *Ṭhāṭ*s in that it omits scale No. A7 but includes *Bhairav ṭhāṭ*.

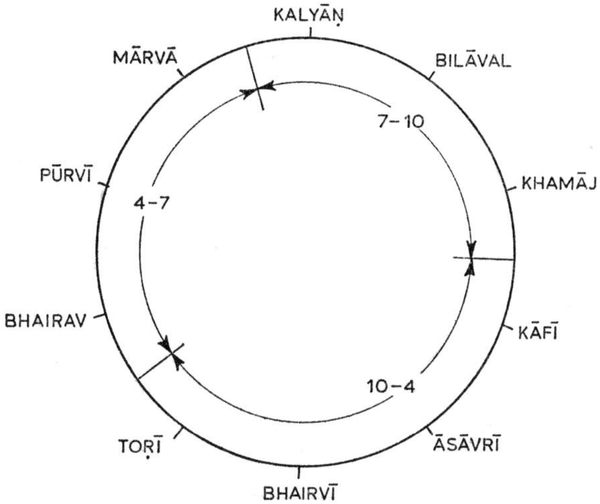

Circle of *Ṭhāṭ*s after Bhātkhaṇḍe's time theory

In this circle *Toṛī* and *Pūrvī* are separated by *Bhairav ṭhāṭ*. Yet Bhātkhaṇḍe clearly mentions the relationship between *Toṛī* and *Pūrvī ṭhāṭ*s in his discussion of the *rāg Multānī*, a *rāg* of *Toṛī ṭhāṭ*, when he says that this *rāg* is '*parmelpraveśak*' (introducing a new group) and is followed by *rāg*s of *Pūrvī ṭhāṭ*.[1] This connection would by-pass *Bhairav* and consequently bring it closer to our Circle of *Ṭhāṭ*s. From the diagram on the following page it will be seen that the fundamentals of Bhātkhaṇḍe's time theory can be coherently related to our Circle of *Ṭhāṭ*s.

The times specified for the performance of *rāg*s are only approximate and in practice there is considerable latitude. It does appear, however, that this theory conforms in a large number of instances to the traditional time of performance of *rāg*s.[2]

The relationship between the scale of a *rāg* and its time of performance has been expressed as follows: 'The principle that really emerges from Bhātkhaṇḍe's theory is nothing but the tendency of *rāga*s to follow the line of least resistance in the easy transition from scale to scale and it is observed to a certain extent by all musicians.'[3] The concept of gradual change is apparent in many aspects of Indian music: in the extension of the range of a *rāg* in the *ālāp* (prelude); in the acceleration of tempo

[1] *H.S.P.* IV, p. 714.

[2] There are a few *rāg*s whose traditional time of performance does not correspond to that which is obtained in relation to the Circle of *Ṭhāṭ*s. The *rāg Toṛī*, for instance, is said to be a morning *rāg*, but in the circle the time of its performance is approximately three a.m. or p.m. *Multānī*, another *rāg* of *Toṛī ṭhāṭ*, is in fact performed at about this time in the afternoon. In a subsequent chapter we shall suggest an explanation for *Toṛī* being one of the exceptions to the time theory.

[3] H. L. Roy, *Problems of Hindustani Music*, p. 82.

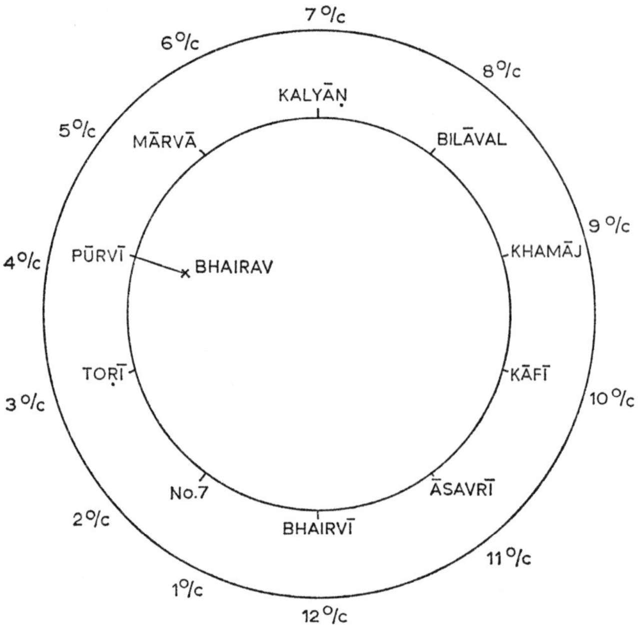

Time theory and the Circle of *Ṭhāṭ*s

during a performance; and in the development of melodic and rhythmic ideas throughout a performance.

The significant feature of the Circle of *Ṭhāṭ*s is that it shows an easy transition from scale to scale, and it is not surprising that the *rāg*s are generally performed in this sequence during the course of each day. There is thus some reason to suppose that the scales may have evolved in this same sequence during the course of the centuries and to say that the daily succession of *rāg*s is, in some respects, a reconstruction of the course of evolution.

In the next chapter we propose to consider the *ṭhāṭ*s from the point of view of musical practice rather than as a matter of musical theory and to attempt to justify the evolution of the Circle of *Ṭhāṭ*s from this standpoint.

IV

The Effect of Drones

A prominent feature of Indian music is the use of a drone, which sounds at least the ground-note, Sa, throughout the whole performance. The ground-note is the point of reference for measuring the intervals used in any *rāg*. It can be said of any modal system, whether or not a drone is used, that the primary significance of the various intervals is their relationship to the ground-note, so that the notes are perceived not in terms of absolute pitch but in terms of this relationship. The particular relationship of any note to the ground-note is responsible for the dynamic quality or function of that note. This quality has been described as the 'particular kind of unfulfilment peculiar to each tone, its desire for completion'.[1] Only the ground-note is at rest and needs no completion. All other intervals manifest instability, each to its own particular degree, and require fulfilment which can only be achieved by a return to the ground-note. The degree of instability and the corresponding tension does not increase in proportion to the distance from the ground-note but is governed to a large extent by the smoothness or roughness (consonance or dissonance) experienced in the relationship of that note with the ground-note. The degree of dissonance of the successive intervals has been calculated by Helmholtz on the basis of two violin tones, one static and the other varying in pitch, as shown in the first diagram on p. 66.[2]

In this diagram the vertical axis represents consonance and dissonance: the deeper the valley, the more consonant the note; the higher the peak, the more dissonant the note. With C as the ground-note (Sa) the F and the G (Ma and Pa) are clearly the most consonant, the A and E (Dha and Ga) next in consonance. The D♭, B, A♭ and F♯ (Re♭, Ni, Dha♭ and Ma♯) are the most dissonant in the series.

This scheme cannot be applied directly to Indian music primarily because a secondary drone is generally used. This is usually the fifth (Pa) but it is sometimes the fourth (Ma), depending largely on the relative importance of these notes in a particular *rāg*. This secondary drone too has its own consonance–dissonance series which must be superimposed on the original series to give a more realistic picture for Indian

[1] V. Zuckerkandl, *Sound and Symbol, Music in the External World,* Bollingen Series, New York 1956, p. 94.

[2] Helmholtz, *Sensations of Tone,* trans. A. J. Ellis, Longmans, Green and Co., London 1875, p. 520.

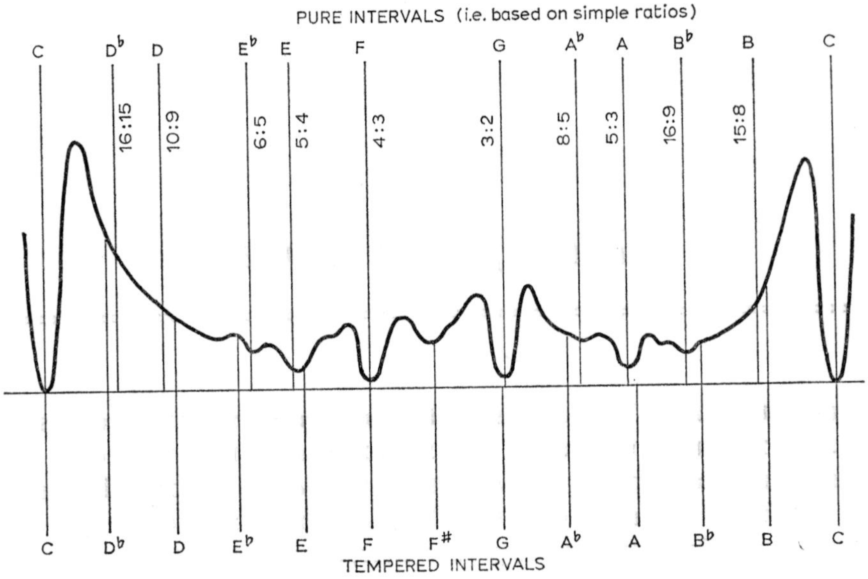

Consonance–Dissonance with C Drone (after Helmholtz)

music. In the diagrams following we have added the effect of the secondary drone, the fifth (Pa) in the first and the fourth (Ma) in the second, working on the assumption that the principal drone (Sa) is twice as prominent as the secondary drone. The dotted lines in both diagrams show Helmholtz's original graph.

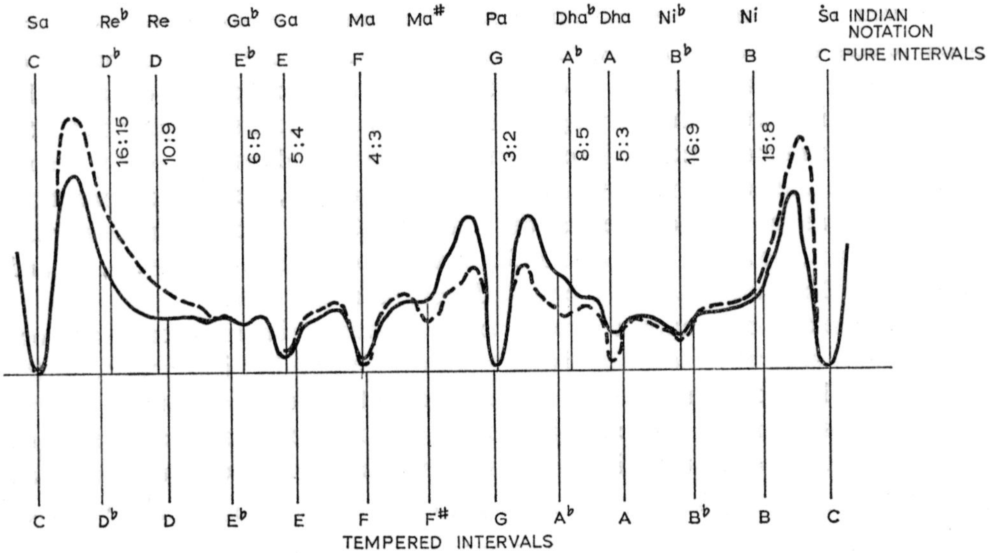

Consonance–Dissonance with Sa Drone twice as prominent as Pa Drone

It will be apparent that the addition of the secondary drone changes the pattern of consonance and dissonance. In both diagrams the ground-note (Sa) is no longer a *perfect* resolution. When Pa is introduced as a secondary drone the most prominent changes are that the Ga is now nearly as consonant as the Ma, while the Dha is much less consonant than it was with merely one drone, and that both the Re♭ and Re♮ are much less dissonant, while the Ma♯ is more dissonant. When Ma is introduced as a secondary drone, both Ga and Pa become less consonant and the Dha, Ni♭ and Ni♮ are now slightly more consonant, as are the Re♭ and Re♮.

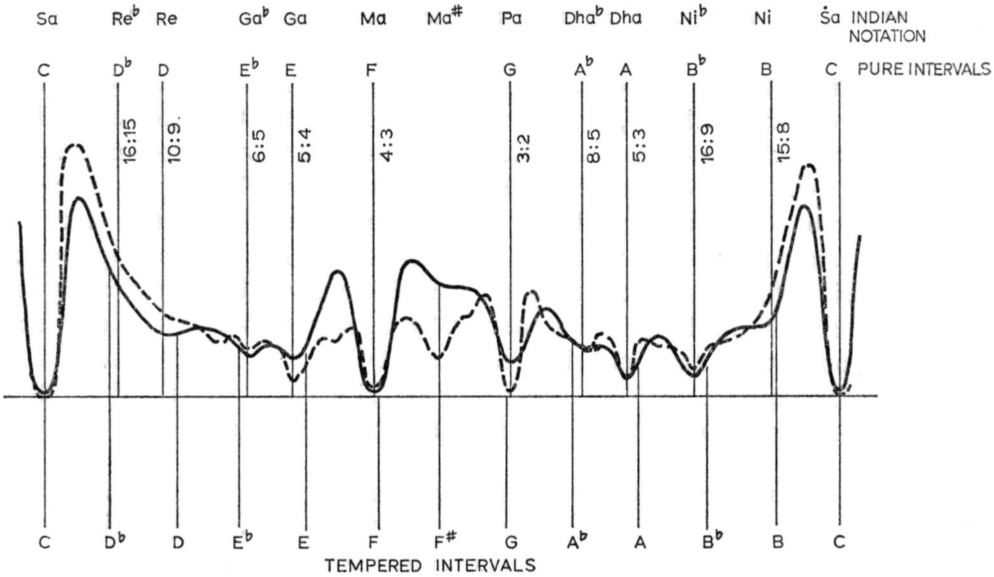

Consonance–Dissonance with Sa Drone twice as prominent as Ma Drone

These diagrams are at best a vague approximation and indicate only the directions in which the consonance–dissonance pattern is altered by the introduction of a secondary drone. There are a number of factors which might affect the real picture. For instance, our calculations are based on Helmholtz's work with two violin tones. Obviously there is a considerable difference in the tone quality of the violin and the usual Indian drone instrument, the *tambūrā*; the latter accentuates different overtones which would alter the consonance–dissonance relationships of the various tones. If the second overtone (sounding Pa) is stronger on the *tambūrā* than on the violin, we may expect the Ma and the Dha to sound slightly rougher against the *tambūrā* drone. The *tambūrā* tone itself is not constant but varies from instrument to instrument, and one must also take into account the particular acoustic quality of the hall or room in which the music is performed. Musicians sometimes add other drone notes[1] which would further alter the graphs. These variables make it impossible to predict an entirely accurate picture of the consonance–dissonance relationships of the tones in any actual performance.

The precise dynamic function of a note varies not only in different performances but, to a lesser extent, even during one performance, as for instance when an instrument goes very slightly out of tune. It will be noticed that most of the 'pure' intervals are located in the bottoms of the troughs or valleys, while the tones of the tempered system are frequently located on the rise or fall and are slightly more dissonant than their 'pure' interval counterparts. This does not necessarily mean that the tempered scale is musically less satisfactory than the 'pure' scale. A musical scale can aptly be described as a scale of dynamic tensions, a gradation of degrees from the most consonant to the most dissonant. There is considerable evidence to indicate that in Western music as well as in Indian music the tensions inherent in either the 'pure' scale or the tempered scale are, by themselves, insufficient for the needs of musical expression. It is well known, for instance, that instruments without fixed intonation as well as the voice tend to sharpen the leading note (Ni♮) even beyond the tempered interval, thereby increasing its already considerable dynamic function and, by contrast, enhancing the effect of resolution on the tonic (Sa). The development of Western music in the past few centuries has been characterised by the increasing use of discords, and, particularly in this century, by experiments with new scales, such as the division of the octave into six equal parts (Debussy's whole-tone scale) and into twenty-four equal parts (Hába's quarter-tone scale). These have served to introduce a greater variety of dynamic functions and to extend the dynamic range of music.

From this evolutionary standpoint we may conclude that the tempered scale was an improvement on the 'pure' scale since it permitted a greater dynamic range. This is particularly evident in the tempered thirds where the slightly increased dissonance gives a vibrant quality to the common major and minor chords. The fact that the intonation in performance does not always follow the tempered intervals indicates that these are by no means perfectly satisfactory. It would seem that the ideal scale is one which permits a certain measure of latitude, so that intonation may vary slightly, depending on the context in which the notes occur and the interpretation of the musician. This, of course, is not generally possible in concerted music, but in Indian music, since it is invariably performed by soloists, flexibility in intonation is quite usual.[2]

In discussing the dynamic function of notes we have so far referred only to the primary level on which this operates, where each note seeks resolution on the ground-note. On a secondary level dissonant notes seek their more consonant neighbours. Here the terms dissonance and consonance must be taken to mean the roughness and smoothness of the notes as modified by the occurrence of a secondary drone. These

[1] See Appendix B, p. 187.
[2] N. A. Jairazbhoy and A. W. Stone, *op. cit.*, p. 130.

two dynamic functions can be shown in schematic form, the solid lines indicating the primary function and the dotted lines the secondary function:

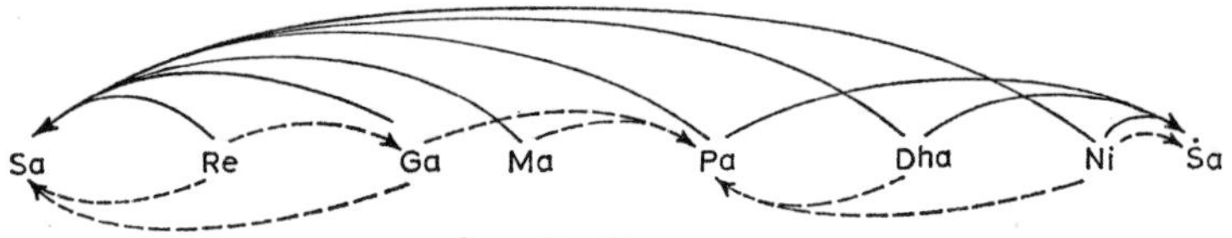

Sa + Pa Drones

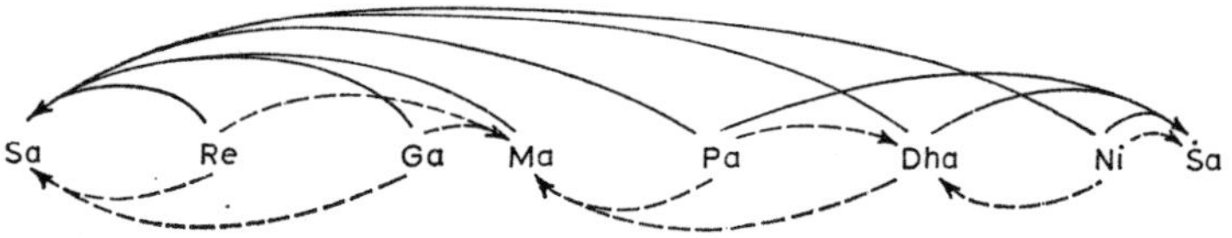

Sa + Ma Drones

In recent times the third (Ga) is often added as a supplementary drone to the Sa + Pa drones[1] resulting in a further modification of the consonance–dissonance pattern of the notes. Here the dynamic function of the notes is similar to that in Western classical harmony where the major triad (Sa, Ga, Pa) is implied and may, for short periods, even function as a drone. The following diagram shows the consonance–dissonance pattern with these three drones, the Sa drone being twice as prominent as the others. The dotted lines once again show Helmholtz's original trace:

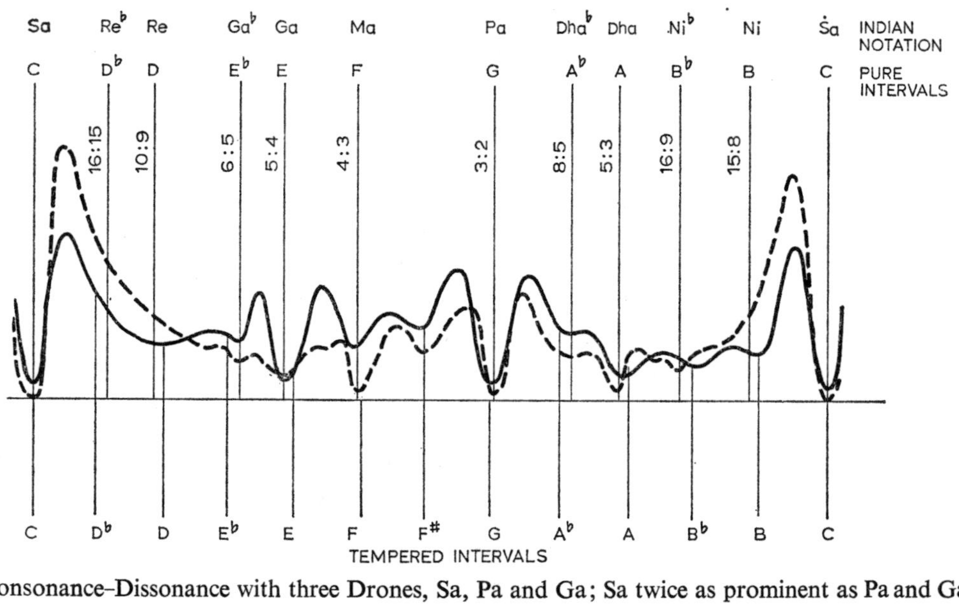

Consonance–Dissonance with three Drones, Sa, Pa and Ga; Sa twice as prominent as Pa and Ga

[1] The principal advocate of this drone accompaniment is *Ustād* Vilayat Khan who also uses other drone combinations to suit particular *rāgs*. Some of these are described in Appendix B on pp. 187, 188 and can be heard on the accompanying record.

The principal modification resulting from the introduction of the Ga drone is that the Ga is much more consonant than the Ma which now has a greatly increased secondary dynamic function in that it leads either to the Ga or the Pa.

We have been discussing the inherent dynamic function of notes which is not derived from their pitch but from their relationship to the ground-note and to the other notes sounded in the drone. There are, however, other factors which also have a very great influence on the function of a note. These arise from the context in which the note is heard and are connected with melody, rhythm and metre. While a full treatment of these factors is beyond the scope of this work, a brief examination of the dynamic function induced by the melodic context is contained in Chapter VIII, pp. 171ff).

A fundamental question arises out of the foregoing discussion. How can we recognise and appreciate a *rāg* when the dynamic function of its notes is variable? The only explanation which appears to fit this condition is that the mind has considerable latitude in the comprehension of musical intervals. This is borne out by the fact that in Indian music the precise intonation of notes also varies from performer to performer, from recital to recital and even within the same recital,[1] and yet the *rāg* being performed is clearly recognised by the audience. Perhaps the best way to understand this is in terms of an analogy. Let us imagine that the consonance–dissonance graphs represent the terrain on which we are walking. As we walk down from a peak into a valley, at a certain point we suddenly recognise the valley and can say this is Dha or this is Ga. The point of lowest potential energy of this valley is at its bottom, but recognition dawns somewhere on the slopes. The analogy must now be carried into three dimensions if we are to convey the dynamic function of the notes, as the particular valley we are concerned with may be located in the mountains, and a river in this valley will run into a lower valley and continue downwards until it finally reaches the ocean. In two dimensions the bottom of the valley appears to be a state of minimum potential energy; in three dimensions, however, it is seen that the bottom of the valley is itself sloping towards a lower valley. The incline is less steep in the valley than on the slopes, thus the kinetic energy, which can be correlated with the dynamic function of the notes, is lower in the valley than on the slopes. Would a musician necessarily choose the point of lowest kinetic energy when he wishes to convey suspense, anticipation or tension? It has been noted that the leading note (Ni) is often sharper in ascent than in descent. Is not this sharpening of the Ni a subconscious device to increase its dynamic value so that it more urgently demands resolution on the tonic (Sa)?

To summarise, music is concerned, from one viewpoint, with states of tension and release, with contrasts of energy levels. Where the musician wishes to convey the feeling of relief from tension, he must seek the bottom of the valley, and particularly those valleys which have a low potential energy level, in other words the more consonant notes. When he aims to convey tension, however, he would not necessarily

[1] *Ibid.*, p. 130–1. There is reason to believe that the same occurs in Western music played on non-keyboard instruments or sung, despite its basis of equal temperament.

seek the *bottom* of the valley of the less consonant notes. Yet he cannot stray too far up the slope, else the note would sound disturbingly out of tune.

While the drone affects the dynamic function of notes, this is by no means its only influence in Indian music. Generally the drone is taken so much for granted and is so much part of the music that the exact nature of its influence is difficult to perceive. Even on the infrequent informal occasions when music is sometimes performed without a drone, it is nevertheless implied, and it is likely that the memory of the drone compensates, to some extent, for its physical absence. However, extraordinary occurrences often enable one to have an insight into normal events. For instance, on a recording by *Ustād* Bismillah Khan[1] playing on the *shahnā'ī*, one of the drone *shahnā'īs* suddenly introduces the third (Ga) as a subsidiary drone note. The result is that the melodic improvisations gravitate to this point and one clearly hears the modal series beginning on Ga rather than the original scale (based on Sa). This is not a transposition, merely a temporary shift of the point of reference and a corresponding shift of tessitura. It is, of course, an unconventional practice, but for this very reason we can clearly appreciate the result. After a short while the Ga drone ceases and the melodic line returns to its original framework.

Another interesting occurrence can be heard on a record of *Ustād* Bundu Khan playing the *sāraṅgī*.[2] Here he plays the pentatonic *rāg Mālkoś* (*Mālkāus*) in which the secondary drone is usually the fourth (Ma). On this occasion the primary Sa drone is abandoned entirely and only the secondary Ma drone is played; on analysis, the proper scale of the *rāg* (Ex. 23a) appears to be inverted so that the Ma now becomes its ground-note (Ex. 23b):

Ex. 23. rāg Mālkoś

(a) (b)

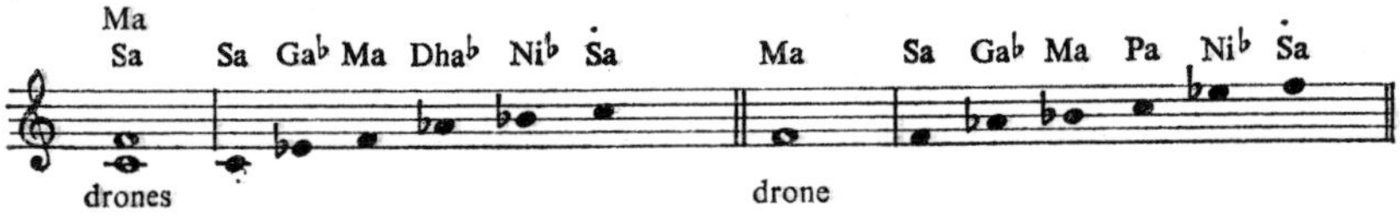

There is, nevertheless, no difficulty in recognising that it is *rāg Mālkoś* which is being performed. This can only be explained if we acknowledge that the series of notes in Ex. 23b, the Ma-inversion provoked by the secondary drone (Ma), is always implicit in this *rāg*.

These two examples suggest the following conclusions: first, that the secondary drone may become the temporary ground-note of the *rāg*, particularly when it is brought forward as it was in the first example by its sudden introduction; and secondly, that the modal sequence starting on the secondary drone is also registered in the mind of the listener, whether overtly realised or not, and is an essential aspect of any *rāg*.

1 H.M.V. N 94755 (78 r.p.m.), side entitled *Kajrī*.
2 H.M.V. HT 83 (78 r.p.m.).

It may be argued, with some justification, that these conclusions need not apply when Pa occurs as the secondary drone since there is a basic acoustic difference between Ma and Pa in this context. Let us go into this matter in some detail.

Analysis of musical tones reveals that no tone produced on a musical instrument is pure, but is composed of a fundamental and, in addition, a number of overtones which are generally much softer than the fundamental. These overtones are explained by the fact that a string on an instrument or a vibrating column of air in a pipe vibrates not only in its full length but also in proportions of its length—half, third, quarter, etc. In theory this overtone series[1] is limitless, but, as each successive overtone is softer (except where one of these is amplified by the shape of the resonating chamber of a particular instrument), for all practical purposes only the first few overtones are musically significant.

We should note that the perfect fourth, Ma, is not one of the notes which is significant in this series.

Ex. 24.

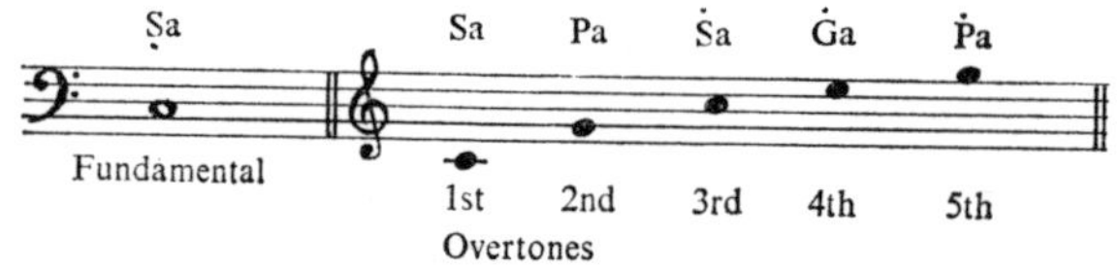

When the Sa drone is sounded, the overtone series is evoked and the first few overtones are often clearly audible. The second overtone, Pa, is usually quite prominent, especially on the *tambūrā*, and is thus always present in Indian music as a secondary drone whether or not it is actually sounded. To a lesser extent this also holds for the fourth overtone, Ga. The addition of Ga, therefore, as an extra drone note is an extension of a natural phenomenon and not a radical development to be associated with Western influence. Ma, however, although consonant to Sa, is alien to the overtone series and is not evoked in the sound of the Sa. On the other hand, Sa is evoked in the sound of Ma since Ṡa is a fifth above Ma and is its second overtone. For this reason it can be argued that the tendency to view Ma as the ground-note has a 'natural' basis. The same cannot be said for Pa as Sa is not part of its overtone series. This thesis can be expressed in the following way: If two drones either a fourth or a fifth apart are sounded, one of these will 'naturally' sound like the primary drone. It is not always the lower of the two which will sound primary, but the one which initiates the overtone series to which the other note (or one of its octaves) belongs. By amplifying a prominent overtone the secondary drone lends support to the primary and intensifies its 'primary' character.

[1] A second system of nomenclature refers to these as the harmonic series, in which the fundamental is the first. The first overtone, i.e. Sa, is the second harmonic; the second overtone, i.e. Pa, is the third harmonic, etc. One advantage of this system is that it permits easy calculation of the intervals between harmonics; for instance, the interval between the ninth harmonic (the eighth overtone) and the eighth harmonic (the seventh overtone) is nine: eight.

Nevertheless, there are instances when Pa also becomes, in effect, the ground-note, evoking its own modal series. Notable examples can be found in the *rāg*s *Pañcam se Pīlū* (lit. *Pīlū* from Pa) and *Pañcam se Gāṛā* (*Gāṛā* from Pa) where the parent *rāg*s *Pīlū* and *Gāṛā* are virtually transposed to the secondary drone, Pa.[1]

That the fifth should evoke its own modal series is not peculiar to Indian music, for the Western Ecclesiastical modes show, in their plagal forms, a similar tendency. This is not exactly the same phenomenon as we have been speaking of in Indian music, for in the plagal modes the *finalis*, which we might equate with the Sa, remained the same as in its authentic mode, and only the ambitus, the range of the octave, was shifted a fourth lower, extending from P̣a to Pa.

It would therefore appear that *rāg*s have a certain measure of dual or even multiple modality. When a secondary drone is brought to the fore, as, for instance, when it serves as the pivot note in a series of melodic phrases, it serves temporarily as the ground-note of the *rāg* and evokes its own particular modal series, which may not, however, be appreciated on a conscious level. In theory this applies to any terminal note but is less significant unless the terminal note is also amplified in the drone.[2] Naturally, the authentic series initiated by the Sa is predominant and the melodic line is inevitably drawn back to this base.

If we accept this hypothesis, it is easy to see how the six primary *ṭhāṭ*s, *Kalyāṇ* to *Bhairvī*, might have evolved without the conscious process of beginning each one on the successive degrees of a primary scale, as was apparently the case in ancient Indian music theory. From each *ṭhāṭ* two modal series are brought to the fore by the two commonly used secondary drones, Pa and Ma. Each of these series can become a scale in its own right when the primary and secondary drones are interchanged, as shown in the table on the following page.

By this process, too, we arrive at the B mode which is not one of the Indian *ṭhāṭ*s, but whose influence can be seen in the *rāg Bhairvī*, where the diminished fifth is sometimes used in descent (see Ex. 14b, p. 50).

It will be noticed that we cannot continue this process beyond the B mode because Pa would be flat here and there could be no secondary Pa drone. In the same way, retracing our steps, beginning each successive scale on the Ma of the previous scale, we finally arrive at *Kalyāṇ*. Here again the process cannot be continued further because *Kalyāṇ* has a Ma♯, and thus a secondary Ma♮ drone is not feasible.

We have been seeking musical justification for some of the theories expressed in the previous chapter, and, in particular, a practical justification for the Circle of *Ṭhāṭ*s. We can now explain how the six primary *ṭhāṭ*s might have arisen out of musical practice, but we have also seen that we can go no further by this process and the

[1] One of the characteristic features of the *rāg*s *Pīlū* and *Gāṛā* is the use of both forms of Ga (III) and Ni (VII). In the 'transposed' *rāg*s these are also a fourth lower (or a fifth higher) and appear as both forms of Ni (VII) and Ma (IV). These *rāg*s can be heard on the two following records: *Pañcam se Pīlū*, played by Vilayat Khan, H.M.V. 7 EPE 59; and *Pañcam se Gāṛā* by Ravi Shankar, H.M.V. N 94754 (78 r.p.m.).

[2] For a further discussion of this, see Appendix B, pp. 188, 189.

remainder of the Circle of *Ṭhāṭs* is still unexplained. Seen in terms of consonant fourths and fifths, the primary *ṭhāṭs* are nearly perfect, each having only one imperfect relationship. The occurrence of the other *ṭhāṭs* in the Circle cannot be justified in terms of consonance as each of these has several imperfect relationships; for instance, *Mārvā ṭhāṭ* has two augmented fourths, Sa–Ma♯ (I–IV♯) and Re♭–Pa (II♭–V), and an augmented fifth, Re♭–Dha (II♭–VI). We have also seen the primary *ṭhāṭs* as a connected series beginning on the successive degrees of a parent heptatonic scale. This is a complete, conscious system and excludes all other *ṭhāṭs*. Lastly, we have seen these primary *ṭhāṭs* growing out of an imperceptible evolutionary process in which the primary and secondary drones are inverted. Here too we have been unable to go beyond the seven serial modes.

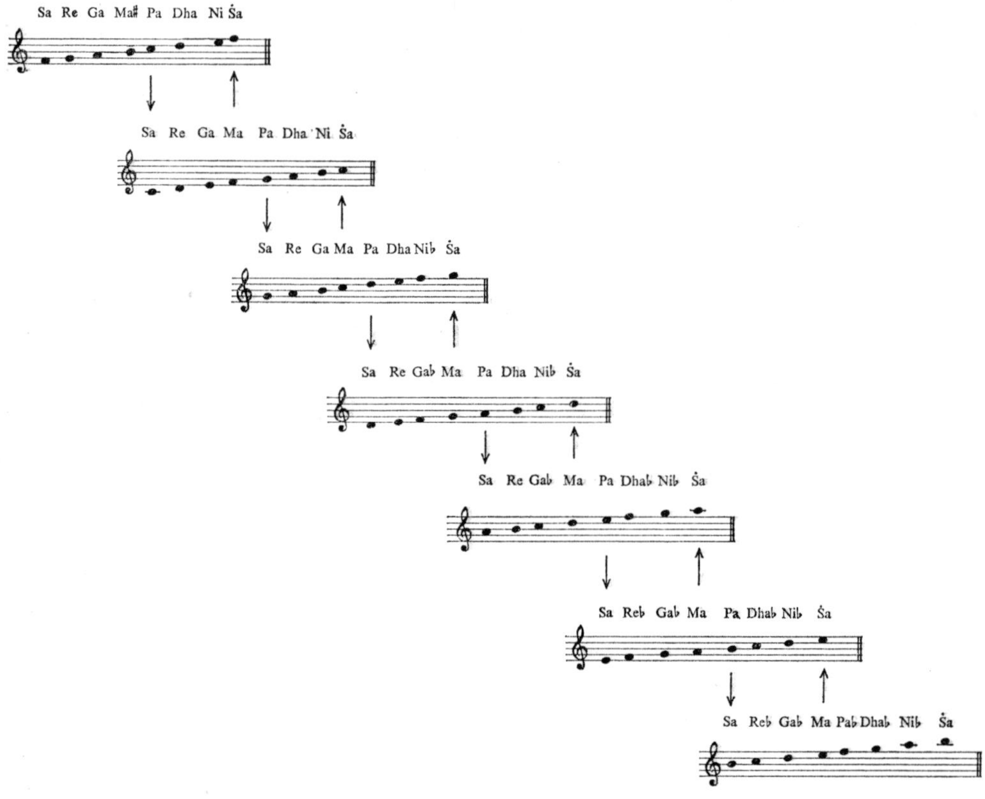

Let us look at our subject once again in a different light. In all our discussion of scales we have taken the upper limit of these scales entirely for granted. The feeling of identity which one experiences in the octave of the ground-note provides a 'natural' opportunity to terminate a scale. It has been said that the Octave has an unique status in the series of notes, comparable to the role of the number One in the set of all numbers.[1] There can, of course, be no denying the exceptional status of the octave;

[1] J. L. Dunk, *The Structure of the Musical Scale*, London 1940, p. 65.

we can, however, question whether the pre-eminence of the octave is a matter of degree or of kind. In other words, we can question whether the identity of the octave with the ground-note is absolute or whether *all* notes can be identified to some extent with the ground-note, while the octave has the highest degree of identity.

Perhaps we can gain an insight into this question by a consideration of what one would actually hear if the ground-note and its octave were sounded loudly and simultaneously. Under normal circumstances, the fundamental notes, Sa and Ṡa, would be the most prominent. One would also hear the overtones of the fundamentals, and, in addition to these, other series of tones produced by the interaction of the two fundamentals and their overtones. These are known as summation and difference tones.

The first summation tone is the sum of the frequencies of the two fundamentals, while the first difference tone is the difference between their frequencies. The relative loudness of the overtones and the summation and difference tones has been calculated by Sir James Jeans.[1] Based on his table, we give in order of diminishing intensity various tones heard when Sa and Ṡa are sounded together:

1.	Sa–Ṡa (I–İ)	The two fundamentals
2.	Ṡa–S̈a (İ–Ï)	The first overtones
	Ṗa (V̇)	The first summation tone
	Sa (I)	The first difference tone
3.	Ṗa–P̈a (V̇–V̈)	The second overtones

If we extend this list we will have, in diminishing intensity, the whole of the overtone series as well as the other summation and difference tones. For our purposes the above is sufficient for we already see the very considerable prominence of Pa in the sound we hear.

In comparison let us see what happens when Sa and Pa are sounded loudly and simultaneously:

1.	Sa–Pa (I–V)	The two fundamentals
2.	Ṡa–Ṗa (İ–V̇)	The first overtones
	Ġa (İII)	The first summation tone
	Ṣa (Ị)	The first difference tone
3.	Ṗa–R̈e (V̇–ÏI)	The second overtones

There is a marked similarity in the two lists. At the same time there are also some differences. Ga (III), which is the first summation tone of the Sa–Pa fundamentals, is only the fourth overtone given by the Sa–Ṡa fundamentals, and consequently will sound more prominent with the Sa–Pa fundamentals. The second overtone of Pa,

[1] *Science and Music*, Cambridge 1937, p. 236.

i.e. Ṙe (İI), appears only as the eighth overtone of Sa, and will certainly be more prominent with Sa–Pa as fundamentals.[1] At the same time the Sa is further strengthened by the first difference tone (Ṣa) of the Sa–Pa fundamentals, and this would tend to enhance the feeling of identity of the Pa with the Sa. This evidence seems to suggest that the difference between the relationship of the octave to the ground-note and the fifth to the ground-note is a matter of degree and not of kind. It is interesting to note that against a Sa drone the octave Ṡa, when sounded, produces Ṗa as a summation tone, while the Pa, when sounded against the same drone, produces Ṣa as a difference tone.

In Indian music particularly, where drones are prominent, the Sa and the Pa tend to acquire a certain ambivalence. The present writer has often noted the difficulty students experience in differentiating between Sa and Pa even when there is a clearly audible conventional drone in which the Sa fundamental is much more prominent than the Pa.

In our discussion of scales we have taken no special account of the Pa, considering it merely as one of the steps, albeit a consonant one, between the ground-note and its octave. It is of importance to note also that we felt no need to go beyond the octave on the presumption that the series of notes would repeat themselves from the octave onwards.[2] However, if the Pa can also be identified with the ground-note Sa, will there not be also a tendency to consider the Pa as the end of a register and the beginning of the next one? If this is so, do we not also expect the intervals to repeat themselves beyond the Pa, just as we expect the intervals to repeat themselves beyond the octave Ṡa?

This raises considerable difficulties, for the Pa does not divide the octave into two musically equal parts, Sa–Pa being a fifth and Pa–Ṡa being a fourth. In spite of this, there is a strong tendency to view the octave in two parallel parts. The half-way point of the twelve semitones of the octave is Ma♯ (IV♯), but the dissonance of this note to the ground-note should preclude its use as the end and beginning of a register. On either side of the Ma♯ are located the two most consonant notes (excluding the octave) i.e. those notes which are most easily identified with the Sa, and it is with these notes that the division of the octave is generally associated.

In ancient Greek musical theory the octave was divided into two tetrachords plus a wholetone. The wholetone could appear between the two tetrachords, Sa–Ma and Pa–Sa (I–IV and V–I), in which case the tetrachords were said to be disjunct, or the wholetone could appear at the end of the two tetrachords to complete the octave, Sa–Ma and Ma–Ni♭ (I–IV and IV–VII♭), and the tetrachords were then said to be conjunct. The octave can also be divided into two overlapping pentachords, or into a pentachord and a tetrachord. These have all been tried at one period or another,

[1] This may help to explain why the Re, which occurs as a terminal note in a number of *rāgs*, does not convey quite the same element of suspense as does the second in Western classical music based on harmony of the triad.

[2] This is not always true in Indian music, notable exceptions being the *rāgs* *Des* and *Soraṭh* of *Khamāj ṭhāṭ* in which some musicians use Ga♭ only in the upper register.

but no perfect division of the octave is possible so long as the consonance of Ma and Pa is recognised. This may explain why, in theoretical systems, the names of the notes do not repeat beyond the Ma or the Pa as they do beyond the octave.

Bhātkhaṇḍe refers to the two parts of the octave as *pūrvāṅg* and *uttrāṅg*, which he sometimes defines as the disjunct tetrachords Sa–Ma and Pa–Ṡa,[1] and at other times as two overlapping pentachords, Sa–Pa and Ma–Ṡa.[2] In Bhātkhaṇḍe's theory the only significance of this sort of division is to provide a basis for determining the time of day at which a *rāg* should be performed. We are suggesting, however, that each successive note in one tetrachord has a certain measure of identity with its counterpart in the other (e.g. Sa with Pa, Re with Dha, etc.) and that this identity is of the same kind, but of a lesser degree, as that which we experience between a note and its octave.

As we have pointed out, there are several possible ways in which the octave can be divided. With Pa as the secondary drone, it would be reasonable to think of the octave as consisting of two disjunct tetrachords, Sa–Ma and Pa–Ṡa[3]—a view which seems particularly reasonable when we consider the scale as an ascending series, with the Pa as the initial of the second tetrachord. In descent, however, this same principle leads to a division of the octave into two conjunct tetrachords, Ṡa–Pa and Pa–Re, with a wholetone, Re–Sa, appearing at the bottom of the scale. From this it becomes immediately apparent that a scale may easily be perceived in the light of more than one tetrachordal scheme, and that there is a certain measure of ambiguity in the location of the wholetone disjunction.

If we now consider the same scale with a secondary Ma drone, where Ma is the initial note of the second tetrachord, we have in ascent two conjunct tetrachords, Sa–Ma and Ma–Ni♭, with the wholetone disjunction, Ni♭–Ṡa, appearing at the top of the scale, whereas in descent we have two disjunct tetrachords, Ṡa–Pa and Ma–Sa, with the wholetone disjunction appearing between Pa and Ma. These four types are shown in the following schema:

Ex. 25. Tetrachord Species

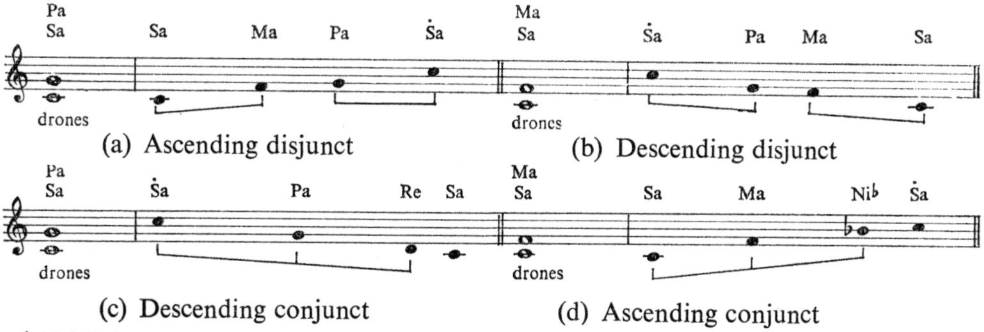

(a) Ascending disjunct (b) Descending disjunct

(c) Descending conjunct (d) Ascending conjunct

[1] *H.S.P.* I, p. 41.

[2] *K.P.M.* V, p. 31.

[3] If one permits the repetition of Pa, one could also consider the octave as a pentachord plus tetrachord, Sa–Pa and Pa–Ṡa. We shall, however, discuss this matter in terms of tetrachords.

It will be noticed that the ascending and descending disjunct tetrachord species are virtually the same, since the disjunction occurs between Ma and Pa.

There is, however, a measure of ambiguity in conjunct and disjunct tetrachord types; conjunct tetrachords become disjunct when extended above or below a single octave register, and vice versa. In musical practice the ascending disjunct tetrachords could be realised as ascending conjunct in the tessitura from P̣a to Pa (or Pa to Ṗa) as in Ex. 26a. Similarly, the other tetrachord types may be realised as in Ex. 26b, c, and d, respectively:

Ex. 26.

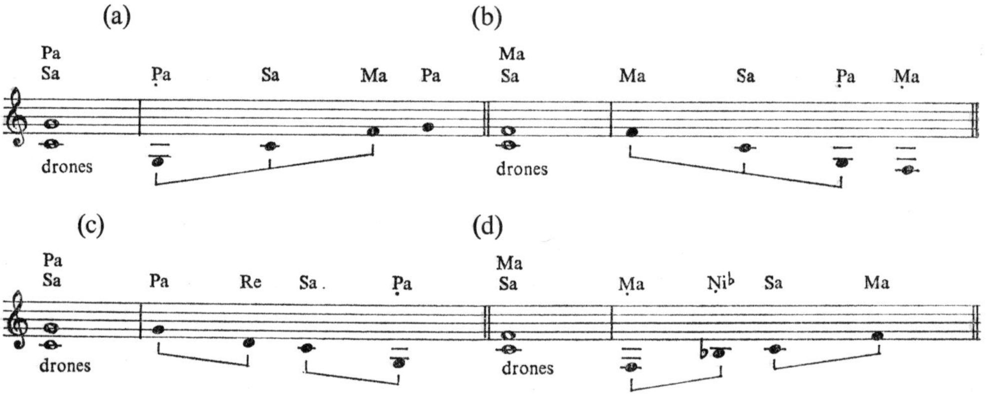

We have expressed these tetrachord types in relation to the drones, but it must be remembered that even when the secondary drone in a *rāg* is Ma, the Pa does have a considerable degree of consonance and may be an important note of that *rāg*. Similarly, when the secondary drone is Pa, the Ma also has a considerable degree of consonance and may also be important. Consequently, the tetrachord types are not always mutually exclusive and there are *rāg*s in which different tetrachord groupings may be emphasised as the *rāg* is developed through its various stages. Later in this chapter we will have occasion to discuss other tetrachordal divisions of the octave.

In analysing the six primary *ṭhāṭ*s we notice that some have parallel ascending disjunct tetrachords (i.e. the successive intervals in the two disjunct tetrachords are identical), while others have parallel descending conjunct tetrachords. Obviously, no scale may be parallel in both respects, for if it is parallel in one, the altered position of the disjunct wholetone ensures that it will be unbalanced in the other.

Inseparable from the consideration of these tetrachord types is the concept of the consonance of fourths and fifths. The successive intervals of two parallel conjunct tetrachords will be a fourth apart, while the successive intervals of two parallel disjunct tetrachords will be a fifth apart. In the primary *ṭhāṭ*s, as we have indicated earlier, there is only one imperfect relationship—one pair of notes bearing the relationship of augmented fourth/diminished fifth. It is this imperfect relationship which destroys the parallelism in one of the tetrachord types. If within the octave register the two notes stand as an augmented fourth, the conjunct tetrachord relationship will be unbalanced while the disjunct tetrachord relationship of fifths will remain perfect and balanced. If, however, the two notes stand as a diminished fifth within the octave register, the disjunct relationship of fifths will be disturbed.

Viewed from the standpoint of musical practice, this discrepancy in the scale could be noticed in two ways, neither of which need be on a conscious level. First, it could be noticed through the absence of a consonant fourth or fifth. This would be particularly significant in a musical system where fourths or fifths might be sounded simultaneously. A good example of this can be found in early Western Church music where the practice of parallel Organum (two voices moving in perfect fourths or fifths, note against note) drew attention to the tritone[1] (augmented fourth) and led to the introduction of accidentals. This is probably not so significant in Indian music where only a single melody line is generally used, and jumps of fourths and fifths are exceptional. Secondly, it could come to notice as the musician tries to repeat a melodic phrase in the second tetrachord register. From our earlier discussion of the identity associated with the successive notes of the tetrachords, it would seem that the inability to repeat a phrase or even an interval in the second tetrachord would be disturbing in the same way, but to a lesser degree, as the inability to repeat a melodic figure or an interval in the next octave register. From the long range evolutionary point of view this disturbance, as we hope to show, provides the vital spur for the evolution of new musical scales.

Let us now consider the application of these principles. In *Bilāval ṭhāṭ* (No. A2) the ascending disjunct tetrachords are parallel, while the descending conjunct tetrachords are unbalanced:

Ex. 27. Bilāval ṭhāṭ

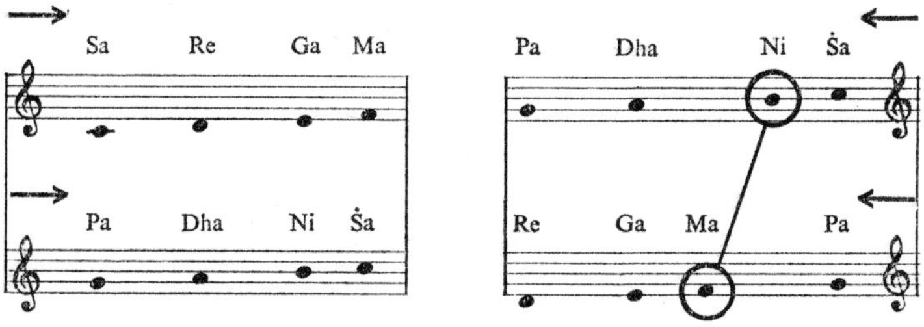

Ascending disjunct tetrachords Descending conjunct tetrachords

In this scale the lack of balance is created by the difference in the first descending steps in the two conjunct tetrachords: the interval between Ṡa and Ni is a semitone, while the interval between Pa and Ma is a wholetone. This is a characteristic feature

[1] In Western plainsong the tritone was forbidden and in early polyphonic music was referred to as *diabolus in musica* (the devil in music).

of *Bilāval ṭhāṭ*; nevertheless, the lack of balance here demands special treatment, and it appears that certain melodic features are directly motivated by this irregularity in the scale and are manifest in many *rāg*s of *Bilāval ṭhāṭ*. Some of these melodic features will be discussed in the chapters that follow.

In general it may be said that these melodic features tend to diminish the disturbing effect of the imbalance, but the final solution is to replace one of the unbalanced notes by a balanced one: in *Bilāval ṭhāṭ*, to replace the Ni♮ by a Ni♭, or the Ma♮ by a Ma♯. The former leads to *Khamāj ṭhāṭ* (No. A3), and the latter to *Kalyāṇ* (No. A1). Both of these have balanced descending conjunct tetrachords, but the balance in the ascending disjunct tetrachords is now disturbed. In these scales too melodic features tend to arise to compensate for the imbalance, but once again the final solution can be achieved only through replacement of one of the unbalanced notes, thus leading to new scales. Passing over *Kalyāṇ ṭhāṭ* for the time being, let us look more closely at *Khamāj ṭhāṭ*:

Ex. 28. Khamāj ṭhāṭ

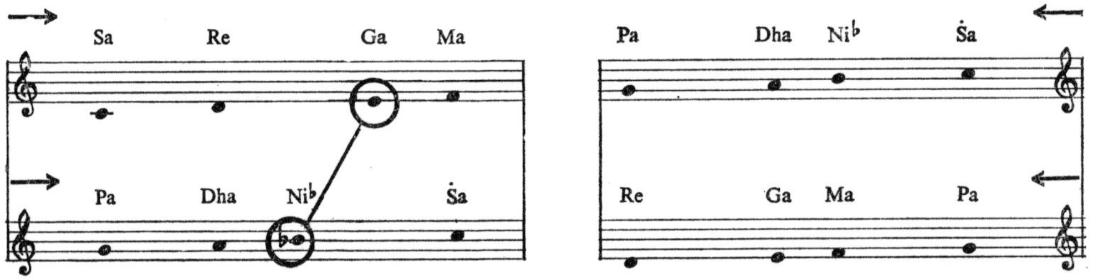

In the ascending disjunct tetrachords of *Khamāj*, the thirds Sa–Ga and Pa–Ni♭ are unbalanced. This can be corrected either by replacing the Ni♭ by a Ni♮, or the Ga♮ by a Ga♭. The former returns to *Bilāval ṭhāṭ*, while the latter leads to *Kāfī ṭhāṭ* (No. A4). Both these have balanced ascending disjunct tetrachords and the imbalance is apparent in their descending conjunct tetrachords.

Ex. 29. Kāfī ṭhāṭ

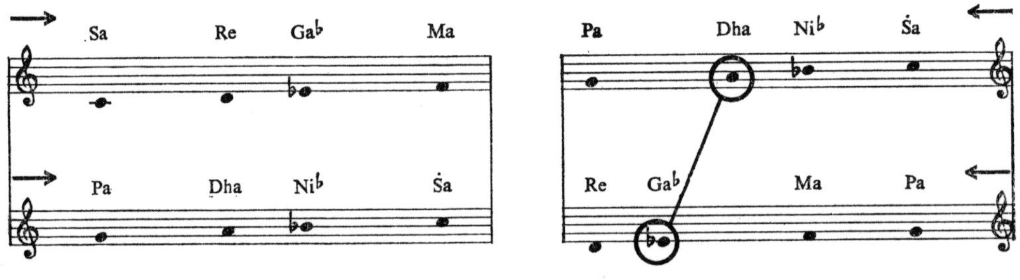

In *Kāfī ṭhāṭ* Ṡa–Dha is a descending minor third, while Pa–Ga♭ is a descending major third. This can be corrected either by replacing the Ga♭ by a Ga♮, or the Dha♮

by a Dha♭. The former returns to *Khamāj ṭhāṭ*, while the latter introduces the new scale *Āsāvrī ṭhāṭ* (No. A5):

Ex. 30. Āsāvrī ṭhāṭ

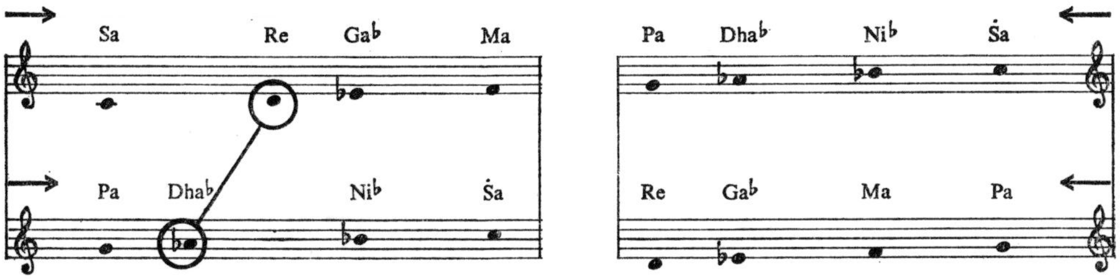

In *Āsāvrī ṭhāṭ* the ascending disjunct tetrachords are unbalanced: Sa–Re is a major second, while Pa–Dha♭ is a minor second. This can be balanced either by replacing the Dha♭ with a Dha♮, or the Re♮ with a Re♭. The former returns to *Kāfī ṭhāṭ*, while the latter leads to *Bhairvī ṭhāṭ* (No. A6):

Ex. 31. Bhairvī ṭhāṭ

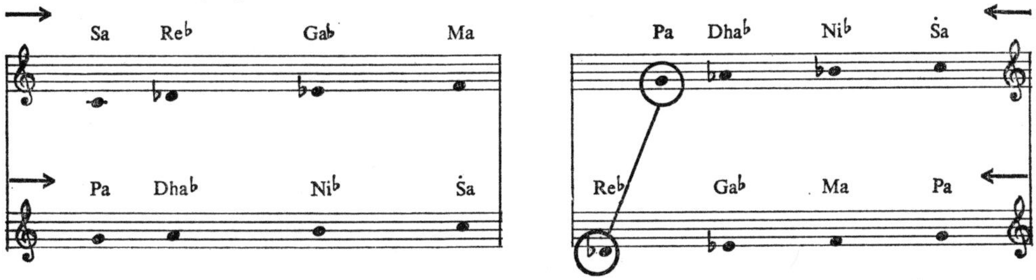

In *Bhairvī ṭhāṭ* the descending conjunct tetrachords are unbalanced; Ṡa–Pa is a descending perfect fourth, while Pa–Re♭ is a descending augmented fourth. This could be balanced either by replacing the Re♭ by a Re♮, or the Pa by a Pa♭. The first course leads us back to *Āsāvrī ṭhāṭ*. In the second instance we are once again confronted with the same difficulty we have faced so many times. The Pa♭ is not permitted in Indian music.

We have once again arrived at a dead end. It will have been noticed that the six scales we have covered are once again the six primary *ṭhāṭ*s. We now return to a consideration of *Kalyāṇ ṭhāṭ*:

Ex. 32. Kalyāṇ ṭhāṭ

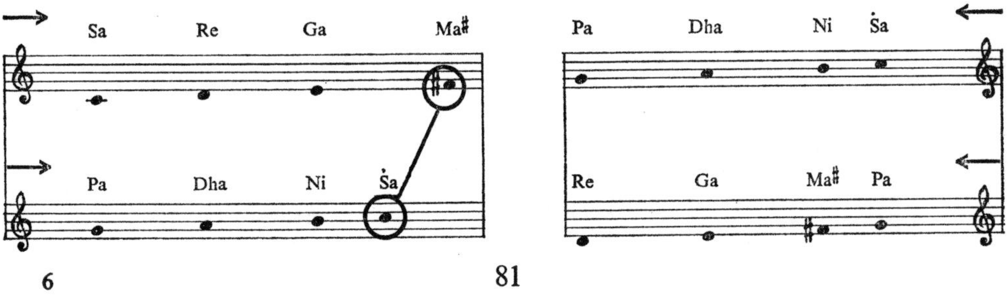

In *Kalyāṇ ṭhāṭ* the ascending disjunct tetrachords are unbalanced: Sa–Ma♯ is an augmented fourth, while Pa–Ṡa is a perfect fourth. This could be corrected either by replacing the Ma♯ by a Ma♮, or by replacing the Sa by a Sa♯. The former leads back to *Bilāval ṭhāṭ*, while the latter is not permissible. Are we once again at a dead end?

The musician, faced with this imbalance between Ma♯ and Sa in the ascending disjunct tetrachords which may not be solved by replacing the Sa with a Sa♯, will naturally try to minimise its effect. One way this can be done is by the omission of one or both of the offending notes, and although the Sa may not be altered, there is no restriction against the temporary omission of it in a particular melodic phrase. Thus in the principal *rāg* of *Kalyāṇ ṭhāṭ*, *Yaman*, Sa is often temporarily omitted in both ascent and descent,[1] and phrases in which the Sa is omitted (see Ex. 33a) are much more characteristic than those including the Sa (Ex. 33b). Once the Sa is omitted, however, the Pa has lost one of its supports, and there is an equal tendency to omit the Pa and phrases parallel to those in which the Sa is omitted are frequently heard (Ex. 33c).

Ex. 33. rāg Yaman

Phrases in which Sa and Pa are omitted are often greatly extended and may encompass a full octave[2] or more:

Ex. 34. rāg Yaman

Let us consider for a moment the balances of the *rāg Yaman* in the phrases where Sa and Pa are omitted:

Ex. 35. rāg Yaman, Kalyāṇ ṭhāṭ [Sa and Pa omitted]

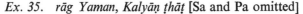

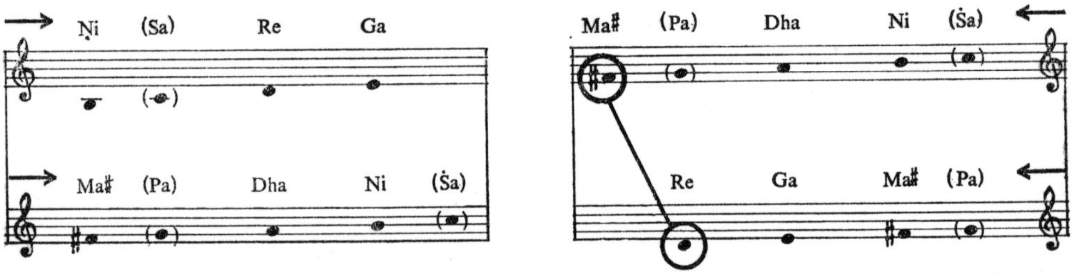

[1] The Ma♯ is also temporarily omitted in *rāg Yaman* and this omission is also characteristic of several other *rāgs* in this *ṭhāṭ*. *Yaman* is played on the accompanying record and is discussed further in Appendix B, pp. 204, 205.

[2] In *Ustād* Vilayat Khan's rendering of *Yaman* on the accompanying record there is no extended passage in which Sa and Pa are omitted. Such passages are quite normal in *Yaman* and are also played by Vilayat Khan, for example on his commercial record, E.M.I. ASD 2425.

When the Sa and Pa are in the scale, the Re balances the Pa, and it is the Sa which is out of balance with the Ma♯. When the Pa is removed from the scale, it could be either Sa or Re which can be said to be out of balance with the Ma♯, but when the Sa is also omitted there is no alternative but to see the Re in relationship with the Ma♯. Now there is only one possibility of creating balance, for the Ma♯ cannot be raised any higher. The Re must be replaced by Re♭. This gives us the scale of *Mārvā ṭhāṭ* (No. A10), and we have finally progressed beyond the primary *ṭhāṭ*s.

Ex. 36. Mārvā ṭhāṭ

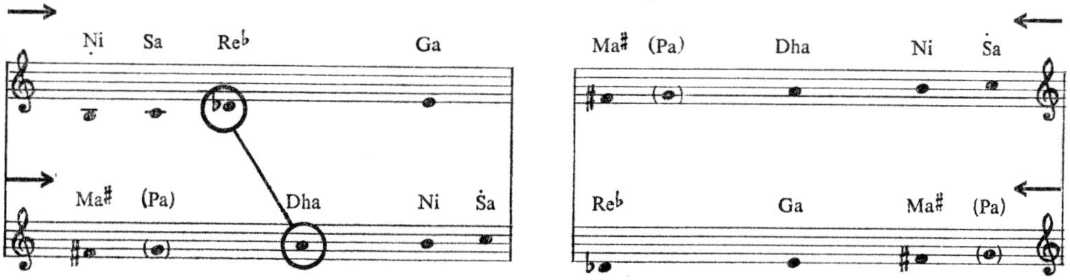

It will be seen that we have put the Pa in brackets; although the Pa is necessary to the definition of *ṭhāṭ* in which each of the seven degrees is required, neither tetrachord will be balanced unless the Pa is omitted. In view of this it is not surprising that many of the *rāg*s in this *ṭhāṭ*, including the *rāg Mārvā* after which the *ṭhāṭ* is named, are hexatonic and omit the Pa. Just as in *Kalyāṇ*, the omission of Pa means that the Sa has lost one of its supports and there is a strong tendency to omit the Sa temporarily in particular phrases. This phenomenon is so characteristic of *rāg Mārvā*, that its ascending and descending lines have been given as follows:[1]

Ex. 37. rāg Mārvā

Earlier we had indicated that the dissonant quality of the Ma♯ tended to prevent the use of this note as the initial of a tetrachord. In view of the fact that the Pa is omitted completely and the Sa is frequently omitted in certain phrases we could consider the parallelism occurring in the descending conjunct tetrachords, Ni–Ma♯ and Ma♯–Re♭, with a semitone disjunction at either end.[2]

Ex. 38.

[1] This is sung in demonstration by Rām Nārāyaṇ, the *sāraṅgī* player, on the long-playing record B.A.M. LD 094.

[2] The conjunct parallelism could also be expressed as being in the two tetrachords Dha–Ga and Ga–Ṇi (VI–III and III–ⱯII).

If we now consider the scale of *rāg Mārvā*, without the Sa and Pa, it will be seen that the ascending disjunct tetrachords are unbalanced due to the augmented fifth relationship of the Re♭ and the Dha. This can be corrected either by replacing the Re♭ with a Re♮ or the Dha♮ with a Dha♭. The former returns to *Kalyāṇ* (see Ex. 32), the latter to the new *ṭhāṭ*, *Pūrvī* (No. A9).

Ex. 39. Pūrvī ṭhāṭ

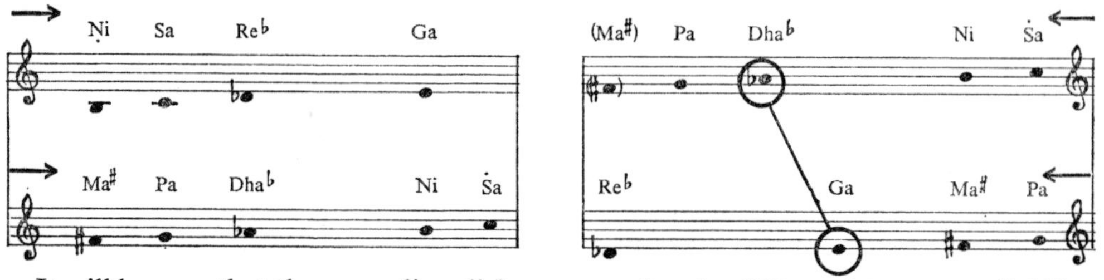

It will be seen that the ascending disjunct tetrachords of *Pūrvī ṭhāṭ* are parallel if we think of them from Ṇi to Ga and from Ma♯ to Ni. If we go further, either the Sa must be omitted temporarily, as is sometimes the case in *rāg*s of this *ṭhāṭ*, or the Ma♯ must be replaced by a Ma♮ (in order to provide balance for the Sa), thus making two parallel ascending disjunct tetrachords, Sa–Ma and Pa–Sa. This leads to *Bhairav ṭhāṭ* (No. C9) which is not part of the Circle of *Ṭhāṭ*s, but is, nevertheless, of great importance in Indian music.

Before discussing *Bhairav ṭhāṭ* in greater detail, we propose to complete our discussion of the Circle of *Ṭhāṭ*s. Returning to a consideration of *Pūrvī ṭhāṭ* (Ex. 39), it will be seen that the descending conjunct tetrachords are unbalanced in two respects: first, the Pa has no perfect fifth to support it, so there is a tendency to omit this note in some *rāg*s of this *ṭhāṭ*, just as in the *rāg*s of *Mārvā ṭhāṭ*; and secondly, the Dha♭ is not balanced by the Ga. This can be corrected either by replacing the Dha♭ with Dha♮, which leads us back to *Mārvā ṭhāṭ*, or by replacing the Ga♮ with Ga♭, leading us to the new *ṭhāṭ* in the Circle, *Toṛī*.

Ex. 40. Toṛī ṭhāṭ

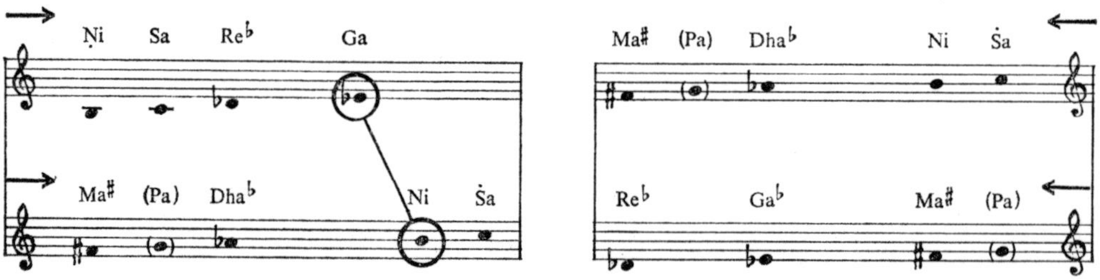

Since the Pa has no support in the descending conjunct tetrachords, it is not surprising that one of the very few *rāg*s in this *ṭhāṭ*, *Gujrī Toṛī*, is hexatonic omitting the Pa. The *rāg Toṛī* (also called *Mīyā̃ Kī Toṛī*), too, manifests this same tendency to omit the Pa in particular phrases, and, correspondingly, to omit the Sa which is unbalanced in the ascending disjunct tetrachords.[1]

The ascending disjunct tetrachords of *Toṛī* are unbalanced in two respects. The Sa has no perfect fourth, and, as we have indicated, is frequently omitted in phrases in the *rāg Toṛī* as well as in *Gujrī Toṛī.* There is not the same urgency as in *Pūrvī ṭhāṭ* to replace the Ma♯ with a Ma♮ to support the Sa, as the ascending disjunct tetrachords will still remain unbalanced due to the augmented fifth relationship of the Ga♭ and Ni♮. This second imbalance can be corrected either by replacing the Ga♭ by a Ga♮, which takes us back to *Pūrvī ṭhāṭ*, or the Ni♮ by a Ni♭, which leads us to the hypothetical *ṭhāṭ* (No. A7) and completes our Circle of *Ṭhāṭs*. Before leaving this Circle, we must consider how the hypothetical *ṭhāṭ* could also have been arrived at from *Bhairvī.* It will be seen from the tetrachord scheme of *Bhairvī* (Ex. 31 on p. 81) that in the descending conjunct tetrachords the Pa and Re♭ are unbalanced. We have already mentioned one possibility of creating balance, that of replacing the Re♭ by a Re♮, and have indicated that the second possibility of replacing the Pa by a Pa♭ is not acceptable in Indian music. In discussing *Kalyāṇ ṭhāṭ*, which has similar problems to those of *Bhairvī*, we had suggested that the musician would naturally try to minimise the effect of this imbalance, and would tend to omit one or both of the offending notes. This is readily apparent in *Bhairvī ṭhāṭ* also, where in the very prominent pentatonic *rāg Mālkoś* just these two notes, the Re♭ and Pa, are omitted. In the *rāg Bhairvī* too, the same tendency is also manifest and the Re♭ and Pa are frequently omitted in particular phrases (see p. 125). Once the Pa is omitted, the Re♭ can only be balanced by changing the Ma♮ to Ma♯, and thus one could arrive at the hypothetical *ṭhāṭ*.

Having argued that the hypothetical scale could have arisen in Indian music, we must now attempt some explanation for its absence in the current repertoire of the musician. In one respect the scale of the hypothetical *ṭhāṭ* is musically unstable.

Ex. 41.

From the consonance–dissonance charts (on p. 66) it will be apparent that the most dynamic notes in the octave are the Re♭ (II♭), Ma♯ (IV♯), Dha♭ (VI♭) and Ni♮ (VII). The Re♭ and the Ni demand resolution in the ground-note, Sa, while the Ma♯ and the Dha♭ demand resolution in its fifth, Pa. When Pa is a secondary drone, the demand for resolution on it is intensified. Three of these dissonant notes, Re♭, Ma♯ and Dha♭, are in the hypothetical *ṭhāṭ*; as there is no Ni♮, only the Re♭ resolves in the Sa, while both Ma♯ and Dha♭ demand resolution on the Pa. As a consequence, it may very easily be that the Pa has a strong tendency to usurp the place of the Sa and lead to a

[1] This *rāg* can be heard on the L.P. record ASD 498 (E.M.I.) played by *Ustād* Imrat Khan on the *surbahār*.

plagal inversion.[1] There would also be a very strong tendency to introduce Ni♮ both as a leading note in ascent[2] and to provide symmetry in the descending conjunct tetrachords.

From the standpoint of balance too, this scale appears to be more unstable than the others. As in *Mārvā, Pūrvī* and *Toṛī ṭhāṭ*s there is a tendency to introduce Ma♮ to balance Sa, but in this *ṭhāṭ* Ma♮ is a double balance note since it also balances Ni♭. Thus there must be a very strong tendency to introduce Ma♮ and move the scale back to *Bhairvī.* If instead Ni♮ were introduced to balance Ma♯, the resulting scale, *Toṛī*, is not nearly so unstable as the Ma♮ would only balance one note, Sa, while putting Ni♮ out of balance.

Ex. 42. Hypothetical ṭhāṭ

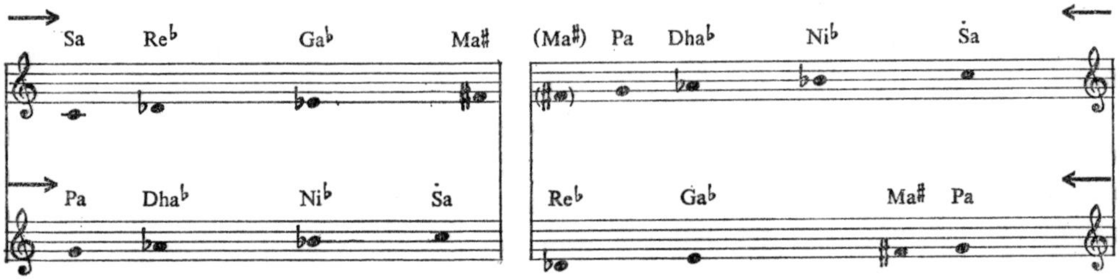

We now return to a further consideration of *Bhairav ṭhāṭ* and the related phenomena which lead to the curious scales of the *Lalit rāg*s, which use both Ma♮ and Ma♯ and are thus outside the thirty-two *ṭhāṭ* system. In the ascending disjunct tetrachords of *Pūrvī* we have already explained how, if we progress beyond the tetrachords Ṇi–Ga and Ma♯–Ni, either the Sa must be omitted or the Ma♯ must be replaced by the Ma♮ forming *Bhairav ṭhāṭ*.

Ex. 43. Bhairav ṭhāṭ

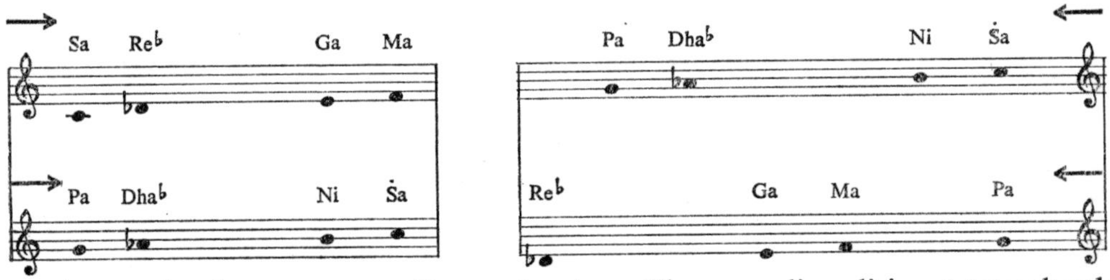

Bhairav ṭhāṭ has an extraordinary structure. The ascending disjunct tetrachords are parallel while the descending conjunct tetrachords are completely unbalanced.

1 In Western terms the Sa lacks a leading note, while the Pa has one and thus tends to receive greater importance than the Sa. The resulting scale:

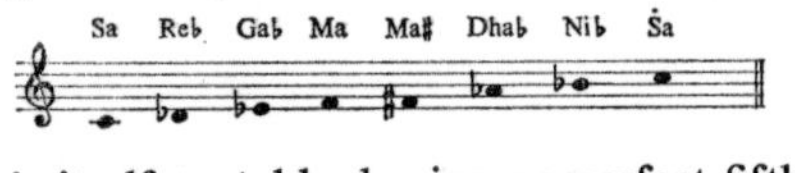

is itself unstable, having no perfect fifth and no semitone leading notes below either the Sa or the Ma. There are at present two *rāg*s in which the Pa has a leading note, while the Sa does not. These two *rāg*s, *Madhukoś* (*Madhukāus*) and *Madhukānt*, are both modern *rāg*s which appear to be evolving rapidly. These are discussed in Chapter VII (pp. 136, 137).

2 See pp. 113, 114.

Perhaps the popularity of this scale can be explained, in part at least, by the fact that there is both simple parallelism in the disjunct tetrachords as well as complete imbalance in the conjunct, thus making for extreme contrasts between symmetry and asymmetry. The imbalance in the descending conjunct tetrachords can lead to the replacement of any of the five movable notes by their chromatic counterparts. Some of the resulting new scales still bear names which hint at their origin, *Ahīr Bhairav*, (No. C3), *Naṭ Bhairav* (No. C2) and *Ānand Bhairav* (No. B10). In fact, all thirty-two *ṭhāṭ*s could eventually be obtained through *Bhairav*.

There is no doubt, however, that Ma♯ is the most prominent alternative note in *Bhairav ṭhāṭ*, and occurs as an accidental in a number of *rāg*s in this *ṭhāṭ* (e.g. *Rāmkalī*, see p. 49). It is probably this impulse which has also led to the introduction of the *rāg Lalit* (No. 34) which appears to be a compromise between *Bhairav* and *Pūrvī ṭhāṭ*s. It can be seen more clearly as a derivative of *Pūrvī*. The Re♭ (II♭) and Pa (V) are unbalanced in this *ṭhāṭ* and we have noted earlier that the Pa is sometimes omitted. Since this leaves the Sa without either a perfect fourth or a perfect fifth it seems very plausible that the Ma♮ (IV♮) is introduced to provide conjunct balance for the Sa. In other circumstances the Ma♯ would probably have been omitted, but here it is supported by both Re♭ and Ni:

Ex. 44. rāg Lalit

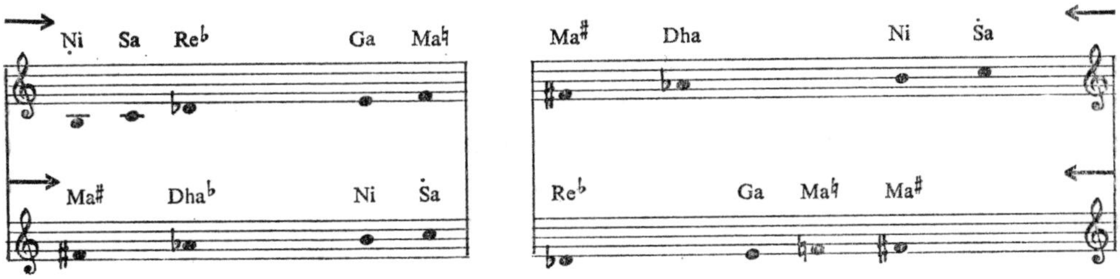

It will be seen that the ascending disjunct tetrachords Ṇi–Ga and Ma♯–Ni are balanced only when the Sa is omitted as is frequently the case in this *rāg*.[1] The version of *Lalit* given by Bhātkhaṇḍe (No. 33) can be derived in a similar manner from *Mārvā ṭhāṭ*, the Pa (V) being omitted as it is unbalanced with the Re♭, the Ma♮ (IV♮) being introduced to balance the Sa, and the Ma♯ (IV♯) being too well supported by the Re♭ (II♭) and the Ni (VII) to be omitted:

Ex. 45. rāg Lalit

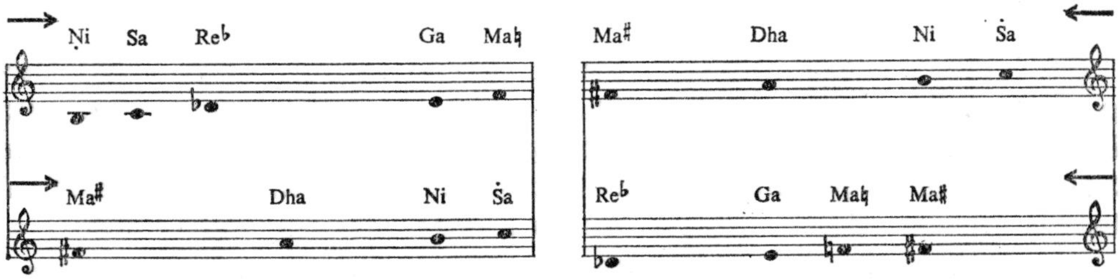

[1] See p. 51.

The *rāg Ahīr Lalit* (No. 35) can be explained as a derivative of this *rāg*, having a further conjunct balance, the Ni♭ being introduced as a support for the Ma♮:

Ex. 46. rāg Ahīr Lalit

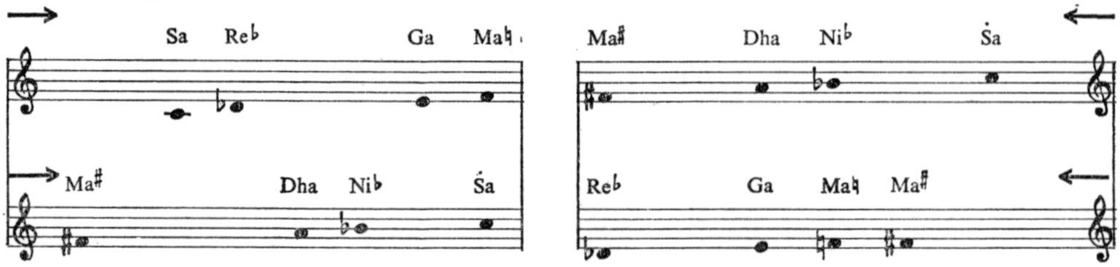

These three *Lalit rāg*s can also be explained in another way as plagal inversions (i.e. the series beginning on Pa) of three *ṭhāṭ*s: the inversion of *Pūrvī* gives Bhātkhaṇḍe's version of *Lalit* (No. 33); the inversion of *Toṛī* gives the commonly heard *Lalit* of today (No. 34) and the inversion of *Bhairav* gives *Ahīr Lalit* (No. 35). This explanation does not appear to be very plausible, particularly in connection with the two *Lalit*s since the Pa is generally weak in the *rāg*s of *Toṛī* and *Pūrvī ṭhāṭ*s and there seems no reason for the plagal inversion. However, *Ahīr Lalit* may well have been derived in this way.

In spite of the strange scale of these *Lalit rāg*s, their musical justification in terms of balanced tetrachords will be evident (in Ex. 45, Dha–Ga and Ga–Ṇi, descending conjunct, are parallel; in Ex. 46, Sa–Ma and Ma–Ni♭, ascending conjunct). However, balanced tetrachords are difficult to achieve in some of the 'isolate' *rāg*s which have recently been introduced into North Indian music. This may indicate that the importance of balanced tetrachords is diminishing. The *rāg Cārukeśī* (No. B3), for example, has unbalanced conjunct as well as disjunct tetrachords:

Ex. 47. rāg Cārukeśī

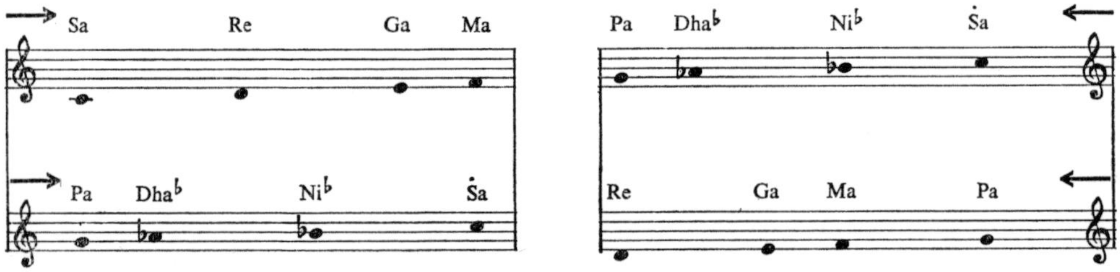

Can it be that one of the fundamental impulses in North Indian music is undergoing change or modification, or will time ensure that balance is somehow created in one of its tetrachords? The pentatonic *rāg Haṃsdhvanī* which was also taken from South Indian music, probably more than forty years ago,[1] now shows signs of artificial balance being introduced to compensate for an inherently unbalanced scale:

[1] Bhātkhaṇḍe described this *rāg* as one which had been introduced from Karnatic music and was quite rare in his time. *K.P.M.* V, p. 255.

Ex. 48. *rāg Haṃsdhvanī*

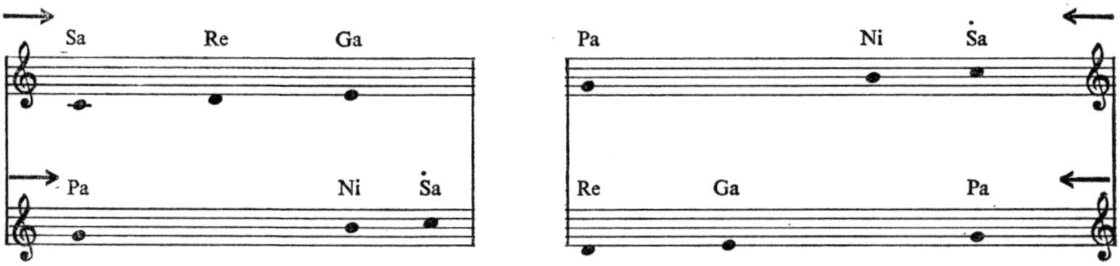

This is accomplished by means of turns in which Sa and Re are temporarily omitted, for example in the following phrases, where in (a) Ga Pa is parallelled by Ni Ṙe, and in (b) Ni Pa is parallelled by Ga Sa.[1]

Ex. 49. *rāg Haṃsdhvanī*

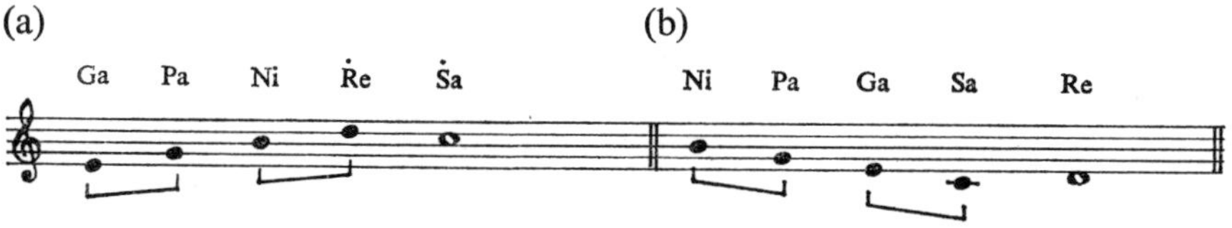

In the *rāg Cārukeśī*, too, there are indications of similar turns which produce a measure of symmetry within the *rāg*, but these are not yet clearly defined. It is too early to tell if the urge to balance tetrachords has now weakened and will finally be lost, or whether it will reassert itself once the novelty of these new scales has worn off.

[1] This can be heard on the recording of the *rāg Haṃsdhvanī* played by Ravi Shankar, E.M.I. ALP 1893.

V

Evolution of the Circle of Ṭhāṭs

While the ten *ṭhāṭ*s of Bhātkhaṇḍe's system are musically coherent through their relationship to each other, the course of their evolution was neither coherent nor systematic. It was frequently diverted by mutations which were either retrogressive or led to blind alleys or were too far in advance of their period to be accepted. So it is not entirely surprising that the *ṭhāṭ*s have not evolved in an orderly manner around the Circle.

Indian music appears to have undergone a fairly radical change probably some time before the 10th century A.D., a change which may have been associated with the replacement of the ancient bow-harp *vīṇā* (which is now obsolete) by stick zithers and long-necked lutes, which are now commonly found in India. In the introductory chapter we outlined the musical system described in the *Nāṭyaśāstra*, perhaps the earliest work on Indian secular music. Here the music was based on seven serial modes (*śuddha jāti*) derived from two very similar parent scales, the *Ṣaḍjagrāma* and the *Madhyamagrāma*.[1]

A system based on serial modes of this nature implies a difference in the pitch of the starting note of each mode, particularly in application to musical instruments. The practice of changing ground-notes for the successive modes can be accomplished easily on bow-harps where, presumably, all the strings are melody strings and are tuned to the successive degrees of the scale. This could, however, cause considerable inconvenience when applied to stick zithers and long-necked lutes where, as today, a number of strings could be used to supply the drone and would have to be retuned for each change of mode. Thus it seems probable that the prominence of the drone[2] is associated with the widespread acceptance of stick zithers and long-necked lutes and that the inconvenience as well as the practical difficulties entailed in retuning the instruments led to the acceptance of a standard ground-note, Sa, to which the modes

[1] A third parent scale, the *Gāndhāragrāma*, mentioned in other early works does not appear to have been significant in Bharata's time, although it is referred to under the section on *Mārjanā* (tuning of drums). *Nāṭyaśāstra*, Chapter XXXII, śl. 37, Bib. Ind. no. 272. The system of 'pure' *jāti*s had already been extended, in the *Nāṭyaśāstra*, to include eleven other 'altered' modes (*vikṛita jāti*).

[2] Unfortunately, the early treatises do not mention the drone and the later treatises follow their pattern. As a consequence, there is even now no commonly accepted term for drone in North India.

were then transposed. As we have indicated earlier, this does not imply a fixed and invariable pitch for the Sa, which merely provides a common frame of reference for the different modes, just as does the Doh in the Western sol-fa system.

When serial modes are transposed to a common tonic, they lose their cyclic significance, and it is neither so obvious nor of particular importance that they are derivatives of a parent scale or scales. The acceptance of a standard tonic, influenced by the requirements of stick zithers, was probably responsible for the loss of distinction between the two ancient parent scales, although it is not until much later that this is clearly admitted.[1] The subtle difference between the four *śruti* major whole-tone, the three *śruti* minor whole-tone and the two *śruti* semitone in the modes of the two parent scales would require about eighteen frets (or stops) in the octave and these would have to be positioned so close to each other as to be impractical.[2]

Six of the seven serial modes of the early period have continued in Indian music to the present time, reflecting the continuity of tradition in India. It must be remembered, however, that these six, the primary *ṭhāṭ*s, are the most consonant possible as they have only one tritone (augmented fourth/diminished fifth relationship), the other fourths and fifths being perfect. Consequently, they might arise in any musical culture in which the consonance of perfect fourths and fifths is recognised. The fact that the seventh mode, the *jāti Dhaivatī* (B mode), prominent in ancient India, is not now used in Indian music is an indication that the seven ancient modes were not held in any great sanctity after the changes had entered the musical system.

Many of the North Indian treatises dating from about the 11th century A.D. describe *rāga*s in terms of the hierarchy, *rāga* (masculine) and *rāginī* (feminine), a fanciful classificatory scheme which was extended to include *putra* (son) and *bhāryā* (wife of the son) as the number of *rāga*s increased.[3] These *rāga-rāginī* classification schemes do not appear to have been based primarily on musical principles. In the most commonly used schemes there are six masculine *rāga*s, each having either five or six *rāginī*s. There are, however, divergent opinions as to which are the six *rāga*s and which are their *rāginī*s. According to Muḥammad Rezā, *c.* 1813, four principal traditions appear to have been current,[4] but Gangoly presents a more realistic view when he draws attention to the 'bewildering variety of catalogues, groups and classifications'.[5]

Concurrent with the *rāga-rāginī* schemes occur the much less fanciful classification systems based on scale, *mela* (present-day *ṭhāṭ*), which presuppose that all scales have been transposed to a common tonic. The majority of the treatises adopting this method appear to have been describing the South Indian musical system. One of the

[1] For instance in the *Rasakaumudī* of Śrī Kaṇṭha (probably 18th century) and *Saṅgītasārāmṛita* of Rājā Tulaja (18th century) in both of which only the *Ṣaḍjagrāma* is said to be in existence.

[2] See p. 21.

[3] *Saṅgītamakaranda* of Nārada which is probably the first text in which the melodic system is classified into three groups, masculine, feminine and neuter. Gangoly, *op. cit.*, p. 23.

[4] Quoted in Gangoly, *op. cit.*, p. 220.

[5] *Ibid.*, p. 92.

earliest North Indian texts of this nature is the *Rāgataraṅgiṇī* written by Locana Kavī (probably 16th or 17th century),[1] a work of considerable importance for evidence of the evolution of modern North Indian *rāgs*.

Locana classifies *rāgas* in terms of the following twelve scales.[2]

Locana's *melas*	Scale	Modern *ṭhāṭ*
Bhairavī		Kāfī (No. A4)
Toṛī		Bhairvī (No. A6)
Gaurī		Bhairav (No. C9)
Karṇāṭa		Khamāj (No. A3)
Kedāra		Bilāval (No. A2)
Imana		Kalyāṇ (No. A1)
Sāraṅga		
Megha		
Dhanāśrī		Pūrvī (No. A9)

[1] The date of this work is discussed on p. 20, f.n.4

[2] These twelve scales are also mentioned in *Hṛidayaprakāśa* of the late 17th century.

Pūravā

Mukhārī

Āsāvrī (No. A5)

Dīpaka no description

It will be apparent that eight of the modern ten *ṭhāṭ*s were in existence at the time of Locana, probably more than three hundred years ago. The *mela*s *Sāraṅga* and *Megha* involve the use of Ga♯ and Dha♯ which is not permissible today, and they would therefore appear to be chromatic scales from the modern point of view. But if we interpret the Ga♯ and Dha♯ as their chromatic counterparts Ma♮ and Ni♭ respectively,[1] the description would then be consistent with the modern *rāg Śuddh Sāraṅg* which is largely pentatonic but uses both alternatives of Ma and Ni. Similarly, *Megha* may be interpreted as a hexatonic scale having both alternatives of Ni. *Pūravā* is, however, a different matter, for according to the *Rāgataraṅgiṇī* the Dha in this scale is raised by one *śruti*.[2] Since *Pūravā* appears to have no counterpart at the present time, it may be described as an unsuccessful mutation.[3]

The modern *Mārvā* (No. A10) and *Toṛī* (No. A8) *ṭhāṭ*s are not among Locana's *mela*s and appear to have evolved since his time. This is a clear indication that the modern *Bhairav* (No. C9) and *Pūrvī* (No. A9) *ṭhāṭ*s did not originate as parts of the Circle of *Ṭhāṭ*s as there are discontinuities in both clockwise and anti-clockwise directions. The following diagram shows the discontinuity of Locana's *mela*s in terms of the Circle of *Ṭhāṭ*s:

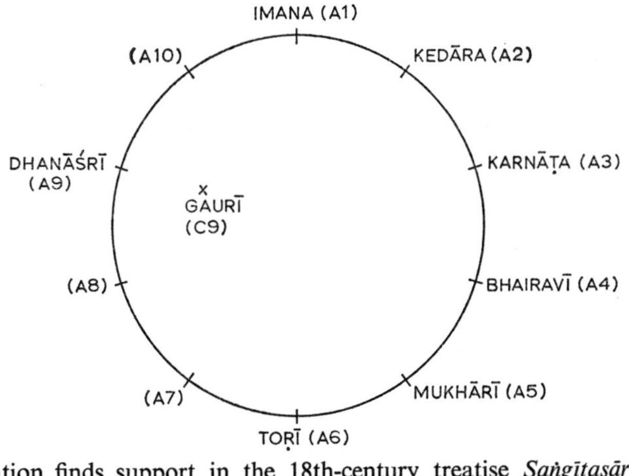

[1] This interpretation finds support in the 18th-century treatise *Saṅgītasārāmṛita*, where the author, Tulaja, discussing *Sāraṅga mela*, equates Ga♯ with Ma♮ (*Music Academy Series*, No. 5, 1942, p. 111).

[2] *Hṛidayaprakāśa* (second half of the 17th century) which follows the same scheme as the *Rāgataraṅgiṇī*, states that the Dha of *Pūravā* is very sharp (*tīvratara*) as are also the Ga and Ma. Quoted by V. N. Bhātkhaṇḍe, *A Comparative Study*, p. 30.

[3] *Pūravā* does not seem to have been a prominent *mela* even in Locana's time, for only one *rāga* is given in it, namely, *Pūravā*.

Evolution of the Circle of Ṭhāṭs

It was suggested by the late Dr. A. A. Bake that the scale of *Bhairav* was first introduced into South India, probably from Persian or Arabic music, under the name of *Hejujī* (*Hejāz*, *Hājiz*, *Hijej*), from whence it spread into North India appropriating the name *Bhairava* from a *rāg* which was then losing popularity.[1] This may be a possible explanation in view of the fact that the *Durrat al-Tāj*, an encyclopaedia in Persian dated *c.* 1300, describes the tetrachord *Hejāz* as having an augmented second interval (i.e. Re♭–Ga) which is characteristic of *Bhairav ṭhāṭ*. This argument is by no means conclusive, for this scale has the most *rāga*s in Locana's system, a fact which would suggest that it had been in existence in India for a considerable period before the 16th century.

Since Locana gives only two *rāga*s in what is modern *Pūrvī ṭhāṭ*, we may deduce that this scale was of more recent origin than *Bhairav* and it is very probable that *Pūrvī* evolved out of *Bhairav*. Locana mentions two versions of the *rāga Dhanāśrī*, one in *Dhanāśrī mela* (modern *Pūrvī ṭhāṭ*) and the other in *Gaurī mela* (modern *Bhairav ṭhāṭ*). This establishes a connection between the two *ṭhāṭ*s[2] but does not help us to determine which of these originated earlier. However, a number of *rāga*s given by Locana in *Gaurī mela* are now classified in *Pūrvī ṭhāṭ*, for example *Mālvī*, *Triveṇī*, (*Pūriyā*) *Dhanāśrī*, *Vasant*, *Revā* and *Jetśrī*. In addition, the *rāg Gaurī* now occurs in two main variants, one in *Pūrvī*, the other in *Bhairav*, while the *rāg Vibhās* occurs in three, one each in *Pūrvī* and *Bhairav* and one in *Mārvā ṭhāṭ* as well. There seems, therefore, to be sufficient evidence to substantiate the theory that the *rāg*s of *Bhairav ṭhāṭ* have a tendency to merge into *Pūrvī ṭhāṭ*,[3] and this, we suggest, may have been responsible for the origin of *Pūrvī ṭhāṭ*.

Some *rāga*s of Locana's *Gaurī mela* are now in modern *Toṛī ṭhāṭ*, the present-day *Multānī* and *Gurjrī* (*Gujrī Toṛī*), for example; others are in modern *Mārvā ṭhāṭ*: *Bhaṭiyār*, one version of *Vibhās*, (*Mālī*) *Gaurā*, and perhaps Locana's *Mālavā* which may be the origin of modern *Mārvā*. Not all the *rāga*s in *Gaurī mela* have changed, however, and the *rāga*s *Gaurī*, *Bhairava*, *Vibhāsa*, *Rāmakalī*, *Guṇakarī* and one version of *Khaṭa* still belong to *Bhairav ṭhāṭ*.

The relationship between Locana's *Gaurī mela rāga*s[4] and their present-day equivalents can be shown more clearly in tabulated form:

[1] That *Hijej* (cf. *Hejujī*) was an importation was first suggested by William Jones in 1799. *Music of India*, Calcutta 1962, p. 94. A further connection between *Bhairav* and *Hejujī* is suggested by the divergent readings in the various manuscripts of the *Kitāb-i-Nauras* composed by Ibrāhīm 'Ādil Ṣhāh II, *c.* 1600. Both *Bhairav* and *Hājiz* (cf. *Hejujī*) are mentioned in some of the manuscripts. In others, however, only one or the other is mentioned; the songs which are said to be sung in *Bhairav* in one manuscript are ascribed to *Hājiz* in others. *Kitāb-i-Nauras* translated by Nazir Ahmed, Delhi 1956, p. 62 f.n.

[2] The occurrence of two variants of a *rāg* may be purely coincidental, i.e. they may have completely different origins. On the other hand, if the two recensions are closely related, it is very probable that one has evolved from the other, the original being preserved perhaps in a different part of the country.

[3] There are, however, also indications that *rāg*s of *Pūrvī ṭhāṭ* merge into *Bhairav ṭhāṭ*.

[4] A full list of Locana's *rāga*s is given in Gangoly, *op. cit.*, p. 196, and in Bhātkhaṇḍe, *A Comparative Study*, p. 21 (in Devnāgrī script). The deviant readings of Locana's *rāga*s in the latter are given in brackets.

Locana's *Gaurī mela rāgas* (modern *Bhairav ṭhāṭ*)	Modern Equivalents (conjectural)	Modern *ṭhāṭs*
Mālava	Mārvā	Mārvā ṭhāṭ (No. A10)
	Mālvī	Pūrvī ṭhāṭ (No. A9)
Trivaṇa	Triveṇī	,, ,, ,,
Dhanāśrī	Pūriyā Dhanāśrī	,, ,, ,,
Vasanta	Vasant	,, ,, ,,
Revā	Revā	,, ,, ,,
Jayantaśrī (Jayataśrī)	Jetśrī	,, ,, ,,
Vibhāsa	Vibhās (1)	,, ,, ,,
	Vibhās (2)	Bhairav (No. C9)
	Vibhās (3)	Mārvā (No. A10)
Gaurā	Gaurī (1)	Pūrvī (No. A9)
	Gaurī (2)	Bhairav (No. C9)
	Māligaurā	Mārvā (No. A10)
Bhairava	Bhairav	Bhairav (No. C9)
Rāmakalī	Rāmkalī	,, ,,
Gunakarī (Guṇakarī)	Guṇkrī (Guṇkalī)	,, ,,
Ṣaḍrāga (Khaṭa)	Khaṭ (1)	,, ,,
	Khaṭ (2)	Āsāvrī (No. A5)
Āsāvarī	Sāverī	Bhairav (No. C9)
	Āsāvrī	Āsāvrī (No. A5)
Bhaṭiyāra	Bhaṭiyār	Mārvā (No. A10)
Mūlatāni (Mulatānī)	Multānī	Toṛī (No. A8)
Gurjarī	Gurjrī (Gujrī)	Toṛī ,,
Deśakāra (Deśakārī)	Deśkār	Bilāval (No. A2)
Devagāndhāra	Devgāndhār	Āsāvrī (No. A5)
Deśī Toṛī	Deśī Toṛī (1)	,, ,, (?)
	,, ,, (2)	Kāfī (No. A4) (?)

Six other *rāgas* mentioned by Locana in this *mela* do not exist today. It will be seen that the *rāgas* of Locana's *Gaurī mela* are distributed principally among the modern *Bhairav, Pūrvī, Mārvā, Toṛī* and *Āsāvrī ṭhāṭs*. The first four of these are obviously related, while *Āsāvrī* is three steps removed from *Bhairav* (see diagram on p. 184). There are indications, however, that the *Āsāvrī ṭhāṭ rāgs* above may have evolved from a different tradition from that which is represented in the *Rāgataraṅgiṇī*. Puṇḍarika Viṭṭhala (late 16th century) gives several versions of the *rāga Devagāndhāra* in his works. In his *Sadrāgacandrodaya* its scale appears to be that of our modern *Bhairav ṭhāṭ*, while in his *Rāgamañjarī* its scale is that of our modern *Kāfī ṭhāṭ*.[1] It is probably from this second version that the existing *Devgāndhār* has descended. Similarly, in *Rāgalakṣaṇa*[2] two variants of *Āsāvarī* (Sāverī) are men-

[1] *H.S.P.* IV, p. 476. [2] *Ibid.*, p. 438.

tioned, one in modern *Bhairav* and the other in modern *Bhairvī*. The former is very commonly heard in South Indian music as the rag *Sāverī* and occasionally in the North, while the latter is probably the ancestor of the modern North Indian *Āsāvrī*.

To recapitulate, it would appear that the early period of the seven serial modes was followed by a period of expansion and exploration in which the modes were altered and mixed and basic changes were accepted within the system. As a result either of this exploration or of foreign influence *Bhairav ṭhāṭ* was introduced and because of its melodic qualities was rapidly absorbed into the system. We have suggested that *Pūrvī ṭhāṭ* may well have evolved out of *Bhairav* which, as we have indicated in the previous chapter, is extremely prone to change. It seems probable too that the scales of *Toṛī* and *Mārvā* also grew out of *Bhairav*. Both of these are two notes removed from *Bhairav*, i.e., for *Bhairav* to evolve into *Toṛī*, two notes must be changed: the Ga♮ must become Ga♭ and the Ma♮ must become Ma♯. Similarly, for *Bhairav* to evolve into *Mārvā*, the Dha♭ must become Dha♮ and the Ma♮ become Ma♯. If the course of evolution is gradual, these changes will take place one at a time, and form in transition one of two possible intermediate scales depending on the note which changes first. In both cases if Ma changes first, the intermediate scale will be *Pūrvī*. If in the process of evolution from *Bhairav* to *Toṛī* the Ga changes first, the intermediate scale will be No. B6 (see p. 184). If in the process of evolution from *Bhairav* to *Mārvā* the Dha changes first, the intermediate scale will be No. B10.

Let us consider the *Toṛī rāgs*, *Gurjrī* and *Multānī*, which are classified by Locana in his *Gaurī mela* (modern *Bhairav ṭhāṭ*) but are now in *Toṛī ṭhāṭ*. Ahobala in the *Saṅgītapārijāta* (second half of the 17th century) describes two forms of *Gurjrī*, *Dakṣiṇa* (Southern) and *Uttara* (Northern).[1] The former has the scale of our *Bhairav*, while the latter has Re♭, Ga♭ and Dha♭ and belongs to scale No. B6. The *rāg Multānī* too seems to have evolved through this same intermediate scale, for Kṣetramohan Goswāmī, in the second half of the 19th century, says that some use the Ma♮ instead of the Ma♯ in *Gurjrī Toṛī*,[2] evidently a reflection of an earlier tradition. Thus the evolution of *Gurjrī* and *Multānī* appear to have proceeded as follows:

Locana's *Gaurī mela rāgas—Gurjrī, Multānī*

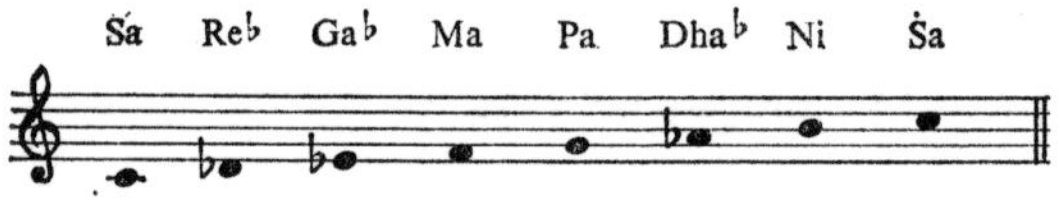

Ahobala's *rāga, Uttara Gurjrī* (17th century)
and Goswāmī's *rāga Multānī* (variant) (19th century)

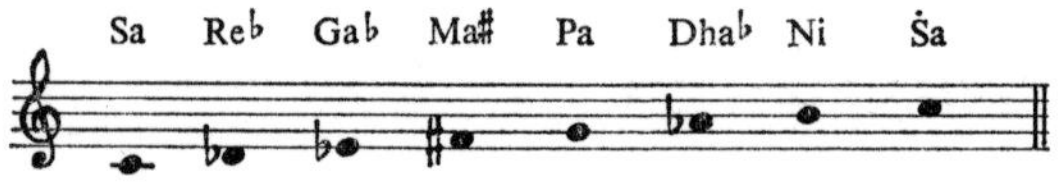

Modern *Gurjrī* and *Multānī*

[1] *H.S.P.* IV. pp. 699–700. [2] *Ibid.*, p. 716.

The evidence for the origin of *Mārvā ṭhāṭ* is not nearly so conclusive, primarily because the many traditions of the *rāg*s in this *ṭhāṭ* are somewhat confused. For instance, the *rāg Mārvā* could have its origin in Locana's *rāga Mālava* of *Gaurī mela*, in his *rāga Māru* of *Karṇāṭa mela* (modern *Khamāj ṭhāṭ*), or in his *rāga Māru* of *Kedāra mela* (modern *Bilāval ṭhāṭ*). The *rāga Vibhāsa* given in Locana's *Gaurī mela* now occurs in three versions, in *Bhairav*, *Pūrvī* and *Mārvā ṭhāṭ*s. This suggests that, in this case at least, *Mārvā ṭhāṭ* may have evolved through the intermediate *Pūrvī* scale. The evidence for the intermediate scale of the present *rāg Bhaṭiyār*, given by Locana in *Gaurī mela* but now occurring in *Mārvā ṭhāṭ*, is also inconclusive. It seems to have maintained its *Bhairav* scale into the second half of the 19th century.[1] Perhaps the only evidence which can be brought to bear on this matter is connected with the present use of the Ma♮ as an accidental in this *rāg* which may be an indication that the process of evolution of the *rāg Bhaṭiyār* from scale No. B10 is not yet complete. The general principles relating accidentals to the evolution of *rāg*s will be discussed in the following chapter.

So far we have been discussing the evidence for the origin of *Toṛī* and *Mārvā ṭhāṭ*s from *Bhairav ṭhāṭ*. This evidence tends to diminish the significance of our Circle of *Ṭhāṭ*s. There is, however, important evidence to prove that both *Toṛī* and *Mārvā ṭhāṭ*s have also been derived around the Circle, the former from *Bhairvī ṭhāṭ*, the latter from *Kalyāṇ*.

Let us first consider the case of *Toṛī*, which from the evolutionary standpoint is one of the most interesting *rāg*s. From the 15th to the end of the 18th century it is said to have had the scale of modern *Bhairvī*, as indeed it still does in South Indian music. This is stated in a number of texts some of which apparently describe South Indian music, e.g. *Rāgavibodha* of Somanātha *c.* 1610, while others such as *Rāgataraṅgiṇī* and *Saṅgītapārijāta* describe the North Indian system. The present-day North Indian *Toṛī* has, of course, a very different scale, and it is usually thought that it represents a different tradition from the earlier *Toṛī*. This, however, does not appear to be so.

In the *Saṅgītsār* compiled in Hindi by Mahārāj Sawai Pratāp Siṃh Dev of Jaipur after a conference of the leading musicians in his court (*c.* 1800 A.D.), several varieties of *Toṛī* are described. Among them we find a *rāg* called *Mārg Toṛī* which has the scale of our hypothetical *ṭhāṭ* (No. A7), and has, in addition, Ma♮ as an oblique descending accidental. The *rāg* is given as hexatonic, the Pa being said to be omitted, but in the example given, Pa occurs in the ascending line.[2] The common *Toṛī* of this period is called *Mīyā̃ kī Toṛī* and still has the scale of the original *Toṛī*, that of our

[1] *H.S.P.* III, p. 330, quoting Goswāmī.

[2] Quoted in *H.S.P.* IV, p. 691. In the *Saṅgītsār* the notations are given in the form of 'magic squares' (*jantr*), in this case consisting of three vertical columns of notes. In the following example, they are transcribed in sequence with the bar lines separating the columns:

Rāg Mārg Toṛī of Saṅgītsār

7

modern *Bhairvī ṭhāṭ*. In *Mārg Toṛī* we can see, however, a departure from this scale towards the present-day North Indian *Toṛī*.

This is not the only available evidence to corroborate this thesis. In a Bengali work by Kṣetramohan Goswāmī (late 19th century) *Toṛī* appears to lie between scale No. A7 and our present *Toṛī*. From the notations given in this work,[1] its ascending and descending lines may be given as follows:

Ex. 50. rāg Toṛī of Goswāmī

In addition, Ni♭ occurs occasionally as an oblique ascending note—perhaps a vestigial reminder of the original scale of the *rāg*.[2]

The connection between *Toṛī* and *Bhairvī ṭhāṭs* can also be established in a different way. Two modern *rāgs*, *Bhūpāl Toṛī* and *Bilāsk͟hānī Toṛī*, are even now classified in *Bhairvī ṭhāṭ*. The former is pentatonic, while the latter is identical in ascent but is heptatonic in descent:

Ex. 51.

(a) *Bhūpāl Toṛī* and *Bilāsk͟hānī Toṛī* (ascent) (b) *Bilāsk͟hānī Toṛī* (descent)

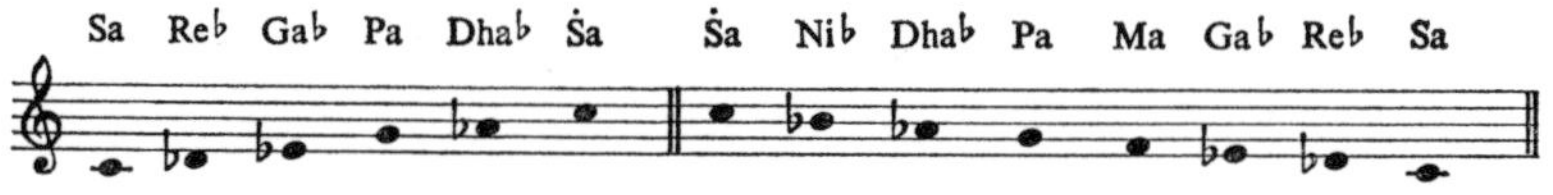

The omitted notes Ma and Ni are, in fact, the very notes which distinguish *Bhairvī ṭhāṭ* from *Toṛī*, and the *rāg Bhūpāl Toṛī* could equally well be classified in modern *Toṛī ṭhāṭ*.

In view of this evidence it seems probable that the *rāg Toṛī* has evolved in the following manner within the past two hundred years:

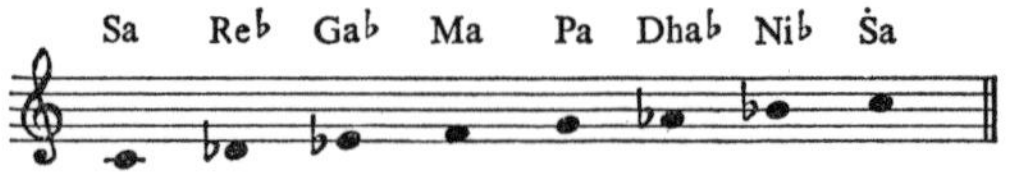

Locana's *Toṛī*, 17th century (modern *Bhairvī ṭhāṭ*)

Pratāp Siṃh's *Mārg Toṛī*, *c.* 1800

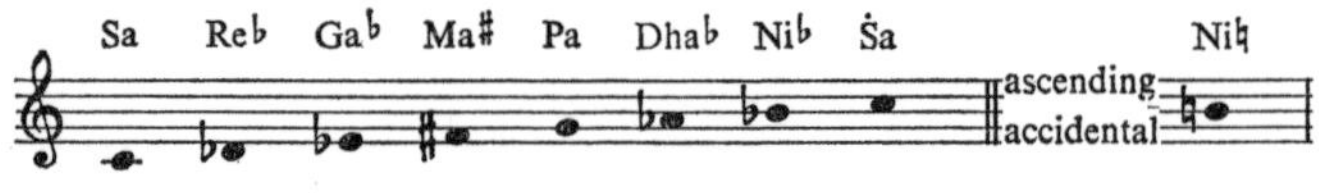

Goswāmī's *Toṛī*, *c.* 1870

[1] Quoted in *H.S.P.* IV, p. 695. Bhātkhaṇḍe does not specify which of Goswāmī's works he is quoting from, his *Saṅgītsār* which appeared in 1868 or his *Saṅgītsārsaṅgrah* which appeared in 1875.

[2] This statement will be clarified in the next chapter.

Modern *Toṛī*

We mentioned earlier (p. 63, f.n. 2) that the *rāg Toṛī* was one of the principal exceptions to the time theory of *rāgs*, as its traditional time of performance was the late morning, whereas according to the time theory it should be performed either at 3 a.m. or 3 p.m. Texts such as the *Rāgavibodha* (*c.* 1610) and Puṇḍarīka's *Rāgamāla* (late 16th century) which state that the *rāga Toṛī* should be performed in the morning are undoubtedly referring to the *Toṛī* of their period which, as we have shown, had the scale of modern *Bhairvī*. The traditional time of performance has remained associated with the name of the *rāg* while its scale has evolved to its present state.[1] This is an excellent example of the imperceptible working of the evolutionary process.

We have now considered the evidence for the evolution of *Toṛī* from *Bhairvī* through the hypothetical *ṭhāṭ*, No. A7, and incidentally provided some justification for the inclusion of the hypothetical *ṭhāṭ* in our Circle of *Ṭhāṭ*s. We now present the evidence which suggests that *Mārvā ṭhāṭ* has evolved from *Kalyāṇ ṭhāṭ* around the Circle in an anti-clockwise direction.

Among the *rāga*s placed by Locana in *Imana mela* (modern *Kalyāṇ ṭhāṭ*) we will first consider the *rāga Pūriyā* which is now in *Mārvā ṭhāṭ*. There can be no doubt that the modern tradition is directly connected with Locana's *Pūriyā*, for in the *Hṛidayaprakāśa* (middle 17th century), a work which closely follows the *Rāgataraṅgiṇī*, there is mention of the *rāga Pūriyā Kalyāṇa* (in *Imana mela*),[2] which also exists in the present period in *Mārvā ṭhāṭ*. The occurrence of the *rāg Pūriyā Kalyāṇ* in *Mārvā ṭhāṭ* obviously suggests its connection with *Kalyāṇ ṭhāṭ*. In the previous chapter we had suggested that *Mārvā ṭhāṭ* might have arisen from *Kalyāṇ* by a comparison of the tetrachords of *Kalyāṇ ṭhāṭ* in which the Sa and Pa had been omitted.[3] This would certainly seem to apply to the *rāg Pūriyā* (the origin of *rāg Mārvā* is uncertain as we have suggested earlier) which, like the *rāg Mārvā*, is hexatonic, omitting the Pa.

The connection between *Kalyāṇ* and *Mārvā ṭhāṭ*s is further suggested by the *rāga Jayata Kalyāṇa* (modern *Jet Kalyāṇ*). Both Locana and Hṛidaya give this *rāga* in *Imana mela* and it does not appear to have changed since it is still classified in *Kalyāṇ*

[1] Some of the other *rāgs* deviating from the time theory may perhaps also be explained in this way. In the diagram showing the time theory in relation to the Circle of *Ṭhāṭs* (p. 64) *Bhairvī ṭhāṭ* is indicated at approximately 12 o'clock. In Locana's system *Bhairvī* had the scale of modern *Kāfī ṭhāṭ* which is indicated at about 10 o'clock. This still does not compare with tradition which ascribes *Bhairvī* to the early morning. It is quite evident that, in the case of some *rāgs* at least, there are other factors involved.

[2] Hṛidaya Nārāyaṇa classifies his *rāgas* in two ways: in the *Hṛidayakautuka* he follows Locana's *melas*, but in the *Hṛidayaprakāśa* he uses *melas* based on the number of altered notes. Thus the term *Imana mela* is taken from the scheme used in the *Kautuka*. It is interesting that, in this *mela*, he mentions the *rāga Pūriyā* in the *Kautuka* and *Pūriyā Kalyāṇ* in the *Prakāśa*, the other three *rāgas* in this *mela* being the same in both works. The full lists of *rāgas* are given in Gangoly, *op. cit.*, pp. 207–8.

[3] See p. 83.

ṭhāṭ. It does appear, however, to be a combination of the modern *rāgs Jet* and (*Śuddh*) *Kalyāṇ*. The former is a *rāg* of *Mārvā ṭhāṭ* in which some musicians, according to Bhātkhaṇḍe, use both alternatives of Re.[1] The Re is, of course, the distinguishing note of the two *ṭhāṭs Mārvā* and *Kalyāṇ*, and the use of the Re♭ as well as the Re♮ in the *rāg Jet* shows a merging of the two *ṭhāṭs*.

Many *rāgs* have undergone change in the past four or five centuries, generally moving from one of these ten *ṭhāṭs* to another. Most of our discussions have been limited to *ṭhāṭs* on the left side of the Circle, from *Kalyāṇ* to *Bhairvī* and including *Bhairav*. It is not only the *rāgs* of these *ṭhāṭs* which have been subject to the process of evolution and before we close this chapter we will briefly consider a few examples from among the six primary *ṭhāṭs*.

The first of these is the very commonly heard *rāg Bhairvī*. Early writers representing both the North Indian school (Locana, for example) and the South Indian school (for example, Rāmāmātya in the *Svaramelakalānidhi*, middle 16th century) give its scale as modern *Kāfī ṭhāṭ* (No. A4). In the 17th century both schools—Ahobala in the *Saṅgītapārijāta* representing the North and Veṅkaṭamakhī in the *Caturdaṇḍiprakāśikā* representing the South—give *Bhairavī* as modern *Āsāvrī ṭhāṭ* (No. A5). This remains the scale of the *rāg Bhairavī* in South India. In North India, however, the evolution of this *rāg* has progressed one step further and Pratāp Siṃh (*c.* 1800) is probably the first writer to give the scale of modern *Bhairvī*. Although the scale of *Bhairvī* has not changed since this period, the occasional use of the Ma♯ (IV♯) as an unconscious diminished fifth indicates that the next evolutionary step, the B mode, has already been considered, a step which may never be completely achieved as the diminished fifth would be in direct relationship with the ground-note.

The *rāga Mālakauśika* (modern *Mālkoś*) is described by Locana as belonging to his *Karṇāṭa mela* (modern *Khamāj ṭhāṭ*, No. A3). This same *rāg* belongs to modern *Kāfī ṭhāṭ* (No. A4) according to the description in *Rāgamañjarī* of Puṇḍarīka Viṭṭhala (late 16th century). *Mālkoś* is now a *rāg* in *Bhairvī ṭhāṭ* (No. A6), and there appears to be no textual evidence to indicate that it has ever been a *rāg* in *Āsāvrī ṭhāṭ* (No. A5) which lies between *Kāfī* and *Bhairvī* in the Circle. This is not entirely surprising in view of the fact that *Mālkoś* is pentatonic, omitting the Pa and the Re—the latter being the distinguishing note of the *ṭhāṭs Āsāvrī* and *Bhairvī*. Thus modern *Mālkoś* could equally well have been classified in *Āsāvrī ṭhāṭ* if judged purely from the point of view of scale.

Of the many other examples which could be discussed, we shall refer only briefly to three other *rāgas* in Locana's *Karṇāṭa mela* (modern *Khamāj ṭhāṭ*, No. A3), *Vāgīśvarī* (modern *Bāgeśvarī*), *Sughrai* and *Aḍānā*. The first two *rāgs* now have Ga♭ and are classified in *Kāfī ṭhāṭ* (No. A4), while *Aḍānā* has evolved even further and is now classified in *Āsāvrī ṭhāṭ* (No. A5).

While the majority of the *rāgas* of Locana's period can be explained in evolutionary terms in relation to the circle of *ṭhāṭs*, a few prominent *rāgas* appear to have under-

[1] *H.S.P.* III, p. 250.

gone sudden and extreme change which is not accounted for in this gradual evolution theory. It will be useful to consider two such instances.

The *rāga Hindola* is given in *Karṇāṭa mela* (modern *Khamāj ṭhāṭ*) by Locana. About two centuries later, in the *Saṅgītapārijāta*, it is given as a pentatonic *rāga* (Ex. 52a). This is still the South Indian version of this *rāga*. In North India, however, *Hindol*, while still remaining pentatonic, now uses all the opposite alternative notes (Ex 52b):

Ex. 52. rāg Hindol

(a) (b)

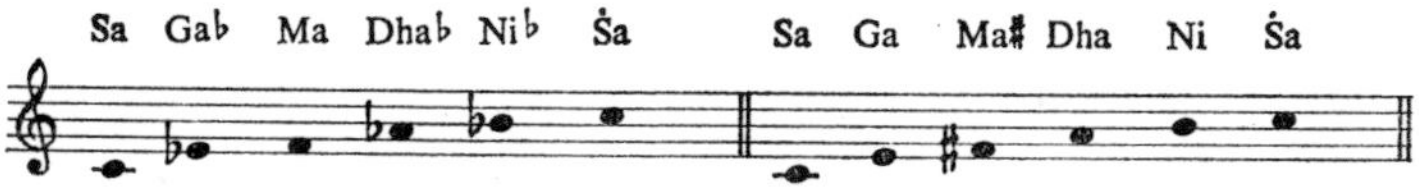

There is no certainty that the modern North Indian tradition is connected with that described in the *Saṅgītapārijāta*. The treatises give no evidence of gradual evolution, and yet the fact that both the ancient *rāga* and the modern *rāg* are pentatonic and omit the Re and the Pa suggests that they are connected. Perhaps, in this instance, we are dealing with a different phenomenon, something in the nature of a semitonal shift of the ground note, which could, in one move, create such a vastly different scale.

Similarly, the *rāga Śrī* is generally described in North Indian treatises (Locana, Ahobala and Puṇḍarīka in *Rāgamañjarī*) as in present-day *Khamāj ṭhāṭ*, while the South Indian writers (Rāmāmātya and Somanātha) describe it as in modern North Indian *Kāfī ṭhāṭ*. The scale of the *rāga Śrī* in South India remains unchanged (Ex. 53a); in North India, however, the *rāg* now belongs to *Pūrvī ṭhāṭ*, and once again, all the alternative notes are reversed (Ex. 53b).

Ex. 53. rāg Śrī

(a) (b)

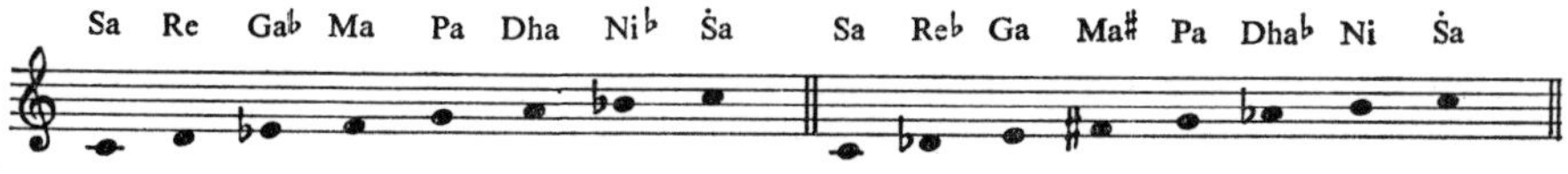

Bhātkhaṇḍe suggests, however, that the modern North Indian *rāg Śrī* may have been descended from the *rāga Śrīgaurī* of Locana's *Gaurī mela* (modern *Bhairav ṭhāṭ*).[1] If this is acceptable, *Śrī* can readily be explained in terms of gradual evolution as *Bhairav* and *Pūrvī ṭhāṭ*s are adjacent in our scheme.

In the previous pages we have been presenting the evidence to show that *rāg*s have tended to evolve around the Circle of *Ṭhāṭ*s. The introduction of *Bhairav ṭhāṭ* was, from the standpoint of the Circle, premature, but has not detracted from the Circle; it appears to have provided a new point of departure which may, in fact, have hastened the completion of the Circle. This analysis should be considered as a tentative beginning, rather than accomplished fact, for there still remain many unknowns.

[1] *H.S.P.* III, p. 62.

VI

Alternative Notes

In the previous chapters we have been discussing Indian musical scales and attempting to connect them in an evolutionary sequence. A discussion of *rāgs* purely on the basis of scales alone cannot obviously be comprehensive; and a case has been made out to minimise the importance of scale as a basis for the classification of *rāgs*.[1] However, in this work we have tried to show that the notes used are much more than a means for classification, and are an important functional element in the evolution of *rāgs*. While it is not surprising that fashions change and new *rāgs* replace old ones, it is remarkable that the scales of many *rāgs* should have been modified over the years apparently without conscious appreciation of this fact. In this chapter we propose to consider why these changes should have come about and how it is that they could pass unnoticed.

There can be no denying that tradition is a powerful conservative factor in Indian music. The inadequacy of the traditional methods of notation, coupled with the intangible structure of *rāgs*, has tended to accentuate the teacher–pupil relationship. This conservative element is, however, more than offset by the creative aspect of improvisation. The pupil can only become a master when he can go beyond what he has been taught and create his own music. The *rāg* is the traditional restraining element within which the creative musician must find the freedom to express himself. In his search for freedom he frequently stretches the bounds of the *rāg* and, as the limits of *rāgs* are never exactly prescribed, we can say they are being re-defined, to some extent at least, in every performance. Under these circumstances change becomes inevitable. There is, of course, a point of endurance in any particular context which the musician may not exceed without violating the traditional basis of the *rāg*; but this does vary, depending on the sensitivity and skill of the performer as well as on the discrimination and receptivity of the audience.

A second conservative influence, which might be expected to retard the rate of evolution, the textual definition (which can be consulted in moments of doubt), has

[1] It has been argued, for instance, that classification according to melodic features—omissions, turns, etc.—may provide a more meaningful basis; but these features can, in any case, often be related to scale.

not been of great importance until this century in North India, for many of the great musicians were illiterate, while others had only been able to consult where and when available the few treatises which had been written in the modern Indian languages.

A characteristic feature of the change we are discussing is that the process is imperceptible. We can see the change in the scale of a *rāg* only by looking back to the description of that *rāg* as it was hundreds of years ago. We may presume, however, that change is not generally noticeable during a musician's lifetime, for if this were so, tradition would assert itself, ensuring that the original *rāg* is preserved and the changed version either discarded or given an independent status. Thus the process by which the scale evolves is gradual, not a sudden replacement of one note by its alternative as it appears on paper. This is accomplished by an intermediate phase in which both the note and its alternative occur in the *rāg*, not as chromatic steps, but each in its own melodic context, the one temporarily replacing the other. With both alternatives of a note in a *rāg*, the shift of emphasis from one to the other can be both gradual and imperceptible. Conversely we can say that the presence of both alternatives of a note in a *rāg* is a manifestation of the process of evolution.

The prime essential in this gradual course of evolution is that the whole process must flow smoothly and without any discontinuity. This being so, we must first attempt to explain how the initial introduction of the accidental can be accomplished with such subtlety that no change is apparent. In Chapter IV we discussed certain concepts of dual tonality initiated by the Sa and Pa drones and the related perception of intervals in terms of tetrachords. We indicated that the unbalanced tetrachord types led to the replacement of one or other of the unbalanced notes, thus producing new scales. This same principle provides the functional *raison d'être* for the introduction of an accidental to produce temporary balance in the tetrachords. This accidental provides an interval which is by no means foreign to the *rāg* for it already occurs in the tonality initiated by one of the two drones. For instance, in *Khamāj*, where the lower of two ascending disjunct tetrachords has a major third, Sa–Ga (I–III), and the upper a minor third, Pa–Ni♭ (V–VII♭), the experience of both the major third and minor third is familiar. The introduction of the minor third, Ga♭ (III♭), into the lower tetrachord or the major third, Ni♮ (VII♮), into the upper merely extends the experience already inherent in *Khamāj*. Initially, this impulse to introduce the accidental may manifest itself as a wavering or an exaggerated vibrato on the nearest diatonic note. This would probably be interpreted as a form of expression on the part of the musician rather than as a separate musical interval and it would only be after a period of acclimatisation that the accidental would gradually emerge as a grace note (*kaṇ svar*). This 'wavering' can even now be heard in a number of *rāgs*. In the *Kānhṛā rāgs*, *Darbārī*, for example, it has become a characteristic and obvious feature of the *rāg* (see p. 162). On a more subtle level, it often occurs in certain *rāgs*, for example the *rāg Kedār*, where some musicians consciously use the Ni♭ (VII♭) as an accidental, while others merely put a slight inflexion on the Dha (VI).[1] From such a modest beginning the accidental may gradually become more prominent at the expense of its chromatic[2] counterpart (the scalar note), until finally the accidental becomes the more important and can be called the scalar note. This process of absorption of the accidental is clearly associated with either the ascending or descending line; if the accidental is lower than its chromatic counterpart it will be, initially, an ornament of the preceding (lower) note of the scale, which is its nearest diatonic neighbour, and will be introduced first into the descending line of the *rāg*. We may here remind the reader that the criterion of both descent and ascent is the position of the succeeding note: if it is higher, then the note is ascending; if lower, the note is descending. In the instance we are considering the accidental will occur as an ornament attached to the lower note, i.e. the ornament will begin on the lower note, rise to the accidental and return to the lower note. It is this descending return which is the determining factor. Similarly, if the accidental is higher than its chromatic counterpart, it will be associated with the following (higher) note of the scale, and will thus be introduced into the ascending line. Thus, if the accidental is Ga♭ (III♭) it will appear as an ornament attached to the Re (II) and if Ga♮ (III♮) will be attached to the Ma.

Ex. 54.

We shall now trace, in hypothesis, the course of the Ga♭ (III♭) from its first introduction as a grace note to its final replacement of the Ga♮ (III♮) as a scalar note. It is convenient to discuss the course of evolution in terms of stages, but it should be understood that there is no precise line of demarcation between these stages, and that they flow smoothly one into another. The first stage can be expressed concisely as follows:

(1) Ascent Ga♮ Descent Ga♮ (+ Ga♭)

The Ga♭ in brackets here indicates that it forms part of an oblique descending line, while the Ga♮ continues to be the direct descending note.[3]

The next evolutionary stage can be said to be reached when the accidental Ga♭ forms a descending line of its own. This may, for instance, be accomplished gradually through an intermediate stage in the following way:

[1] A particularly good example of this can be found on the record of *Kedār* (*Raag Kidara*), CLP 1514, sung by Roshanārā Begam. About 1 min. 20 secs. from the beginning, the Dha (VI) is sustained, first as a steady note, then there are two slight inflexions suggesting the Ni♭ (VII♭). This can also be heard in *rāg Kedār* on the accompanying record.

[2] Chromatic is not used here in the usual Western sense—see p. 48.

[3] The terms 'oblique' and 'direct' are defined on pp. 40, 41.

Ex. 55.

(a)

(b)

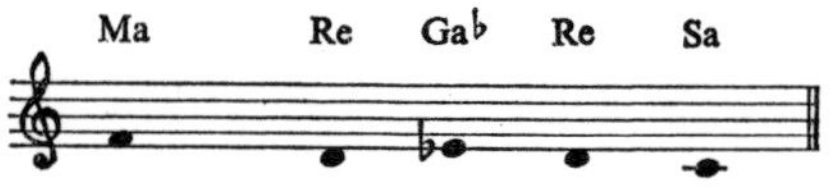

(c)

It frequently happens, however, that the original descending line containing the Ga♮ will continue to exist alongside the new descending line, and there will be two alternative forms of descent. At first, the new descending line may be used only occasionally and the traditional method of descent will be dominant. In the course of time, however, the new descending line with the Ga♭ may supersede it. This second stage can be expressed as follows:

(2) Ascent Ga♮ Descent Ga♮ + Ga♭

With the predominance of the descending line containing the Ga♭, the importance of the original descending line diminishes until, finally, the Ga♮ may no longer appear in a full descending line but, as a vestigial reminder of the original descending line, remain as a discontinuous descending note, as in the example below:

Ex. 56.

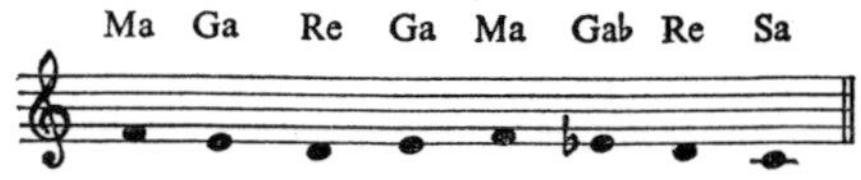

This third stage can be expressed as follows:

(3) Ascent Ga♮ Descent Ga♭ (+ Ga♮)

Next, this vestigial figure in the descending line may become progressively shorter until it is completely dropped and only the Ga♭ occurs in the descending line. At this point the *rāg* is exactly half-way between two *ṭhāṭ*s, for the ascending line contains the Ga♮ and the descending line the Ga♭:

(4) Ascent Ga♮ Descent Ga♭

The Ga♭ would now begin to cast its influence on the ascending line. In the next stage it may occur, at first, as a small discontinuous ascending figure which would gradually become longer and more important without actually forming a full ascending line:

Ex. 57.

This stage is exactly parallel to stage 3 and if we were considering the evolutionary steps of the Ga♮ accidental instead of the Ga♭ accidental, this would indeed have been stage 3 in which the Ga♭ is only a discontinuous ascending note and a vestigial reminder of the original ascending line. To return to our original scheme, this stage can be expressed as:

(5) Ascent Ga♮ (+ Ga♭)   Descent Ga♭

The Ga♭ would next form an ascending line which appears as an alternative to the original ascending line with the Ga♮. This new ascending line may gradually gain prominence at the expense of the original ascending line. This stage can be expressed as:

(6) Ascent Ga♮ + Ga♭   Descent Ga♭

The original ascending line which contained the Ga♮ may then, as it gradually falls into disuse, become oblique and the Ga♮ remain merely as an ornament around the Ma:

(7) Ascent Ga♭ (+ Ga♮)   Descent Ga♭

The change of scale would be complete when, finally, the Ga♮ is no longer used in the *rāg*.

These would be the evolutionary steps of a *rāg* as a note of its scale changes from Ga♮ to Ga♭. If the change were from Ga♭ to Ga♮, the steps would have been exactly reversed. The changes would first occur in the ascending line until the half-way point, stage 4, where the ascending line contains the Ga♮ and the descending line the Ga♭; thereafter, the changes would take place in the descending line until finally there remained no sign of the Ga♭.

We must underline that this is only a hypothetical scheme and need not apply in any particular instance. We have been concerned with the kind of process by which the scale of a *rāg* may, without intent, change over a period of time. In the course of its evolution a *rāg* may retrogress or find a considerable degree of stability and remain in a particular stage, perhaps for several hundred years. On the other hand, it may go through a period of relatively rapid change within a few generations, and may possibly omit some of these intermediate stages. The uneven tempo of this change is reflected in the diverse renderings of the same *rāg* in the different geographical regions of North India, and explains the differences in interpretation in the various musical traditions (*gharānā*), some of which have been more conservative than others. There has, however, been a considerable amount of interchange between these traditions and consequently their interpretations of the details are, in most cases, not so widely divergent as one might expect in view of the size of the country and the difficulties of communication which have existed until the modern period.

There are many *rāg*s which do not appear to have changed in scale, at least since Locana's *Rāgataraṅgiṇī*. Does this mean that certain *rāg*s are less subject to evolutionary forces than others? This is not necessarily so. It is probable that they have also evolved, but their new forms have at some stage received recognition. The new forms have here not replaced the old, but have been granted independent status and been given their own names. The names of such *rāg*s often give an indication of their origin. Thus, *Alhaiyā Bilāval*, *Śukl Bilāval* and *Devgirī Bilāval* all suggest that they have evolved out of *Bilāval*. Sometimes they are differentiated from the parent *rāg* in the notes of emphasis, or in the ascending and descending lines in which the accidentals may have reached a different stage of evolution. The evolutionary process has, in some instances, progressed so far that the derivatives can no longer be classified in the same scale.

It seems probable that the pattern of evolution may be very much the same whether a *rāg* evolves from one scale to another, or other *rāg*s evolve from it. In the former instance there remains no memory of the original state of the *rāg* and no record is left of the various evolutionary stages except those which we can glean from the treatises of the different periods. These texts, however, are generally not detailed enough to permit us to establish positively the various subtle differences between one evolutionary stage and the next. In the latter instance the original *rāg* continues to exist alongside the new *rāg*s which are left as milestones in the path of evolution. Consequently we should be able to find evidence for the various stages of evolution among the *rāg*s which exist at the present time.

We shall now consider the *rāg*s of *Bilāval* (No. A2) and *Khamāj ṭhāṭ*s (No. A3) in order to show that there are, in fact, *rāg*s which corroborate most of the seven intermediate evolutionary stages between these two *ṭhāṭ*s. The following examples are taken from Bhātkhaṇḍe's notations.

1. Beginning from *Bilāval ṭhāṭ*, the first stage is the introduction of the Ni♭ (VII♭), initially as an ornament around the Dha, later used more freely but always remaining an oblique descending note. The *rāg Alhaiyā Bilāval* is an excellent illustration of this stage of development. In Bhātkhaṇḍe's tradition the Ni♮ is found in both the direct ascending and descending lines, while the Ni♭ occurs only in an oblique descending line marked *x*:[1]

Ex. 58. rāg Alhaiyā Bilāval

[1] *K.P.M.* II, p. 75.

2. In the second stage the descending line, with the Ni♭, is completed and there are now two concurrent descending lines as seen, for instance, in the *rāg Śukl Bilāval*:[1]

Ex. 59. rāg Śukl Bilāval

(a)

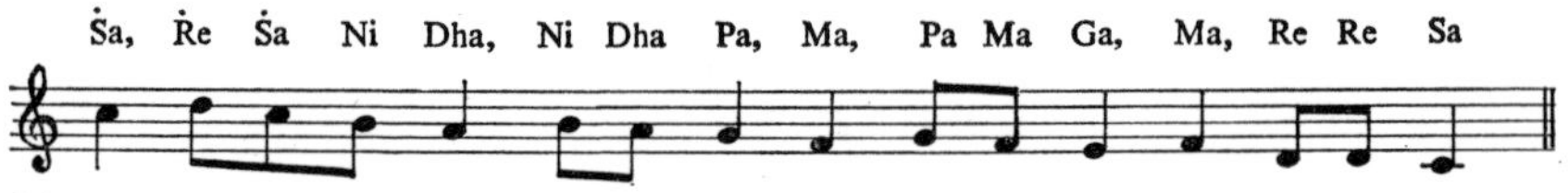

(b)

3. In the third stage the descending line with the Ni♭ has become dominant and the original descending line containing the Ni♮ is now discontinuous, remaining as a vestigial reminder of the original. This is apparent in the *rāg Bihāgṛā* where Ni♭ is freely used in the descending line. The Ni♮ is occasionally used in a discontinuous descent, but is followed inevitably by a descent in which the Ni♭ is used.

This will be evident from the following examples:[2]

Ex. 60. rāg Bihāgṛā

(a)

(b)

4. In the fourth stage the Ni♮ no longer appears in the descending line. The *rāg Des*, as it is usually performed, illustrates this stage. The Ni♮ occurs in the ascent, while the Ni♭ is used in the descent:[3]

Ex. 61. rāg Des

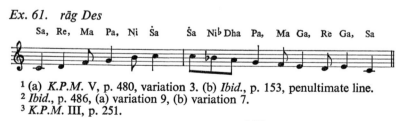

[1] (a) *K.P.M.* V, p. 480, variation 3. (b) *Ibid.*, p. 153, penultimate line.
[2] *Ibid.*, p. 486, (a) variation 9, (b) variation 7.
[3] *K.P.M.* III, p. 251.

5. In the next stage the Ni♭ is used as a discontinuous ascending note. This is sometimes done in the *rāg Des* where the phrase (a) may sometimes be followed by (b):[1]

Ex. 62. rāg Des

(a) (b)

6. In the sixth stage the Ni♭ forms a separate alternative ascending line. The *rāg Khamāj* is an example of this stage of development. The most commonly heard ascent has Ni♮ (a), but occasionally the Ni♭ is used (b):

Ex. 63. rāg Khamāj

(a) (b)

Bhātkhaṇḍe gives the latter[2] but prefers to use the Ni♮ in his *svarvistār* of the *rāg*.[3] There is also corroboration of the ascending use of the Ni♭ in Bhātkhaṇḍe's notations of songs, where this occasionally occurs.[4] The Ni♭ as an ascending note is, however, rarely used, but this has an independent explanation which we shall consider later in this chapter.

7. In the seventh stage the Ni♮ is used only as an incomplete ascending note, as in the following phrase:

Ex. 64.

In fact, there is no *rāg* in either *Bilāval* or *Khamāj ṭhāṭ* in which this occurs. Once again the explanation for this will appear later. This stage can, however, be illustrated

[1] *K.P.M.* III, p. 761, variation 10. It will be noticed in the phrase above that we have called the Ni♭ a discontinuous ascending note in spite of the fact that the phrase proceeds to the upper Sa. An essential requirement of a direct ascending note, in our interpretation, is that the movement above should not be restrictive and normally, a note which permits access to the Sa would not be so. In this exceptional instance, however, the ascent to the Sa following a Ni♭ does not permit free access into the upper register but is invariably followed by a descent. The explanation probably lies in the fact that the leading note, Ni♮, in *Des* paves the way for the Sa, but the Ni♭ does not convey the same sense of anticipation for the ground note and the Ṡa is then treated as an appendage of the Ni♭. This *rāg* can be heard on the accompanying record and is discussed further in Appendix B.

[2] *K.P.M.* II, p. 122.

[3] *K.P.M.* II, p. 490.

[4] For instance in the song, *K.P.M.* II, p. 124.

from a corresponding position between two other *ṭhāṭ*s, for instance *Bilāval* (No. A2) and *Kalyāṇ* (No. A1), in which the two alternatives of Ma are involved. Here we would need a *rāg* in which the Ma♯ (IV♯) occurs as an incomplete ascending note, while the Ma♮ (IV♮) forms the complete ascending line. This stage is illustrated by the *rāg Hamīr*, in which the Ma♯ appears only as an incomplete ascending note, as in the phrase *x* below, while the ascending line has the Ma♮:[1]

Ex. 65. rāg Hamīr

These are then the seven principal stages between two adjacent *ṭhāṭs*. They can be seen more clearly in the following diagrammatic form:

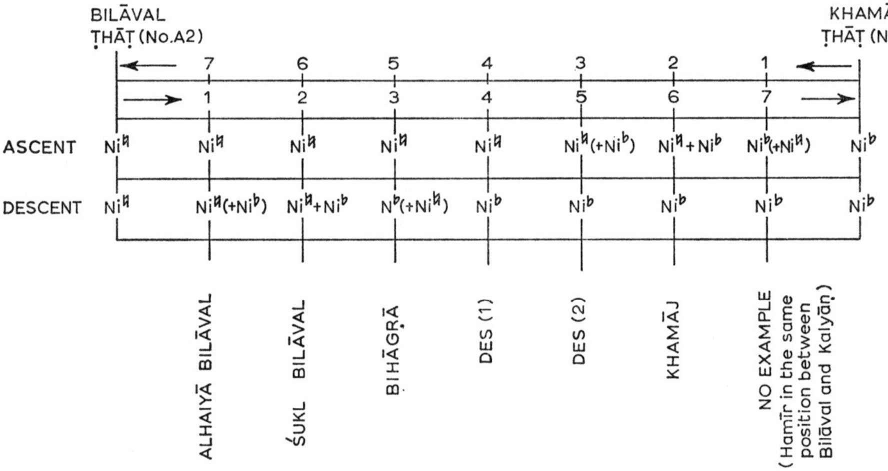

Although these seven stages should apply between each *ṭhāṭ* and its neighbour, it is not always possible to find *rāg*s to corroborate all these intermediate stages. In *Toṛī ṭhāṭ*, for example, there are only three commonly known *rāgs*,[2] and none of these has any accidentals, while in *Bhairvī ṭhāṭ*, in which once again there are very few *rāgs*, the *rāg Bhairvī* permits a great deal of freedom, not only in the way an accidental is used (see p. 120) but also in the number of accidentals permitted.

In the previous chapter we showed that Locana's *Bhairavī* was similar to our modern *Kāfī ṭhāṭ* (No. A4), whereas it now includes, in addition to the Ga♭ (III♭) and Ni♭ (VII♭) of *Kāfī*, Re♭ (II♭) and Dha♭ (VI♭). The two most prominent accidentals

[1] *K.P.M.* III, p. 68.

[2] Bhātkhaṇḍe gives seven *rāgs*, but four of these, *Lācārī Toṛī*, *Lakṣmī Toṛī*, *Bahādurī Toṛī* and *Añjnī Toṛī*, are seldom heard, and with the exception of *Bahādurī Toṛī* do not really belong in the modern *Toṛī ṭhāṭ* since they have Ma♮ as a scalar note.

in the *rāg Bhairvī* are, however, the Re♮ (II♮) and the Dha♮ (VI♮), remaining as if they were a memory of its original form.

This hypothetical scheme may be of value in the clarification of the evolutionary process; it does not, however, help us to determine whether a particular *rāg* in one of these evolutionary stages has evolved from its neighbouring *ṭhāṭ* in a clockwise or an anti-clockwise direction round the Circle of *ṭhāṭ*s, as both are equally possible. In most instances there does not appear to be any musical criterion for determining the *ṭhāṭ* of origin and the only clear evidence sometimes occurs in the name of the *rāg*; thus we can be fairly certain, as we have suggested earlier, that *Śukl Bilāval* has originated from the *rāg Bilāval*. Nor does this scheme automatically resolve the problems in classifying *rāg*s in terms of *ṭhāṭ*s. The obvious difficulty lies in determining the parent *ṭhāṭ* of a *rāg* which is exactly half-way between two *ṭhāṭ*s and would be classified in stage 4 of our evolutionary scheme. This may perhaps be resolved on the grounds that the descending line, on which the perfect cadence is generally constructed, is the more important. A much more serious difficulty is caused by the fact that many *rāg*s have more than one accidental.

We have, so far, been speaking of only one kind of accidental, that which grows out of the unbalanced tetrachords of a scale. This type of accidental can be called a first order balance note, as it creates a temporary balance in the scale. In *Bilāval ṭhāṭ* for instance, where the descending conjunct tetrachords are unbalanced, the introduction of either the Ni♭ (VII♭) or the Ma♯ (IV♯) will temporarily achieve this end. As the Ni♭ occurs initially in the descending line and the Ma♯ in the ascending line, these are not mutually exclusive and there are several *rāg*s in which both of these accidentals are used. This complicates our simple evolutionary pattern for it can be said that these *rāg*s are evolving in both directions at the same time: the Ni♭ leading towards *Khamāj ṭhāṭ*, the Ma♯ towards *Kalyāṇ*.

The introduction of the first order balance note may create temporary balance in the descending conjunct tetrachords of *Bilāval*, but at the same time, it disturbs the balance in the ascending disjunct tetrachords. This can manifest itself in the introduction of a second order balance note which would temporarily restore the balance in the disjunct tetrachords which has been disturbed by the first accidental. For instance in the *rāg Bhairvī* (No. A6) the Re♮ (II♮) may occur as a first order balance note which restores the balance in the descending conjunct tetrachords, Ṡa–Pa (İ–V) and Pa–Re (V–II). However, it destroys the balance in the ascending disjunct tetrachord, Sa–Ma (I–IV) and Pa–Ṡa (V–İ). This might then lead to the introduction of the second order balance note, Dha♮ (VI♮), which will then temporarily create ascending disjunct balance. This process could, of course, be extended further to include third, fourth and fifth order balance notes. There are, however, at least two first order balance notes in every scale and from each stems a second order, so that four of the five possible accidentals can be obtained without proceeding beyond the second order. The remaining accidental which belongs to the third order does not appear to be significant in North Indian music. In *Bhairvī ṭhāṭ*, for instance, the first order accidentals would be Re♮ (II♮) and Ma♯ or rather Pa♭ (IV♯ or V♭); the second order accidentals, Dha♮ (VI♮) and Ni♮ or rather Sa♭ (VII♮ or I♭); the third order accidental, Ga♮ (III♮). In the *rāg Bhairvī* it is commonly understood that all the five possible accidentals may be used, but in fact the third order accidental, the Ga♮, is very rarely used.

Second order accidentals too are relatively infrequently used. This is not an easy matter to establish for it is dependent on the determination of the *ṭhāṭ* to which a particular *rāg* belongs. The *rāg Kedār*, for example, is ascribed by Bhātkhaṇḍe to *Kalyāṇ ṭhāṭ*. In this *rāg* the two alternatives of Ma (IV) and Ni (VII) are used. If we accept Bhātkhaṇḍe's classification of this *rāg* in *Kalyāṇ ṭhāṭ*, then the Ma♮ and Ni♭ are accidentals for these are chromatic alterations of the parent scale *Kalyāṇ* (No. A1). The Ma♮ will be a first order accidental, the Ni♭ a second order. Earlier[1] we had suggested that there was little justification for classifying the *rāg Kedār* in *Kalyāṇ ṭhāṭ*, in view of the fact that Bhātkhaṇḍe himself gives Ma♮ as the *vādī* (important note) of this *rāg*. If this *rāg* is classified in *Bilāval ṭhāṭ*, the accidentals would be Ma♯ and Ni♭, both of which would then be first order balance notes.

The number of first order accidentals depends on the number of unbalanced intervals in the two tetrachords, in other words, the number of imperfect fourths and fifths in the scale concerned. In *Bhairav ṭhāṭ* all the five possible alternatives can be achieved as first order accidentals since the descending conjunct tetrachords are completely unbalanced. In *Mārvā*, *Pūrvī* and *Toṛī ṭhāṭ*s there can be four possible first order accidentals (three in *Mārvā* since Re♮ occurs twice). These first order accidentals are shown in square brackets below:

Ex. 66.

(a) *Mārvā ṭhāṭ*

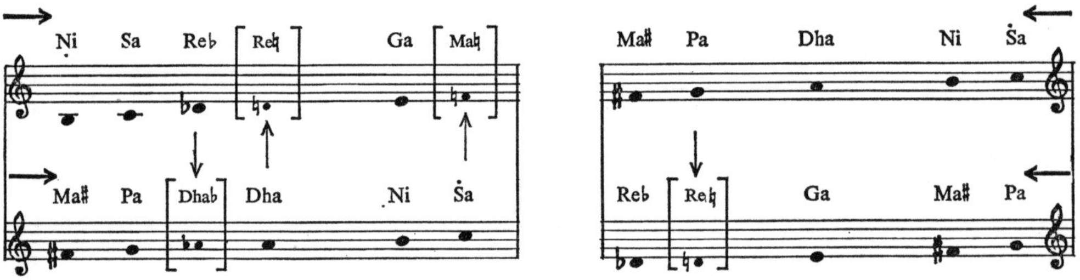

(*b*) *Pūrvī ṭhāṭ*

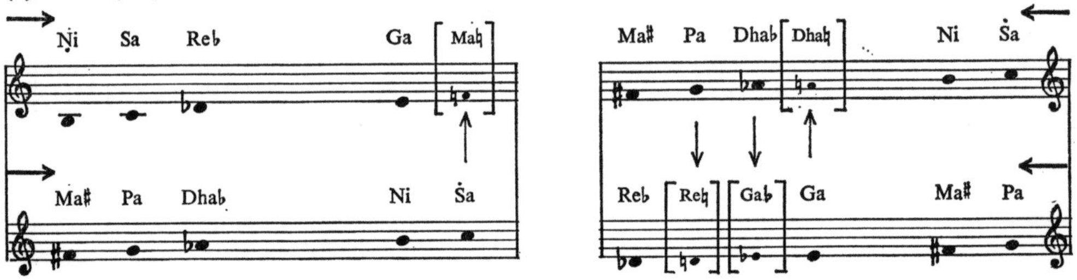

[1] See p. 53.

(c) *Toṛī ṭhāṭ*

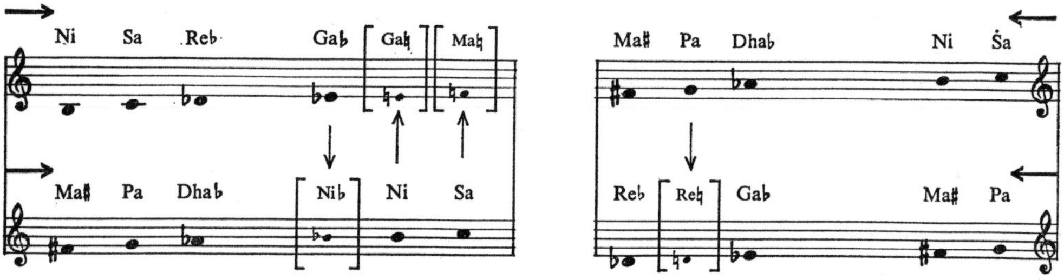

(d) *Bhairav ṭhāṭ*

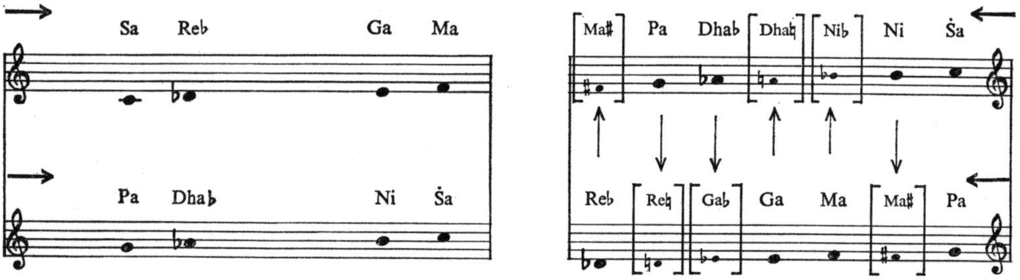

Two of the accidentals in the three *ṭhāṭ*s, *Mārvā*, *Pūrvī* and *Toṛī*, are constant, the Re♮ and the Ma♮. In many of the *rāg*s in these *ṭhāṭ*s, as we have previously indicated, the Pa is either very weak or completely omitted. Consequently, the Re♮, which would, in the *ṭhāṭ*, balance the Pa, is, except in one instance, not actually found as an accidental in the *rāg*s of these *ṭhāṭ*s. On the other hand the Ma♮ which balances the Sa is a very prominent accidental in the *rāg*s of these *ṭhāṭ*s, for although there is a tendency to omit the Sa in the phrases of many of these *rāg*s, the importance of the fundamental note of the system cannot be entirely suppressed. For all practical purposes, then, these *ṭhāṭ*s have three first order balance notes. In *Mārvā ṭhāṭ* the Re♮ occurs twice as a first order balance note. There is, however, only one instance of its occurrence as an accidental, as will be noticed in the table which is given later in this chapter.

Not all the accidentals used in the *rāg*s of North Indian classical music can be accounted for in terms of balance. The other accidentals, with perhaps one or two exceptions, can all be explained as leading notes. This concept, familiar to Western musical theory, is based on the principle that the extreme dissonance of the major seventh (Ni♮) demands resolution in the ground-note and conveys, in the resolution, a considerable measure of finality. The Ni♮ appears to be used in a number of *rāg*s in just this manner, as an accidental in the ascending line (even when it is not an immediate balance note) showing the way to the Sa. Of the ten principal *ṭhāṭ*s only four have Ni♭, and it is obviously in these four, *Khamāj* (No. A3), *Kāfī* (No. A4), *Āsāvrī* (No. A5) and *Bhairvī* (No. A6) *ṭhāṭ*s, that the leading note, Ni♮, occurs as an accidental. In *Khamāj* the Ni♮ is also a first order balance note and it is not surprising that this note is found in all the heptatonic *rāg*s of this *ṭhāṭ*. This explains why, in our illustration of the seven intermediate stages between *Bilāval* and *Khamāj ṭhāṭ*s, we were unable to give an example of stage 7 in which Ni♭ would have been a direct ascending note, with the Ni♮ only an oblique ascending note. In *Kāfī ṭhāṭ* the Ni♮ is a second order balance note which can only be significant if the first order accidental, Ga♮ (III♮), is used in the *rāg*. In fact the Ni♮ occurs much more often than the Ga♮ in the *rāg*s of this *ṭhāṭ*, a fact which clearly indicates that the importance of the Ni♮ is not primarily as a balance note. From Bhātkhaṇḍe's notations it is apparent that the use of this leading note in some of the *rāg*s in this *ṭhāṭ* is not accepted in all the musical traditions.[1]

The prominence of the leading note in *Khamāj* and *Kāfī ṭhāṭ*s may possibly suggest a survival of the early musical system of India, in which the two parent scales, the *Ṣaḍjagrāma* (similar to modern *Kāfī ṭhāṭ*) and the *Madhyamagrāma* (similar to *Khamāj ṭhāṭ*), were each permitted an accidental. These accidentals, the *kākalī* Ni in the former and the *antara* Ga in the latter, were in fact leading notes in the parent scales and could only be used in ascent.[2] In application to *Khamāj* and *Kāfī ṭhāṭ*s, at least, the use of the leading note is a long venerated tradition in India.

In *Āsāvrī* and *Bhairvī ṭhāṭ*s the leading-note accidental is much less common. Sometimes, as in the *rāg Aḍānā* of *Āsāvrī ṭhāṭ*, the occurrence of Ni♮ is a matter of controversy, and although Bhātkhaṇḍe does not draw attention to this in his works there are at present a number of musicians who do not use the Ni♮ in this *rāg*, but show, nevertheless, a tendency to sharpen the Ni♭ slightly in ascent.[3] In *Bhairvī ṭhāṭ* the Ni♮ is even less frequently used, though it occurs occasionally in the little-known *rāg*, *Moṭkī*,[4] and of course in the *rāg Bhairvī*, where accidentals are used quite freely.

While there would appear to be no doubt that the Ni♮ occurs in a number of *rāg*s as an accidental leading to the Sa, it should not be presumed that the Ni♮, where it occurs as a scalar note, is invariably used in this way. In the *ṭhāṭ*s on the left of the Circle, *Mārvā*, *Pūrvī*, and *Toṛī*, which have Ni♮ as a scalar note, the Re♭ (II♭) very frequently serves as a leading note to the Sa. There are probably several explanations for this. The Re♭ is perhaps even more dissonant than the Ni♮ (depending, of course, on the accompanying drones) and consequently we may expect the resolution in the Sa to be even more satisfying. In addition, the final cadence of most *rāg*s is generally descending, a fact which would tend to give prominence to Re♭ as a leading note. Finally, in a number of *rāg*s in these *ṭhāṭ*s, there is a tendency to omit the Sa, often in both ascent and descent, as in the *rāg Mārvā*, where the Ni, in some traditions, does not lead directly to the Sa, but either to the Re♭ or the Dha and thence to the Sa:

[1] For instance in the *rāg Bhīmplāsī*, some songs have Ni♭ in ascent, e.g. *K.P.M.* III, p. 564, others Ni♮, e.g. *ibid.*, p. 573-4.

[2] *Nāṭyaśāstra*, 'Kashi Sanskrit Series' (No. 60), prose, p. 321.

[3] Some musicians refer to the slightly raised ascending Ni♭ as *caṛhī* or *sākārī*. This can be heard on the accompanying record in the *rāg*s *Darbārī* and *Sūhā* and is discussed in Appendix B. It may be this note which Bhātkhaṇḍe has notated as Ni♮.

[4] *K.P.M.* VI, p. 438.

Ex. 67. rāg Mārvā

The balance-note accidentals are a manifestation of the same inherent instability of musical scales which, as we have suggested earlier, is a fundamental factor in the evolution of the musical system. On the other hand, leading-note accidentals do not appear to have influenced the course of evolution to any great extent. There are, however, two or three *rāg*s which may be exceptions. The *rāg Pīlū,* in which accidentals are freely permitted, is given in *Kāfī ṭhāṭ* (No. A4) by Bhātkhaṇḍe. This *rāg* has a very prominent leading note (Ni♮) which often serves as a terminal note. Perhaps because of its importance in the *rāg* the Ni♮ is sometimes also used in descent.[1]

Ex. 68. rāg Pīlū

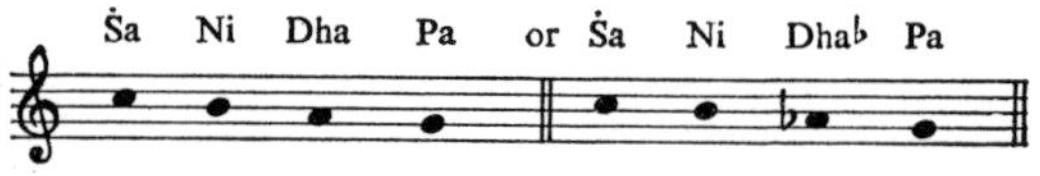

Similarly, in one version of the *rāg Paṭdīp* (this tradition is not mentioned by Bhātkhaṇḍe, but is frequently heard at the present time) the scale could be given as follows:

Ex. 69. rāg Paṭdīp

In both these instances the importance of the Ni♮, probably initially introduced as a leading-note accidental in either *Kāfī* or *Āsāvrī ṭhāṭ,* may finally have led to its acceptance in the descending line as well.[2]

There are indications that the accidental Ga♮ (III♮) may be used as leading note to the Ma (IV) in one or two *rāg*s. The *rāg Devgāndhār* is a case in point. Bhātkhaṇḍe refers to two versions of this *rāg*, both in *Āsāvrī ṭhāṭ* (No. A5). In one of these the Ga♮ occurs as the only accidental, while the other has no accidentals. The scalar Ga♭ is, however, perfectly balanced, having both a perfect fourth, Dha♭, and a perfect fifth, Ni♭. In the normal ascending line of the former the Ga is generally omitted (Ex. 70a); the Ga♮ only occurs in the phrase leading to the Ma, which is then generally sustained (Ex. 70b)[3]:

[1] The scale of *Pīlū,* given by Grosset, is in fact our No. C5 with Ga♭ (III♭) and Dha♭ (VI♭), but with Ni♮, as we have indicated.
[2] The *rāg Candrkoś,* discussed on p. 136, may be a third instance.
[3] *K.P.M.* IV, p. 383.

Ex. 70. *rāg Devgāndhār*

(a) (b)

Similarly, the Ga♮ as a leading note also occurs in one version of the *rāg Paṭdīpkī* (*Pradīpkī*) as given by Bhātkhaṇḍe. This *rāg* is in *Kāfī ṭhāṭ* (No. A4) and the use of the Ga♮ could be explained as a balance for the Dha♮. It is used also, as in the *rāg Devgāndhār*, as a leading note to the Ma. Here the Ga♮ occurs as an incomplete ascending note, while the Ga♭ occurs in the complete descending line as in the following phrases:[1]

Ex. 71. *rāg Devgāndhār*

The use of the Ga♮ as a leading note occurs in a very limited number of *rāg*s, and is only possible in those *rāg*s in which the Ma may be used as a terminal note. In the same way the Ma♯ (IV♯) may also be used as a leading note to the Pa (V) in several *rāg*s. There are, however, no instances of the use of the Ma♯ in a *rāg* where it is not explicable as a balance note.

It is quite clear that the accidentals used in the *rāg*s of North Indian classical music are not fortuitous, but can be explained on musical grounds, either as balance notes or as leading notes. Further, the consistent occurrence of the same accidental or accidentals in many *rāg*s of the same *ṭhāṭ* indicates that they are primarily influenced by the scale of the *rāg*. The occurrence of these accidentals can be conveniently summarised in statistical form. This summary is based on Bhātkhaṇḍe's notations as found in both his works, *K.P.M.* and *H.S.P.* For the purpose of these statistics we have only taken into consideration the heptatonic *rāg*s, except in *Toṛī*, *Pūrvī* and *Mārvā ṭhāṭ*s, in which hexatonic *rāg*s are basic. In the case of divergent traditions of the same *rāg*, we have chosen that tradition in which one or more accidentals are used. These are not necessarily traditions which are preferred by Bhātkhaṇḍe, nor are they necessarily those which are commonly heard today. It was our concern,

[1] *K.P.M.* VI, p. 479, variation 3.

however, to show that even among the lesser-known traditions the use of accidentals appears to be governed by the musical principles indicated.

	Number of heptatonic *rāgs*	First-order clockwise	First-order anticlockwise	Second-order clockwise	Second-order anticlockwise	Other	Observations
Kalyāṇ		Ma♮	Re♭	Ni♭	Dha♭	Ga♭	The *rāgs* with two accidentals, Ma♮ and Ni♭, first and second order clockwise respectively, would be more reasonably considered in *Bilāval ṭhāṭ*, where the accidentals would then be Ni♭ and Ma♯, first-order clockwise and anticlockwise respectively—see discussion of *rāg Kedār*, p. 53. The only example of a *rāg* with Re♭ is given in *Mārvā ṭhāṭ*, where the accidental occurs as Re♮.
No accidentals	2	—	—	—	—	—	
One accidental	3	X	—	—	—	—	
Two accidentals	6	X	—	X	—	—	
Total No. of *rāgs*	11						
Bilāval		Ni♭	Ma♯	Ga♭	Re♭	Dha♭	
No accidentals	2	—	—	—	—	—	
One accidental	14	X	—	—	—	—	
One accidental	3	—	X	—	—	—	
Two accidentals	3	X	X	—	—	—	
Total No. of *rāgs*	22						
Khamāj		Ga♭	Ni♮	Dha♭	Ma♯	Re♭	The Ni♮ occurs as a leading note in all the *rāgs* of this *ṭhāṭ*. Consequently, there are neither *rāgs* with no accidentals, nor *rāgs* with just Ga♭ accidental.
No accidentals	0	—	—	—	—	—	
One accidental	5	—	X	—	—	—	
Two accidentals	4	X	X	—	—	—	
Total No. of *rāgs*	9						
Kāfī		Dha♭	Ga♮	Re♭	Ni♮	Ma♯	In these *rāgs* too the prominence of the leading note, Ni♮, is very marked. Some of the *rāgs* of *Kāfī ṭhāṭ* are commonly heard without the Ni♮, but in all of these there are divergent traditions found among Bhātkhaṇḍe's notations of songs in which the Ni♮ is used as a leading note. The *rāg* with all accidentals permitted is the *rāg Pīlū*.
No accidentals	0	—	—	—	—	—	
One accidental	16	—	—	—	X	—	
Two accidentals	8	—	X	—	X	—	
Three accidentals	3	X	X	—	X	—	
Five accidentals	1	X	X	X	X	X	
Total No. of *rāgs*	28						

	Number of heptatonic *rāgs*	First-order clockwise	First-order anticlockwise	Second-order clockwise	Second-order anticlockwise	Other	Observations
Āsāvrī		Re♭	Dha♮	Ma♯	Ga♮	Ni♮	The leading note is not quite so prominent in this *ṭhāṭ*. The *rāg* with Ga♮ accidental is the *rāg Dev-gāndhār* in which it occurs as a leading note to the Ma (see text, p. 116). The importance of the first order balance notes in *Āsāvrī* and *Khamāj ṭhāṭ*s can be appreciated if the leading-note accidentals are ignored.
No accidentals	3	—	—	—	—	—	
One accidental	1	—	—	—	—	X	
One accidental	1	—	—	—	X	—	
Two accidentals	1	X	—	—	—	X	
Two accidentals	1	—	X	—	—	X	
Two accidentals	1	X	X	—	—	—	
Four accidentals	3	X	X	—	X	X	
Total No. of *rāgs*	11						
Bhairvī		Ma♯	Re♮	Ni♮	Dha♮	Ga♮	The *rāg* with four accidentals is the *rāg Bhairvī* in which all accidentals are said to be permitted. In Bhāt-khaṇḍe's notations, however, there is no indication of Ga♮.
No accidentals	3	—	—	—	—	—	
Two accidentals	1	X	X	—	—	—	
Four accidentals	1	X	X	X	X	—	
Total No. of *rāgs*	5						

All First-Order Balance

Bhairav		Re♮	Ga♭	Ma♯	Dha♮	Ni♭	No clear pattern emerges from the use of accidentals in the *rāgs* of *Bhairav ṭhāṭ*. The Ni♭ and the Ma♯ occur most frequently. The latter indicates the connection with *Pūrvī ṭhāṭ*. The absence of the Re♮ as an accidental may seem surprising in view of the fact that it is a balance for the Pa. However, this could be appreciated only by a comparison of conjunct tetrachords (since Re–Pa is a fourth) which are in Bhairav completely unbalanced. Evidence for the influence of Re♮ may be seen in the *rāg Naṭ Bhairav* (No. C2).
No accidentals	0	—	—	—	—	—	
One accidental	4	—	—	X	—	—	
One accidental	2	—	—	—	X	—	
One accidental	4	—	—	—	—	X	
Two accidentals	1	—	—	X	—	X	
Two accidentals	1	—	X	—	—	X	
Two accidentals	1	—	—	—	X	X	
Total No. of *rāgs*	13						

	Number of hexatonic and heptatonic *rāgs*	First-order clockwise	First-order anticlockwise	Second-order clockwise	Second-order anticlockwise	Other first-order	Other first-order	Observations
Toṛī		Ga♮	Ni♭	Dha♮	(Ma♮)	Re♮	Ma♮	In *Toṛī*, *Pūrvī* and *Mārvā ṭhāṭ*s, hexatonic *rāg*s have been included in the tables. Several other varieties of *Toṛī* are mentioned by Bhātkhaṇḍe. He does not, however, describe them in any detail, as they are very rarely heard and, from the scalar point of view, do not belong in *Toṛī ṭhāṭ*.
No accidentals	3	—	—	—	—	—	—	
Total No. of *rāg*s	3							
Pūrvī		Dha♮	Ga♭	(Re♮)	Ni♭	Re♮	Ma♮	The first-order clockwise (Dha♮) and anticlockwise (Ga♭) do not appear to be used as accidentals. This is, indeed, the case with respect to the Ga♭. There are, however, several *rāg*s which could be indicated in *Pūrvī ṭhāṭ* with Dha♮ as accidental, but these are given in *Mārvā ṭhāṭ*, with Dha♭ as accidental, by Bhātkhaṇḍe.
No accidentals	7	—	—	—	—	—	—	
One accidental	5	—	—	—	—	—	X	
Total No. of *rāg*s	12							
Mārvā		Re♮	Dha♭	(Ma♮)	Ga♭	(Re♮)	Ma♮	The Re♮ is the connecting link with *Kalyāṇ*, and thus with the serial *ṭhāṭ*s. This link is undoubtedly weak and the Re♮ occurs in only one version of the *rāg Jet*. Ni♭, not given in this table, is neither first- nor second-order, and is not used as an accidental in any *rāg* of this *ṭhāṭ*.
No accidentals	4	—	—	—	—	—	—	
One accidental	3	—	X	—	—	—	—	
One accidental	4	—	—	—	—	—	X	
Two accidentals	1	X	X	—	—	—	—	
Two accidentals	3	—	X	—	—	—	X	
Total No. of *rāg*s	15							

These tables show that the first order balance notes are of prime importance in the system, and that leading-note accidentals have considerable effect in some of the *ṭhāṭ*s. Second-order balance notes can, to some extent, be eliminated by the re-classification of certain *rāg*s. There are, however, a few *rāg*s in which these would still be significant. In these, for instance *Bhairvī* and *Pīlū*, the accidentals are used more as a temporary change of scale rather than as ascending or descending melodic features. This temporary change of scale is characteristic of the *ṭhumrī*, a form of song in which the use of accidentals is considered desirable provided the transition from one scale to the next is accomplished smoothly. This is another instance of the re-creation of the evolutionary pattern which also depends on the smooth transition from one scale to the next. Thus, in the *rāg Bhairvī*, the accidental Re♮ is not introduced merely into the ascending line, but may completely replace the Re♭ until the final cadence at the end of a variation as in the following example:

Ex. 72. *rāg Bhairvī*

It is primarily in those *rāgs* in which the first order balance accidental may be used so extensively, that the second order accidental becomes significant. In *Bhairvī,* the Dha♮ can be used in a similar manner:

Ex. 73. *rāg Bhairvī*

The following diagram is designed to provide a convenient reference for the order of accidentals in the *ṭhāṭs*. The ten radial lines here represent the ten movable notes. The *ṭhāṭs* are represented as segments of a circle, each crossing five of these lines which are the constituent movable notes of that *ṭhāṭ*. Thus this diagram shows the scale of each *ṭhāṭ* (not including *Bhairav*) when the immovable Sa and Pa are added. The first radial beyond the segment representing the *ṭhāṭ* is the first order clockwise balance note. The following radial in the same direction is the second order clockwise. Similarly, the two radials beyond the segment in the anticlockwise direction, are the first and second order anticlockwise balance notes. In the diagram we have also added two more radials in dotted lines to indicate that the *ṭhāṭs* crossed by these lines are those affected by the leading note, Ni♮; and the first order balance note, Ma♮.

Although our prime purpose in this work is to further the understanding of Indian music rather than to suggest the reform of musical theory, certain principles for the classification of heptatonic and the 'functional' hexatonic *rāg*s of *Mārvā, Pūrvī* and

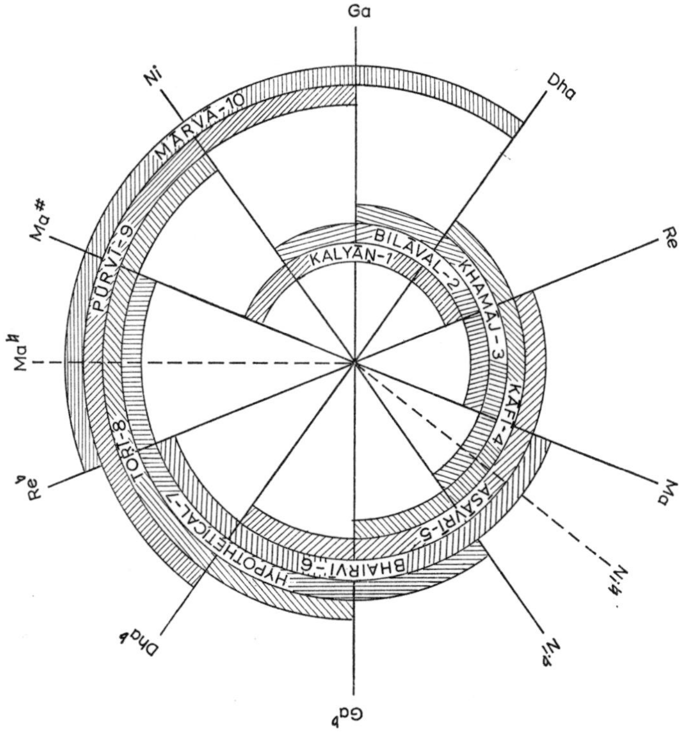

*Toṛī ṭhāṭ*s become evident from our analysis. These can be expressed briefly as follows:

1. For the purpose of classification leading notes may be ignored.
2. A *rāg* in which one pair of alternatives is used should be classified according to the way in which the alternatives are used with reference to the seven stages between two *ṭhāṭ*s. If the usage is such as to be exactly half-way between two *ṭhāṭ*s (stage 4), then the *rāg* could be classified, perhaps somewhat arbitrarily, according to its descending line.
3. If two pairs of alternatives (excluding the leading note) are used, the *rāg* should be classified in that *ṭhāṭ* in which the alternatives occur as first-order balance notes, irrespective of the way in which the alternatives are used.
4. If more than two alternatives are used, i.e. second-order balance notes are clearly significant, then the *rāg* should be classified according to the cadence or cadences.

VII

Transilient Scales

The Indian term for a heptatonic series, *sampūrṇ* (lit. complete), suggests that hexatonic and pentatonic series are incomplete, lacking either one or two notes. This provides justification for the use of the term transilient (or gapped) scales for the hexatonic and pentatonic series in Indian classical music. The heptatonic series has been the basis of the musical system from a very early period.[1] The *grāma-jāti* system of the *Nāṭyaśāstra* is, of course, also based on the heptatonic series and there are instructions given for the creation of transilient forms by the omission of specific notes from the heptatonic *jāti*s.

In the Muslim period, however, the pentatonic series appears to have been given a measure of importance in the *rāga-rāginī* schemes of classification which were then in vogue. In these schemes the masculine *rāga*s were frequently pentatonic, with the implication that the system was based on the pentatonic series. This was a period when poetic imagination had free rein and *rāga*s were associated with the Hindu deities, colours, stars and other natural and supernatural phenomena, culminating in the *rāga-mālā* paintings in which the *rāga*s and *rāginī*s are represented in their visual symbolic form. There is no reason to suppose, however, that the association of pentatonality with the masculine *rāga* at this time reflects the real origins of art music and it is much more probable that the connection between the two was based on aesthetics.[2]

In the modern period the heptatonic series is thought of as the parent of the hexatonic and the pentatonic. Bhātkhaṇḍe says that pentatonic, hexatonic and heptatonic *rāg*s are all produced from *ṭhāṭ*s, and consequently each *ṭhāṭ* must necessarily have seven notes.[3] From one heptatonic series of notes Bhātkhaṇḍe derives 484 possible combinations of penta-, hexa- and heptatonic forms, his calculations being based on the independence of the ascending and descending lines as follows:

[1] *Ṛik Prātiśākhya*, a Vedic text of about the 4th century B.C. dealing with phonetics, mentions seven notes (*yama*) and three registers (*sthāna*).

[2] That this association of *rāga* with pentatonality is largely subjective is emphasised by Bhātkhaṇḍe when he quotes an opinion that *rāga*, being male, will have a serious character, be sung in a leisurely and grand manner and be *heptatonic*. *H.S.P.* III, p. 36.

[3] *K.P.M.* II, p. 14.

Transilient Scales

Ascent	Descent	Number of possible forms
heptatonic	heptatonic	1
heptatonic	hexatonic	6
heptatonic	pentatonic	15
hexatonic	heptatonic	6
hexatonic	hexatonic	36
hexatonic	pentatonic	90
pentatonic	heptatonic	15
pentatonic	hexatonic	90
pentatonic	pentatonic	225
	Total ..	484

These combinations, each of which could provide the basis for at least one *rāg*, are all derived from just one heptatonic *ṭhāṭ*. To impress the reader still further, Bhātkhaṇḍe multiplies this number by the seventy-two *mel*s (*mela*s) of the South Indian system, arriving at a grand total of 34,848. But even this figure does not exhaust all the possible *rāg*s, for it does not take into account the differentiation of one *rāg* from another on the basis of altering important notes, i.e. *vādī* and *samvādī*.[1] Bhātkhaṇḍe does not, however, place too much importance on these theoretical possibilities for he recognises that in current practice there do not appear to be many more than 200 *rāg*s in all.

Transilient *rāg*s could obviously have been derived from heptatonic scales by a similar intellectual process, but in fact there is little reason to believe that this has actually occurred, except perhaps in a few isolated instances. Whereas the intellect can conceive hundreds of transilient scales, only a very small percentage is actually in use; for instance, among Bhātkhaṇḍe's notations there are only twenty-seven *rāg*s pentatonic in both ascent and descent. This enormous discrepancy between theory and practice is explained by Bhātkhaṇḍe on the grounds that *rāg*s must have the capacity to give pleasure and, by implication, only a few of these combinations have this capacity. Our experience with heptatonic scales indicates that the prominent scales have evolved within the system in a logical subconscious process, and only a few modern *rāg*s have been borrowed or created intellectually. It would not be unreasonable to expect the transilient scales to follow this same pattern and to be closely related to the ten heptatonic *ṭhāṭ*s.

The concept of balance has been seen to be a fundamental aspect of the heptatonic *ṭhāṭ*s and appears to be of equal importance in transilient scales. The inherent imperfection of heptatonic scales, where at least one pair of notes stands in an augmented

[1] *K.P.M.* III, pp. 13 and 14.

fourth/diminished fifth relationship, precludes the possibility of producing a perfectly balanced scale. This imperfection, we suggested in the previous chapter, was the prime instigation for the introduction of accidentals which then supply temporary balance in the scales. A second obvious solution is to omit one or both of the notes which cause this imperfection. This has already been mentioned in our discussion of the *rāg Mārvā* (see pp. 82, 83), where we suggested that the omission of the Pa was a necessary device in order to create balance in the *rāg*. The tendency to omit the unbalanced notes in a heptatonic scale is readily demonstrated in those *rāg*s for which there are few prescribed rules of movement, where musicians are relatively free to use virtually any combinations of the notes and, in the process, to omit notes according to their inclinations. Even in these *rāg*s certain conventional phrases have evolved and are very commonly heard, while other theoretical possibilities are used much less frequently or not at all.

In the *rāg Bhairvī*, for instance, the correlation between the first-order accidentals and the commonly omitted notes is clearly apparent. The unbalanced intervals are the Re♭ (II♭) and the Pa (V), and the first order balance notes are the Re♮ (II♮) and the Pa♭ (V♭), called Ma♯ (IV♯). Both the scalar note Re♭ and the accidental Re♮, may be used in ascent, but a third ascending line in which the Re is omitted is equally as prominent. All three of these ascending lines are found among Bhātkhaṇḍe's notations:

Ex. 74. rāg Bhairvī

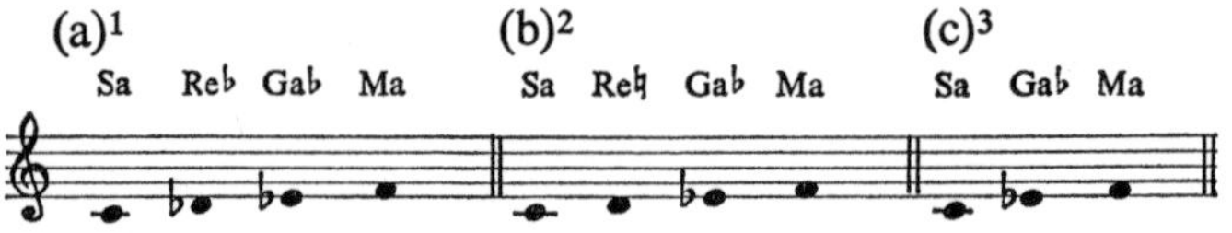

Similarly, the Pa may either be included in the ascending line or omitted. The Pa♭, or rather Ma♯ as it is called, occurs however only in the descending line:

Ex. 75. rāg Bhairvī

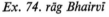

In *rāg Bhairvī* two characteristic symmetrical, gapped phrases are apparent. In the first (Ex. 76a), Re is omitted, in the second (b), Pa. Some musicians also introduce a

[1] *K.P.M.* II, p. 498, variation 10.
[2] *K.P.M.* II, song, on p. 400.
[3] *K.P.M.* II, p. 498, variation 3.
[4] *K.P.M.* II, p. 498, variation 6.
[5] *K.P.M.* II, p. 498, variation 6.
[6] *K.P.M.* II, p. 427, song.

third gapped phrase (c) which provides disjunct symmetry to (a) in spite of the fact that this tends to place emphasis on Re♮ which is really an accidental in *Bhairvī ṭhāṭ*:

Ex. 76. rāg Bhairvī (a)

Neither of these omissions is essential in *Bhairvī*, and theoretically there would be no objection to the omission of other notes, for instance, the Ga♭, but in fact this occurs very seldom.

Our second example is the *rāg Pīlū*, where in several songs given by Bhātkhaṇḍe our argument is well illustrated, as in the following:[1]

Ex. 77. rāg Pīlū—tritāl

Bhātkhaṇḍe ascribes this *rāg* to *Kāfī ṭhāṭ*, but in this song the Ni♮ is used in both ascent and descent, the Ni♭ appearing only once in oblique descent in the second part of the song (*antrā*) in the following fragment:

Ex. 78. rāg Pīlū

In Ex. 77 we are concerned with the three possibilities: the occurrence of the scalar Ga♭, the occurrence of its alternative Ga♮ (probably introduced to balance the Ni♮

[1] *K.P.M.* III, pp. 615–16, *sthāyī* and *antrā*.

and used as a leading note to the Ma) and the omission of the Ga altogether. In the second line of the *sthāyī* (main verse) the Ga♭ is clearly established as an ascending note in the figure marked *x*. In the first bar of the next line the accidental Ga♮ is used in ascent as a leading note to the Ma, marked *y*. In the following bar, however, the Ga is omitted in the ascending phrase, marked *z*.

In the *rāgs Bhairvī* and *Pīlū* the omitted note is correlated with the first order accidentals. The tendency to omit the unbalanced notes does not, however, depend on the use of accidentals. In the *rāg Yaman* (*Kalyāṇ ṭhāṭ*, No. A1) the notes of the ascending and descending lines are given as consecutive sequences but, in fact, any combinations of the notes of *Kalyāṇ ṭhāṭ* are permissible.[1] The absence of precise rules of ascent and descent permits us to note trends which have entered in the performance of this *rāg*. Of these, the four most prominent are:

(1) The tendency to omit the Sa:[2]

Ex. 79. rāg Yaman

(2) The tendency to omit the Ma♯ and the Ni:[3]

Ex. 80.

(3) The tendency to omit the Ma♯ and the Ga in a descending cadence:[4]

Ex. 81.

(4) The tendency to omit the Pa:[5]

Ex. 82.

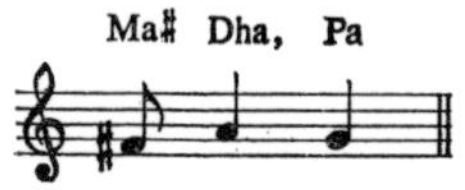

[1] *H.S.P.* I, p. 51.
[2] *K.P.M.* II, p. 487, variation 2.
[3] *Ibid.*, p. 488, variation 11.
[4] *Ibid.*, p. 488, variation 11.
[5] *Ibid.*, p. 488, variation 10. The omission of Pa in *Yaman* is not so prominent in Bhātkhaṇḍe's notations but is very much in evidence at the present time.

In *Kalyāṇ ṭhāṭ* the Sa (I) and Ma♯ (IV♯) are unbalanced (see p. 81) and here we see evidence of the omission of both these notes. These omissions can be called 'first order' to be consistent with the terms used in the previous chapter on alternative notes. However, once the Sa or the Ma♯ are omitted there is a tendency to make a second order omission of Pa (V) and Ni (VII) respectively. Thus the Ma♯ and the Ni are omitted in the same phrase (as in Ex. 80 above). The Sa and Pa may also be omitted in one phrase as follows, although this does not occur in Bhātkhaṇḍe's notations:

Ex. 83.

The notes Sa and Pa are, however, omitted in exactly parallel phrases (see phrase in Ex. 79 marked *x* and Ex. 82). *Kalyāṇ ṭhāṭ* is in some ways an exceptional case, for the second order omissions are of greater importance than is usually the case. This can perhaps be explained by the fact that the first order omissions, Sa and Ma♯, which have such an extreme contrast of dynamic functions, are not usually thought of as a pair. Although a comparison of the ascending conjunct tetrachords is not feasible owing to the absence of the Ma♮ (IV♮), the descending conjunct tetrachords, Ṡa–Pa (İ–V) and Pa–Re (V–II), are not only comparable but parallel in *Kalyāṇ ṭhāṭ*. This tetrachord scheme is emphasised in the two cadences, Pa–Ṡa in Ex. 80 above and Pa–Re–Sa in Ex. 81, and this may explain the omission of the Ma♯ (IV♯) and Ga (III) in the descending cadence.[1]

In these examples from the *rāgs Bhairvī, Pīlū* and *Yaman*, we have attempted to demonstrate that it is, in fact, the unbalanced notes that tend to be omitted. As the heptatonic *ṭhāṭs*, excluding *Mārvā, Pūrvī* and *Toṛī*, are balanced in one tetrachord scheme, either conjunct or disjunct, the omission of one note is bound to disrupt the balance. In *Mārvā* and *Toṛī*, however, the omission of one note, the Pa, is essential to produce balance, so that these two *ṭhāṭs* are, in this respect, exceptional. On the other hand, balance can be preserved in pentatonic scales if the omitted notes are in corresponding positions in the two tetrachords. Thus for a scale in which notes I, II, III, and IV are balanced by V, VI, VII, and İ respectively, the omission of II and VI will still leave I, III, and IV balanced by V, VII, and İ. From the standpoint of balance, therefore, pentatonic scales are generally much more satisfactory than hexatonic scales.

In *Bilāval ṭhāṭ* the omission of one of the two unbalanced notes, either Ma (IV) or Ni (VII), will disturb the ascending disjunct balance which is characteristic of this *ṭhāṭ*. This does not mean that there can be no hexatonic *rāgs* in *Bilāval ṭhāṭ*, but that balance is not inherent in these hexatonic scales and may have to be achieved in some

[1] This *rāg* can be heard on the accompanying record and is discussed further in Appendix B, p. 204.

manner in the *rāgs* themselves. Therefore, we propose to discuss pentatonic scales first and to consider the omissions in pairs.

In *Khamāj ṭhāṭ* the corresponding pairs of notes can be seen vertically:

Ex. 84. Khamāj ṭhāṭ

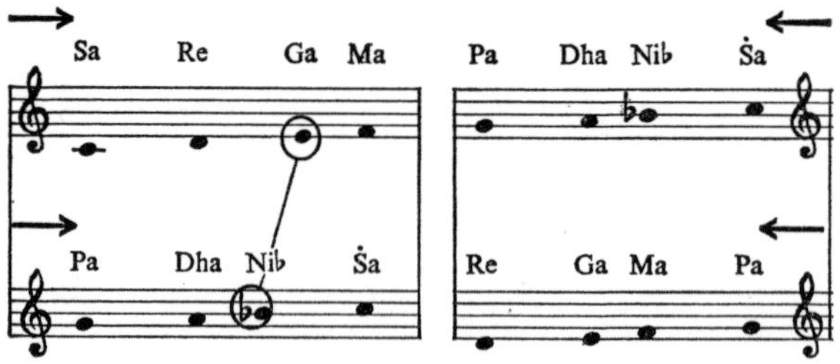

Here the Ga and Ni♭ are the first order omissions. If these are omitted, the ascending disjunct tetrachord will become balanced, while the balance of the original descending conjunct tetrachord scheme will be disrupted, as the Ga will no longer be there to balance the Dha and, similarly, the Ni♭ will not be there to balance the Ma. The resulting scale will be quite satisfactory as one tetrachord scheme will be balanced. There is also a certain justification for omitting the pairs Ga–Dha or Ni♭–Ma, first and second order omissions clockwise and anticlockwise respectively round the Circle (see p. 59). These would leave the descending conjunct tetrachords balanced and cause no great disturbance in the scale. There is, however, no functional need to omit these notes, for in the descending conjunct scheme of *Khamāj* they are already balanced. These two pairs are the first order omission notes of the adjacent *ṭhāṭ*s, Ni and Ma in *Bilāval*, Ga♭ and Dha in *Kāfī*, where the need to omit them is functional.

Ex. 85. Bilāval ṭhāṭ

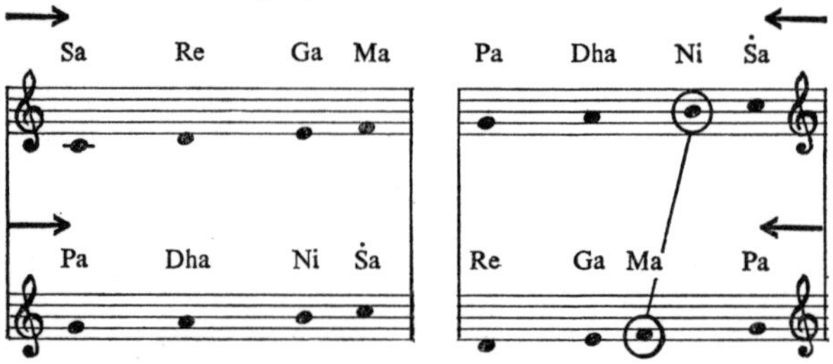

Ex. 86. Kāfī ṭhāṭ

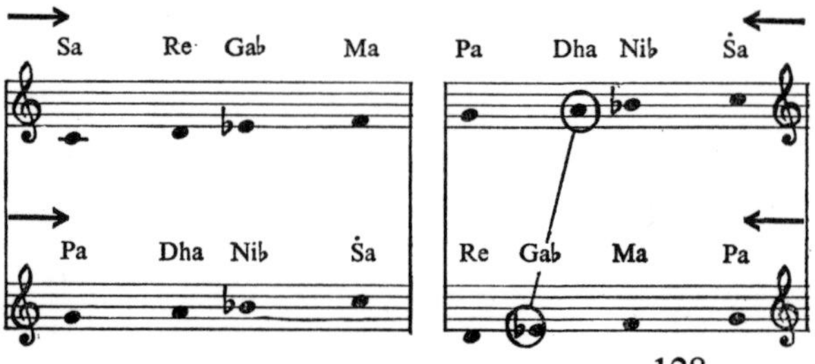

The resulting pentatonic scale whether derived from *Khamāj* or *Bilāval* will naturally be the same, for the note which distinguishes *Khamāj* from *Bilāval*, the Ni, is one of the two notes omitted. Consequently, the pentatonic scales derived from omitting the respective first and second order notes from any *ṭhāṭ* are identical with the scales derived from their adjacent *ṭhāṭs* by the omission of the two first order unbalanced notes.

There still remain two other pairs in *Khamāj* which could be omitted, Re–Dha (II–VI) and Re–Pa (II–V). (The pairs in which the Sa is one of the notes may not be omitted.) The omission of the former destroys the parallelism in both tetrachord types, but the omission of Re and Pa still leaves the possibility of parallelism in ascending conjunct tetrachords, Sa–Ga–Ma (I–III–IV) and Ma–Dha–Ni♭ (IV–VI–VII♭). Here again, there is no reason why these notes should not be omitted but there is no functional need for doing so.

It must be stressed that none of the pentatonic scales are perfectly balanced in both conjunct and disjunct tetrachords, and in this respect they are no better than heptatonic scales. In *Bilāval ṭhāṭ*, for instance, if the first order unbalanced notes, Ma (IV) and Ni (VII), are omitted, the original unbalanced descending conjunct tetrachords of *Bilāval* will become balanced, but the ascending disjunct tetrachords will now be unbalanced:

Ex. 87. *Bilāval* Pentatonic

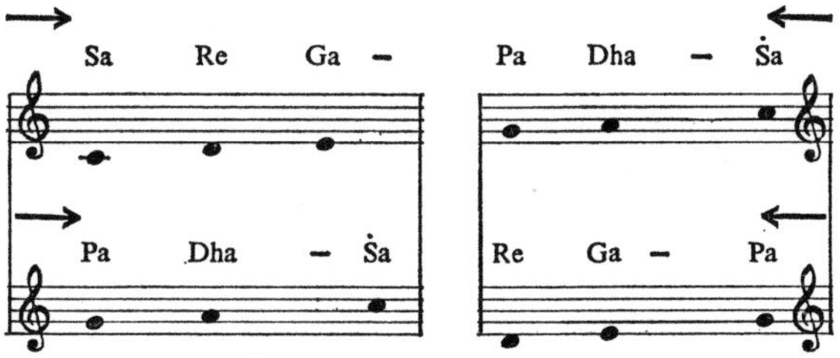

The Ga and the Sa are unbalanced in the ascending disjunct tetrachords. If the process of omitting the unbalanced notes is carried further and the Ga omitted, this will remove the balance for the Dha in the descending conjunct. The omission of this Dha would remove the support for the Re, and if the Re were omitted this would in turn have an effect on the Pa and through this on the Sa. That this tendency is not without substantiation in North Indian music will be shown later in this chapter when the *rāg Mālśrī* is discussed. The reverse process, that of adding the balancing notes (i.e. perfect fourths and fifths), has equal justification. The scales of the six serial *ṭhāṭs*, which are the foundations of the Indian system, can be constructed by successions of fourths and fifths.[1] These are, in fact, the intervals which separate conjunct

[1] For instance, *Kāfī ṭhāṭ*, by three consecutive upper perfect fifths from Sa, giving Pa (V), Re (II) and Dha (VI), and three upper perfect fourths from Sa, giving Ma (IV), Ni♭ (VII♭) and Ga♭ (III♭). Similarly, *Kalyāṇ ṭhāṭ* could be constructed by a succession of six upper perfect fifths, and *Bhairvī* by a succession of five upper perfect fourths and one upper perfect fifth.

and disjunct tetrachords. The heptatonic scale is readily obtained from its related pentatonic scale merely by adding the balance notes—in the above example, Ni (VII) to balance the Ga (III) and Ma (IV) to balance the Sa (I). This being so, it does not make much difference whether the Indian system originated from a heptatonic or a pentatonic base, for they are complementary. To be consistent with the modern Indian tradition, however, we shall discuss transilient scales in terms of their heptatonic 'parents'.[1]

From each of the ten *ṭhāṭ*s in the Circle of *Ṭhāṭ*s, a pentatonic scale can be derived by the omission of the two unbalanced notes. The derivatives of five of the six serial *ṭhāṭ*s are quite regular and are given below, where the unbalanced notes of the *ṭhāṭ* to be omitted in the pentatonic derivative are shown in brackets:

Ex. 88.

Ṭhāṭ		Representative *rāg*
Bilāval (No. A2)		*Bhūpālī*
Khamāj (No. A3)		*Durgā*
Kāfī (No. A4)		*Sāraṅg*
Āsāvrī (No. A5)		*Dhānī*
Bhairvī (No. A6)		*Mālkoś*

These are the five most common pentatonic scales whose occurrence is not limited to India alone. A characteristic feature of these scales is that they have no semitones and, for this reason, are sometimes called anhemitonic.

The pentatonic derivative of *Kalyāṇ ṭhāṭ* is not so easily resolved, for Sa is one of the unbalanced notes and may not be omitted. We have, however, already referred to

[1] This terminology follows Bhātkhaṇḍe who says, for instance, that the pentatonic *rāg Bhūpālī* is born of *Kalyāṇ ṭhāṭ* (*bhūpālī rāg kalyāṇ ṭhāṭ se utpann hotā hai*). *K.P.M.* III, p. 23.

the enharmonic compromise growing out of the temporary omission of Sa, as a result of which Re (II) is seen in relation to Ma♯ (IV♯). This, we have suggested, was the basis of *Mārvā ṭhāṭ*. In the same way, we can derive a pentatonic form related to *Kalyāṇ ṭhāṭ* by the omission of Re and Ma♯ instead of Sa and Ma♯:

Ex. 89.

Kalyāṇ (No. A1)

Śaṅkrā[1]

In our Circle of *Ṭhāṭs* we had accepted a second enharmonic compromise, that between *Bhairvī* and the hypothetical *ṭhāṭ* where the Pa♭ (V♭) is interpreted as a Ma♯ (IV♯). For the derivation of a pentatonic scale from *Bhairvī ṭhāṭ*, this compromise is unnecessary since the omission of Pa is not forbidden. Thus the pentatonic derivative of *Bhairvī*, *Mālkoś*, is formed by the omission of Re♭ (II♭) and Pa (V), the unbalanced notes.

The *ṭhāṭs* on the left side of the Circle, *Mārvā*, *Pūrvī* and *Toṛī*, could each have more than one derivative as more than one pair of notes are unbalanced. The derivatives around the Circle are as follows:

Ex. 90. Representative *rāg*

Mārvā (No. A10)

Mālśrī

Pūrvī (No. A9)

—

Toṛī (No. A8)

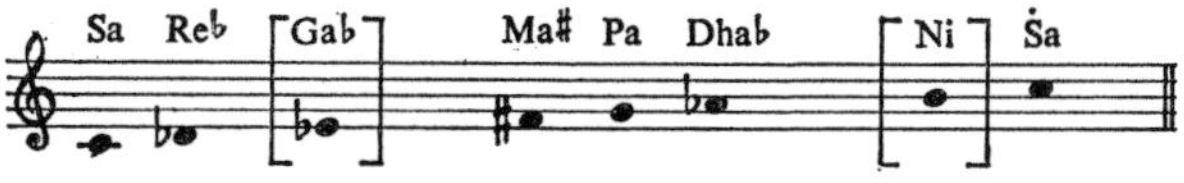

—

(No. A7)

Bhūpāl Toṛī

It will be seen that the derivatives of *Pūrvī* and *Toṛī* are not in common use at the present time. However, the *rāg Śrī* shows, in its pentatonic ascent, a close connection with the pentatonic *Pūrvī* derivative, while the derivative of *Toṛī* does apparently

[1] There are two main versions of *rāg Śaṅkrā*. One is pentatonic as above, while the other is hexatonic, Ma being the only omitted note (*K.P.M.* IV, p. 208). This second version can be heard on the accompanying record and is discussed in Appendix B, p. 206.

occur in a very seldom heard *rāg* called *Yaśā Rañjnī.*[1] Neither of these two derivatives has either conjunct or disjunct balance, a fact which may help to explain why these pentatonic forms are so rare.[2] The pentatonic derivatives of the Circle of *Ṭhāṭ*s are shown in the following diagram, where dotted lines indicate the notes which are unbalanced and therefore omitted:

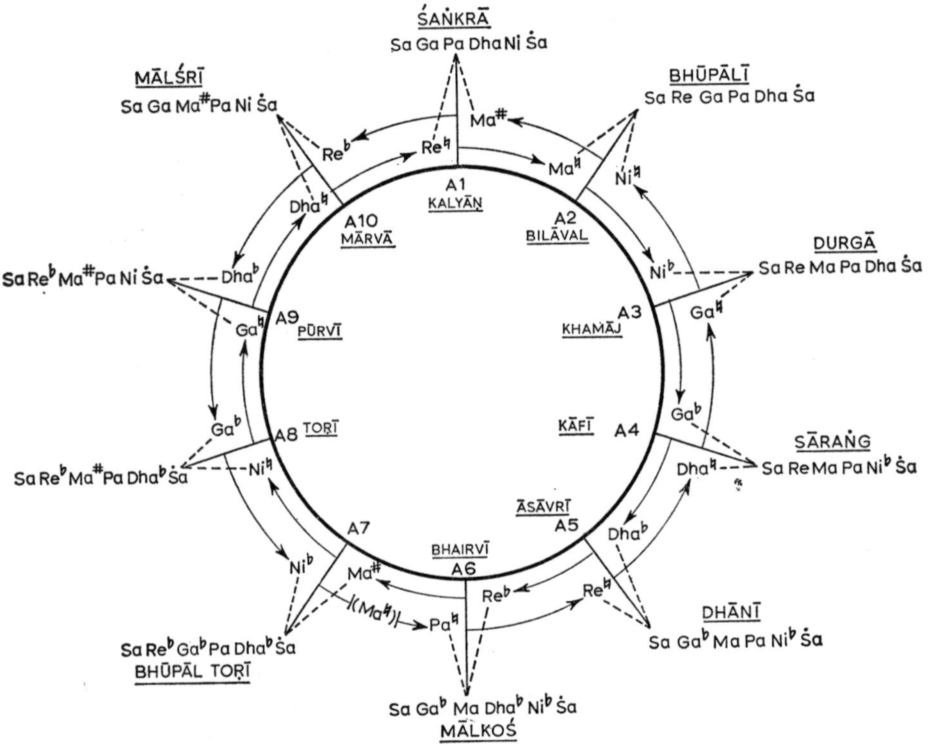

Mārvā ṭhāṭ has a second possible pentatonic derivative if Re♭ and Pa are seen as the unbalanced notes. The omission of these results in the *rāg Hindol*:

Ex. 91.

Mārvā (No. A10)

Hindol

There are three possible pentatonic derivatives of *Bhairav ṭhāṭ* since the three pairs of notes, Re♭–Pa (II♭–V), Ga–Dha♭ (III–VI♭), and Ni–Ma (VII–IV), are unbalanced

[1] Vasant, *Rāg Koś*, Hathras 1962, p. 21.

[2] Several commonly heard pentatonic *rāg*s are, however, also basically unbalanced, and yet an element of symmetry is produced in them. Some examples of these are discussed later in this chapter.

in the descending conjunct tetrachords. Of these, only one pair appears to be significant. In the previous chapter we had noted that Ma♯ (IV♯) and Ni♭ (VII♭) were the most commonly used accidentals in *Bhairav ṭhāṭ* (see table p. 119). The omission of the two unbalanced notes, Ma and Ni, results in the commonly heard pentatonic *rāg Vibhās*:

Ex. 92.

Bhairav (No. C9)

Vibhās

Another pentatonic *rāg*, *Guṇkrī*, ascribed by Bhātkhaṇḍe to *Bhairav ṭhāṭ*, is better discussed as a derivative of the *rāg Vasant Mukhārī* (No. C6). According to Bhātkhaṇḍe the latter has been introduced from the South Indian system,[1] but it would appear that the impulse to produce this scale must be indigenous to North Indian music since the introduction of Ni♭ (VII♭) as an accidental into *Bhairav ṭhāṭ* suggests it. It will be noticed below that neither the ascending disjunct nor the descending conjunct tetrachords in this scale are balanced, a fact which may explain why it has no lengthy tradition in North Indian music:

Ex. 93. Vasant Mukhārī

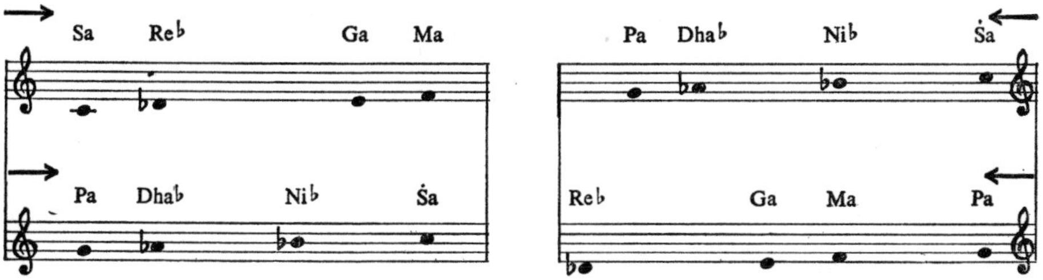

The pentatonic *rāg Guṇkrī* can be derived from this by the omission of the two unbalanced notes, Ga and Ni♭, in the ascending disjunct tetrachords of *Vasant Mukhārī*, leaving two parallel disjunct, gapped tetrachords:

Ex. 94.

Vasant Mukhārī (No. C6)

Guṇkrī

The scale of *Vasant Mukhārī* provides a link between *Bhairav* (No. C9) and *Bhairvī* (No. A6) in the Circle of *Ṭhāṭs*. There are indications of similar connections between *Bhairav* and other *ṭhāṭs* of the Circle—the connection with *Mārvā* (No.

[1] *K.P.M.* VI, p. 446.

A10) through the intermediate *Ānand Bhairav* (No. B10), with *Bilāval* (No. A2) through *Naṭ Bhairav* (No. C2), and with *Khamāj* (No. A3) through the two intermediate scales *Ānand Bhairav* (No. B10) and *Ahīr Bhairav* (No. C3). These connections cannot, however, be established conclusively.

Of the twenty-seven pentatonic *rāg*s discussed by Bhātkhaṇḍe, sixteen appear to be derivatives of the Circle of *Ṭhāṭ*s and two others of *Bhairav ṭhāṭ*. This still leaves a significant percentage of the pentatonic *rāg*s unexplained. Three others clearly have their origin in South Indian music, a fact which is acknowledged by Bhātkhaṇḍe: *Haṃsdhvanī* (Ex. 95a), *Ābhogī* (b) and *Devrañjnī* (c). In addition, *Meghrañjnī* (Ex. 95d) appears either to have been imported from South India or to be the modal series from the fifth of *Devrañjnī* with Ni♮ instead of the Ni♭,[1] and these four *rāg*s do not appear to represent evolution within the system.

Ex. 95.

(a) *rāg Haṃsdhvanī* (b) *rāg Ābhogī*

(c) *rāg Devrañjnī* (d) *rāg Meghrañjnī*

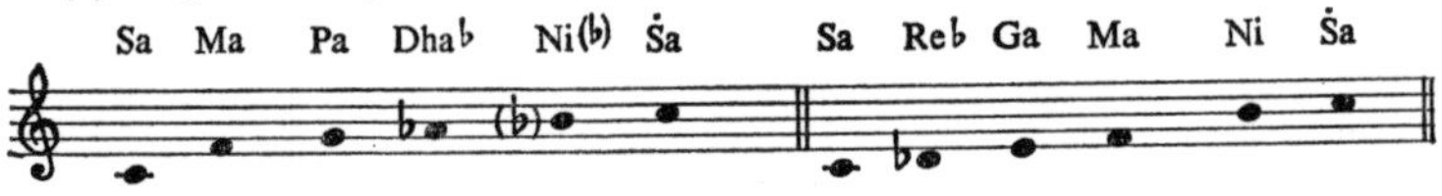

There still remain five pentatonic *rāg*s which have apparently originated within the North Indian system but do not seem to be connected with the derived pentatonic scales we have discussed. On the assumption that the omitted notes are first order unbalanced notes, we can attempt to reconstruct the heptatonic scales of origin of these *rāg*s. In the following table the unbalanced notes to be added to the pentatonic *rāg* are shown in brackets:

Ex. 96.

Pentatonic *rāg*		Conjectural Heptatonic Parent
Guṇkrī	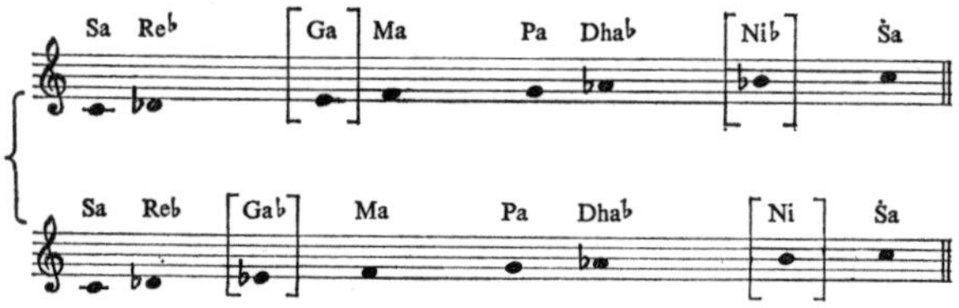	*Vasant Mukhārī* (No. C6) — (No. B6)

[1] *Meghrañjnī* and *Devrañjnī* are the only two *rāg*s in which consecutive notes are omitted and it seems probable that they are connected.

Transilient Scales

Pentatonic *rāg* | Conjectural Heptatonic Parent

Tilang

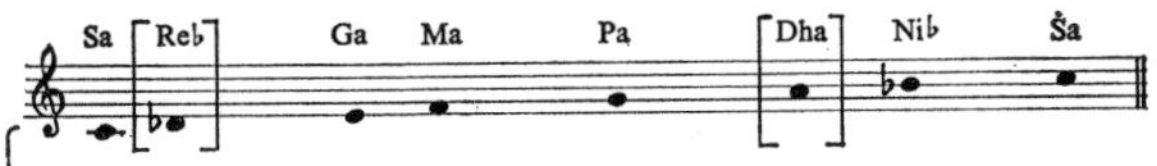

Ahīr Bhairav (No. C3)

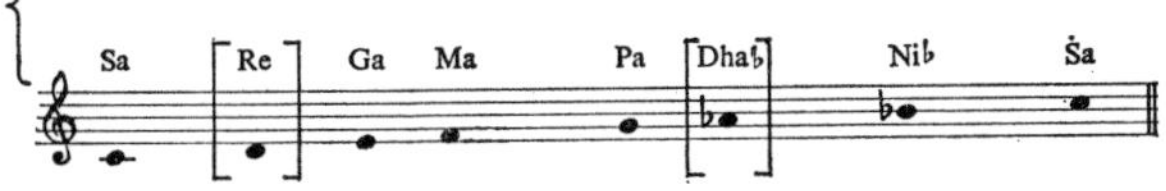

Cārukeśī (No. B3)

Durgā (2nd tradition)

Ahīr Bhairav (No. C3)

Jet (*Mārvā ṭhāṭ*)

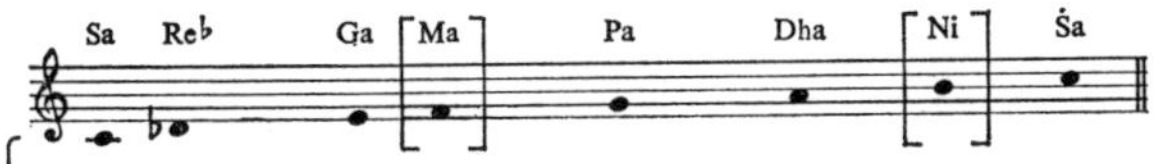

Ānand Bhairav (No. B10)

— (No. C10)

Candrkoś (Bhātkhaṇḍe's tradition)

— (No. B4)

The first four of these *rāgs* could have been derived from off-shoots of *Bhairav ṭhāṭ*, *Vasant Mukhārī*, *Ahīr Bhairav* or *Ānand Bhairav*. There is, however, no conclusive evidence which can be brought to bear on this matter. The connection between *Ahīr Bhairav* and *Khamāj ṭhāṭ* is apparent in certain traditions where the Re♮ is sometimes used in ascent in *Ahīr Bhairav*;[1] there is, however, no indication of a tendency to omit the Re♭ in the notations of this *rāg*. There appears to be no justification for the assumption that the above *Candrkoś*, which is now extremely rare, may have originated from a heptatonic scale. The explanation that it is a combination of the *rāgs* *Mālkoś* and *Bāgeśrī*[2] may very well apply in this case.

It will be seen, however, that the majority of Bhātkhaṇḍe's pentatonic *rāgs* appear to have been derived from the heptatonic *ṭhāṭs* or from the heptatonic derivatives of *Bhairav*, while only a small proportion are either borrowed from outside the North

[1] *K.P.M.* V, p. 346, and in songs on pp. 348, 349 and 351.

[2] This is a *rāg* of *Kāfī ṭhāṭ* whose ascending and descending lines are given by Bhātkhaṇḍe (*K.P.M.* III, p. 444) as follows:

rāg Bāgeśrī

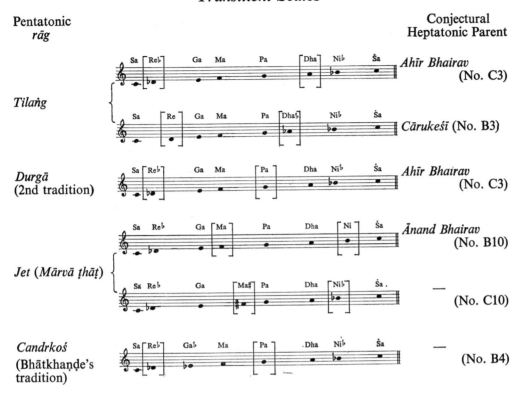

Indian system or intellectually created. In present-day practice there are several other pentatonic *rāg*s which have not been mentioned in Bhātkhaṇḍe's works: *Madhukoś* (*Madhukãus*), *Kalāvtī*,[1] *Śivrañjnī*, and another version of *Candrkoś* (*Candrkãus*):

Ex. 97.

(a) *rāg Madhukoś* (b) *rāg Kalāvtī*

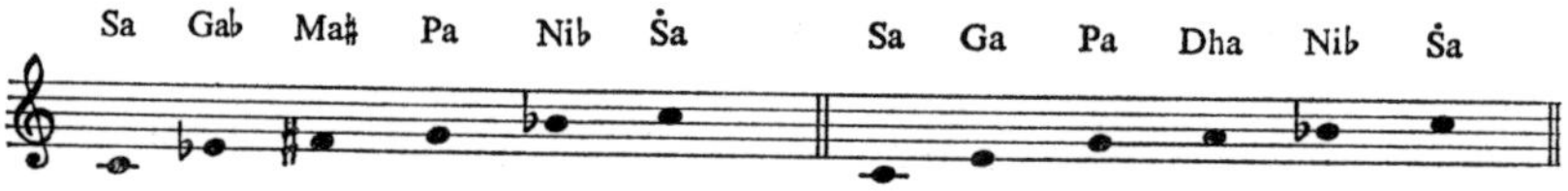

(c) *rāg Śivrañjnī* (d) *rāg Candrkoś*

Since these *rāg*s are not mentioned by Bhātkhaṇḍe they would appear to be recent innovations. In spite of this, their origins are not clearly known. The second version of *Candrkoś* is very likely derived from *Mālkoś* with the leading note Ni♮ replacing the Ni♭ in both ascent and descent. This would not be the only instance of the ascending leading note becoming a scalar note, for this also appears to occur in the *rāg Pīlū* where Ni♮ is frequently used in descent (the scalar Ni♭ occurs in the more usual descending line) and in the *rāg Paṭdīp* in which this is carried further to the complete exclusion of the Ni♭.[2] The *rāg Madhukoś* is the modal series beginning on the fourth of this version of *Candrkoś*. This series would naturally be prominent in *Candrkoś* as the secondary drone would be tuned to Ma (IV), there being no fifth in the *rāg*. The *rāg Madhukoś* appears to be unstable, however, as the Ma♯ leads to the Pa while there is no comparable pull from the Ṇi♭ (ṾII♭) to the Sa (I). Thus there will be a tendency to shift back to *Candrkoś* which is the series from its Pa. *Madhukoś* is, however, clearly connected with the heptatonic *Madhukānt* (No. C4), and if indeed *Madhukoś* has its origin in *Candrkoś*, the heptatonic *Madhukānt* has been derived from it by the addition of the Re (II) and Dha (VI), first and second order balance notes respectively. *Madhukānt*, too, appears to be unstable as it also has a Ma♯ and Ni♭. This may account for the heptatonic *rāg Madhuvantī* (No. C1) in which the Ni♮ has replaced the Ni♭ of *Madhukānt*. From *Madhukānt* too the pentatonic *rāg Śivrañjnī* may have been derived by the omission of both Ma♯ and Ni♭. This possible chain is schematised below:

[1] This *rāg* may also be of South Indian origin.

[2] In Bhātkhaṇḍe's time this *rāg*, called *Paṭdīpkī*, generally had Ni♮ in ascent and Ni♭ in descent. Since then it appears that the Ni♭ has gradually been replaced by Ni♮ in descent.

Ex. 98.

This is, perhaps, an oversimplification of the evolutionary process, and it may never be possible to establish conclusively the validity of this sequence. That this whole process has taken a relatively short time, perhaps less than fifty years, can be explained by the fact that all these derivatives of *Mālkoś* are essentially unbalanced scales. This does not necessarily mean that they are musically unsatisfactory, although balance appears to be an extremely important aspect of the scales which have withstood the test of time. There are, however, pentatonic scales even among the derivatives of the Circle of *Ṭhāṭ*s which are not, in themselves, balanced.

The five anhemitonic scales have simple balanced tetrachords either conjunct or disjunct. These five are related to each other serially in exactly the same way as are the seven primary heptatonic scales in that they too can be derived by starting on the successive degrees of any one of the five scales. They can also be derived in succession by redressing the balance in each of the scales. In the example overleaf the arrows show the notes introduced to create each new balance.

It will be apparent that the series is discontinuous at both ends as the next step would require in each case the omission of the Sa. If this series is to be continued beyond *Bhūpālī* the Ni replaces not the Sa, but its neighbour, the Re; and beyond *Mālkoś* the Re♭ must replace the Ni♭. The changing notes in this series of pentatonic scales are a succession of perfect fourths (or fifths) as in the Circle of *Ṭhāṭ*s. If this pentatonic Circle is to be completed, a similar enharmonic compromise is necessary, occurring between *Bhairvī* and the hypothetical *ṭhāṭ* where the Pa♭ (V♭) is interpreted as Ma♯ (IV♯), and between *Kalyāṇ* and *Mārvā* where Sa♯ (I♯) is interpreted as Re♭ (II♭).

Ex. 99.

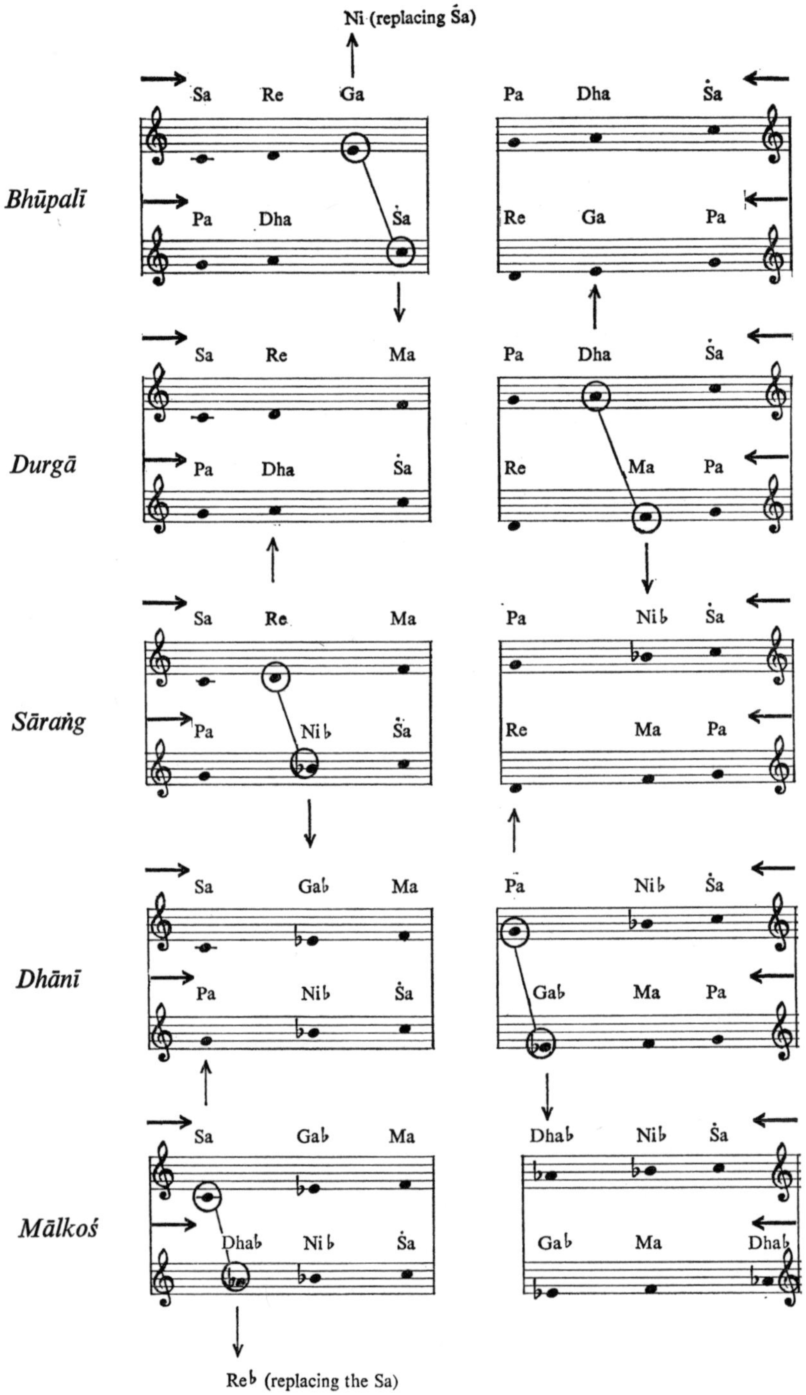

The scales of *Śaṅkrā* (pentatonic version)[1] and *Hindol* are unbalanced both as conjunct as well as disjunct tetrachords:

Ex. 100.

(a) *Śaṅkrā*

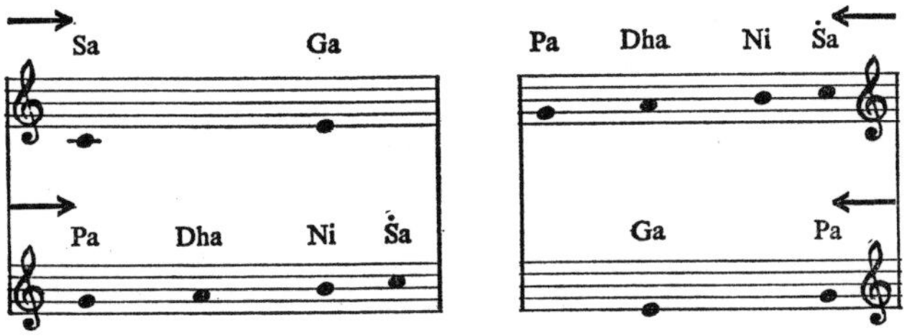

(b) *Hindol*

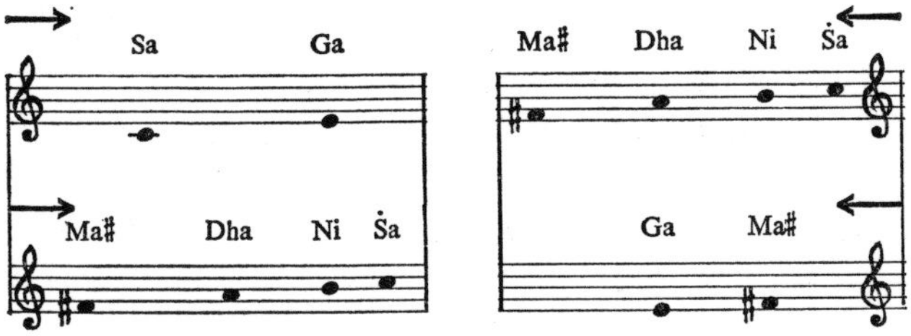

Although these scales are clearly unbalanced, a measure of symmetry is nevertheless produced within the *rāgs* themselves. In *Śaṅkrā* this is accomplished, to some extent, by frequently omitting the Dha and making the Ni oblique (*vakr*) in ascent. Bhātkhaṇḍe gives its ascending line as follows:[2]

Ex. 101. rāg Śaṅkrā

This twist in the ascending movement is an unconscious but functional element for this enables the major third *x* and the minor third *y* to be balanced in the upper tetrachord, the former disjunct, the latter conjunct. In descent the Dha is generally omitted, accentuating the major third, Ni–Pa, which is finally balanced by the other major third, Ga–Sa.[3]

[1] Bhātkhaṇḍe also mentions the fairly common occurrence of a second version of *rāg Śaṅkrā* which is hexatonic. It is this hexatonic version which is played by *Ustād* Vilayat Khan on the accompanying record and is discussed in Appendix B, p. 206.

[2] *K.P.M.* IV, p. 208.

[3] These turns, slightly modified, are well illustrated on the accompanying record.

Similarly, in the *rāg Hindol* an element of symmetry is also created by an oblique movement. Bhātkhaṇḍe gives the ascending line as follows:[1]

Ex. 102. rāg Hindol

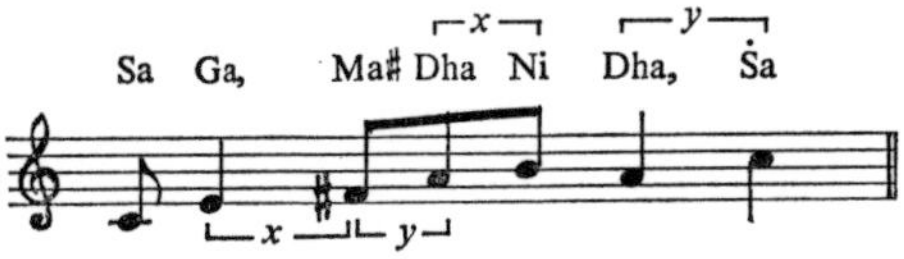

Here the wholetone *x* and the minor third *y* are repeated in the upper tetrachord. Although Ma♯–Dha and Dha–Ṡa are not parallel in the tetrachordal sense, they do, nevertheless, convey an illusion of symmetry. The significance of this oblique movement is not, however, appreciated on a conscious level. Bhātkhaṇḍe states that the Ni in *Hindol* is oblique in ascent and adds that the less the Ni is used the more clearly is the *rāg* delineated. His explanation for this is that excessive use of the Ni will evoke the *rāg Sohnī*.[2] This is not a very convincing argument in view of the fact that *Sohnī*, a *rāg* of *Mārvā ṭhāṭ*, is hexatonic and has a very prominent Re♭ (II♭), and is thus easily distinguished from *Hindol*. The frequent omission of the Ni in the ascent of *Hindol* (in spite of its function as a leading note) and its descent can be reasonably explained as an unconscious attempt to produce symmetry in a *rāg* whose scale is clearly unbalanced. Non-tetrachordal symmetry may be more readily acceptable in this scale where both the Ma♮ (IV♮) and the Pa (V), the initial degrees of the second tetrachord conjunct and disjunct, are absent.

The *rāg Mālśrī* is perhaps the most extraordinary of the pentatonic *rāg*s. From the standpoint of symmetry the scale of *Mālśrī* is not nearly so awkward as *Hindol* and *Śaṅkrā*, Ṇi–Sa–Ga being balanced by Ma♯–Pa–Ni (ascending disjunct in the octave from Ṇi to Ni):

Ex. 103. rāg Mālśrī

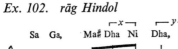

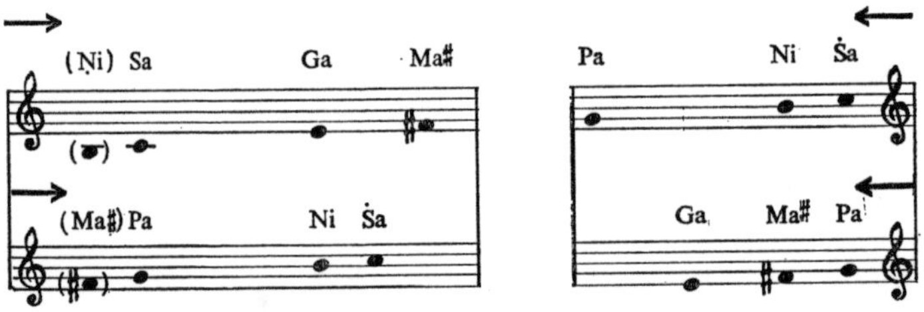

However, the expression of this symmetry is by no means characteristic of the *rāg*, although the parallelism between the major thirds Sa–Ga and Pa–Ni is sometimes brought into focus. Apparently, Sa and Pa are so strong here that they do not permit the octave to be viewed as a range from Ṇi to Ni as is characteristic of *Mārvā*, *Pūrvī* and *Toṛī ṭhāṭ*s. The absence of the Re in *Mālśrī* focuses attention on the fact that the Ma♯ and the Sa are unbalanced, with the consequence that the Ma♯ is also frequently

[1] *K.P.M.* IV, p. 176.
[2] *Ibid.*, p. 176.

omitted. This omission is then countered by the temporary omission of the Ni. According to Bhātkhaṇḍe, some musicians say that *Mālśrī* should have only three notes, Sa, Ga and Pa,[1] and this is certainly evident in some of the songs in this *rāg*.[2] In the following example the Ma♯ and Ni are used merely as grace notes:[3]

Ex. 104. rāg Mālśrī—Jhaptāl[4]

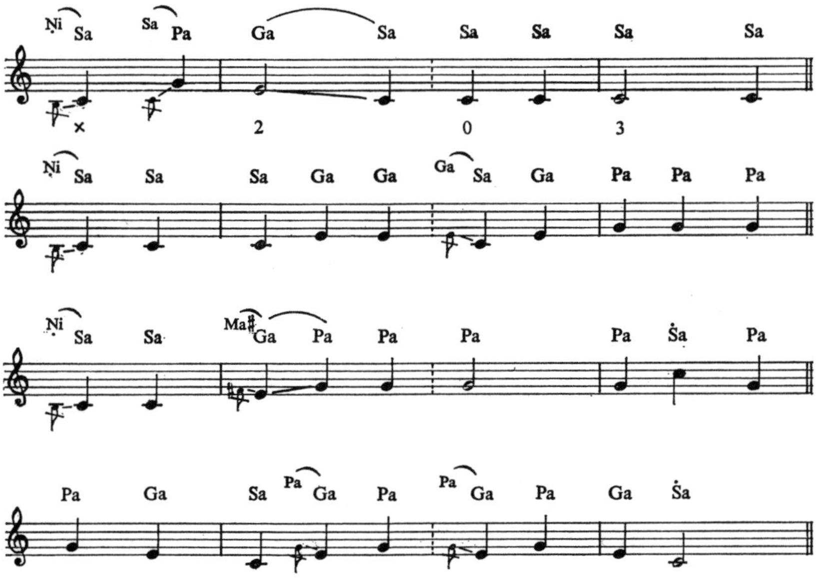

In Bhātkhaṇḍe's system, however, no *rāg*s may have less than five notes, thus a small measure of symmetry is still maintained.

In the *rāg Bhūpāl Toṛī* once again the simple tetrachord schemes beginning on Sa and Pa (I and V) or Sa and Ma (I and IV) must be disturbed if symmetry is to be produced, for the parallelism in the scale of this *rāg* lies between Ḍha♭–Sa–Re♭ and Ga♭–Pa–Dha♭ (ascending disjunct in the octave from Ḍha♭ to Dha♭), in both instances a semitone following a major third:

Ex. 105. rāg Bhūpāl Toṛī

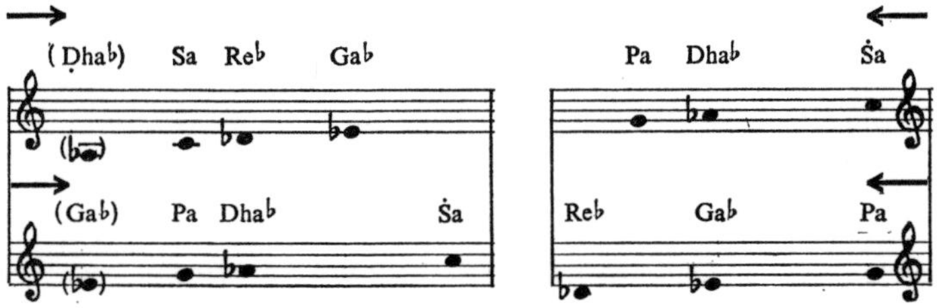

[1] *Op. cit.* V, p. 78.
[2] *K.P.M.* V, pp. 93–4.
[3] *Ibid.*, p. 91—*sthāyī.*
[4] *Jhaptāl* is a time measure of ten units, subdivided into four groups, 2 + 3 + 2 + 3.

This scheme is, in fact, followed in the *rāg* and phrases frequently begin on Dha♭ and Ga♭,[1] as is well illustrated in the following song.[2] In the second line of this song the parallelism is also apparent.

Ex. 106. rāg Bhūpāl Toṛī—Dādrā

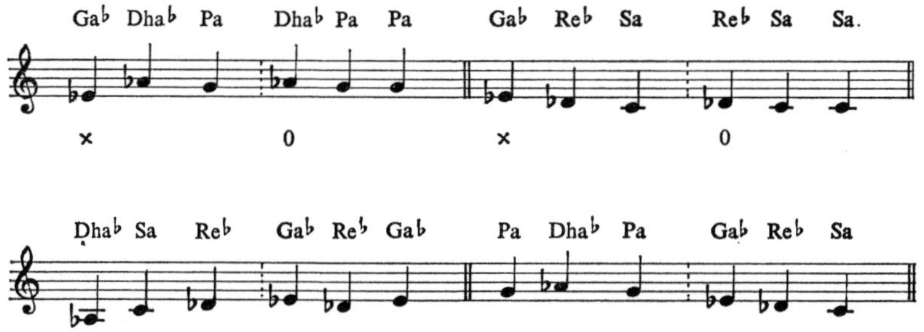

The *vādī* and *saṃvādī* of *Bhūpāl Toṛī*, Dha♭ and Ga♭ respectively in Bhātkhaṇḍe's system, also give an indication of their parallel roles in the *rāg*, for these are the two notes which initiate the parallel movements. In spite of the fact that Bhātkhaṇḍe's choice of *vādī* and *saṃvādī* is not always based on objective musical principles, they often provide a clue to the symmetry within a *rāg*. In the *rāg Śaṅkrā* (see p. 206), Bhātkhaṇḍe gives Ga and Ni as the *vādī* and *saṃvādī*. These are the upper notes of the parallel thirds Sa–Ga and Pa–Ni (Dha being an oblique ascending note is approached from the Ni), or the initiators of the parallel descending thirds, Ni–Pa (Dha is generally omitted in descent) and Ga–Sa. He also mentions a second tradition in which Sa and Pa are recognised as *vādī* and *saṃvādī* in this *rāg*;[3] these are, in fact, the lower notes of the parallel thirds. In the *rāg Hindol* Dha and Ga are given as *vādī* and *saṃvādī*—the two notes at which we have suggested the parallelism is initiated. In the *rāg Mālśrī* too the *vādī* and *saṃvādī*, Pa and Sa, are the initiators of the parallel ascending thirds. Unfortunately, this kind of relationship does not always hold.

It will be observed that even the pentatonic scales derived from the Circle of *Ṭhāṭs* are not always balanced. The *rāg Vibhās*, a derivative of *Bhairav*, also has unbalanced conjunct and disjunct tetrachords:

Ex. 107. Vibhās

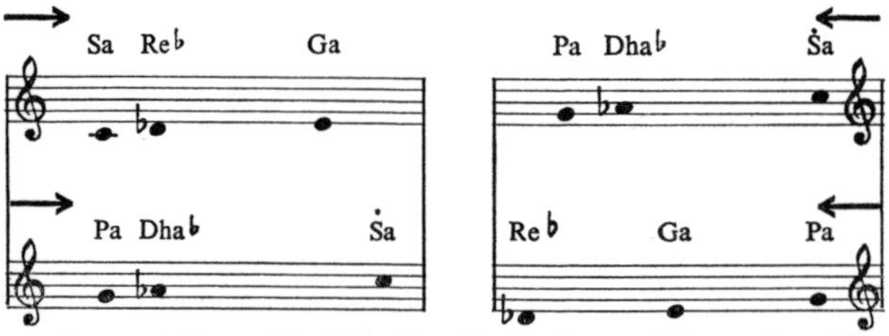

[1] *Op. cit.* VI, p. 441. Bhātkhaṇḍe begins on Dha♭ when illustrating the usual movement (*sādhāraṇ calan*) in this *rāg*.

[2] *Bhairav ṭhāṭ aṅk*, Special publication of '*Saṅgīt*', Hathras, January 1962, p. 114, *sthāyī* of song by Yeśvant D. Bhatt. *Dādrā* is a type of song based on *Dādrā tāl*, a time measure of six units, subdivided into two equal parts.

[3] *K.P.M.* IV, p. 207.

No clear solution to this problem is yet apparent in this *rāg*. There is definitely a tendency to introduce the Ni (VII) to balance Ga (III), particularly in descent[1] where it generally occurs as a grace note. This produces a measure of disjunct balance Ni–Dha♭–Pa and Ga–Re♭–Sa. There is also a tendency to produce a non-tetrachordal balance by omitting the Re♭ in ascent[2] leaving two major thirds, Sa–Ga and Dha♭–Ṡa. Perhaps the justification for this *rāg* may lie in the inverted symmetry occurring in the two segments Sa–Re♭–Ga, semitone and augmented second, and Ga–Pa–Dha♭, augmented second (minor third in a heptatonic series) and semitone.[3] In *Vibhās* this inverted symmetry appears to be a feature of considerable importance and can be heard frequently in the characteristic phrase (*pakaṛ*):

Ex. 108. rāg Vibhās

In the *rāg Guṇkrī* the disjunct parallelism is quite clear:

Ex. 109. Guṇkrī

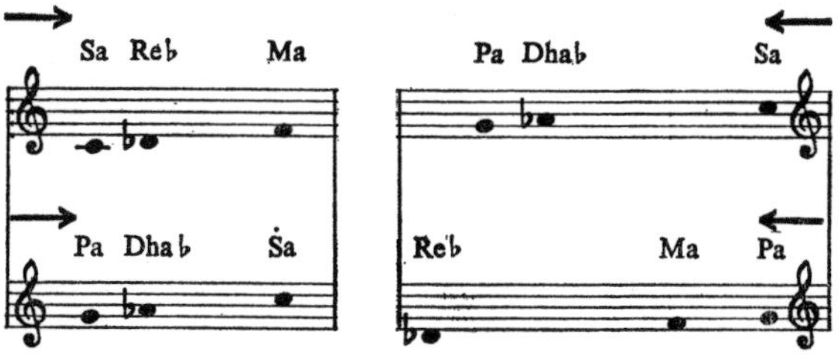

Ex. 110. Tilaṅg

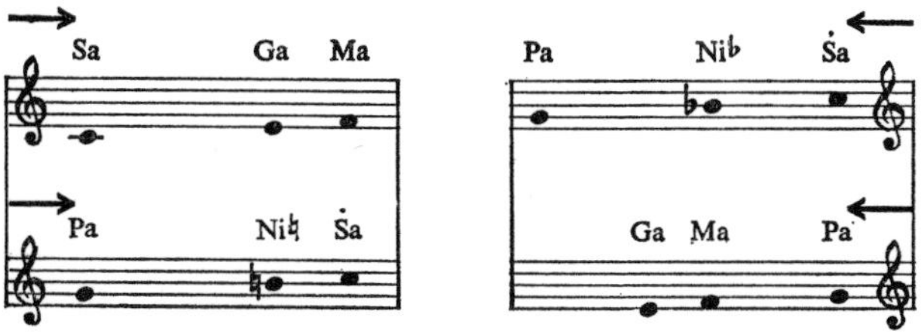

In *Tilaṅg*, however, the scale is unbalanced, but a considerable measure of symmetry is produced within the *rāg*. In ascent, the leading note, Ni♮, is commonly used, thus

[1] *K.P.M.* V, songs on pp. 392–9 and 402.

[2] *K.P.M.* V, songs on pp. 392 and 397–9.

[3] There is a second *rāg*, *Revā*, which has this same scale, but is classified by Bhātkhaṇḍe in *Pūrvī ṭhāṭ* because its *vādī* is in the lower tetrachord while the *vādī* of *Vibhās* is in the upper tetrachord. This, according to his time theory, determines that *Revā* is sung in the second half of the day, a common characteristic of *Pūrvī ṭhāṭ rāg*s, while *Vibhās* is sung in the first half of the day, a feature of *Bhairav ṭhāṭ rāg*s. *Revā* is, however, a rare *rāg* and Bhātkhaṇḍe gives only one song from which no conclusions can be drawn.

producing parallel ascending disjunct tetrachords Sa–Ga–Ma and Pa–Ni♮–Ṡa. In descent, however, the Ni♭ destroys this parallelism and both conjunct and disjunct tetrachords are unbalanced. It is not surprising, therefore, that a descent of continuous steps is seldom heard although it is not prohibited. Instead, the usual descent is as follows:[1]

Ex. 111. rāg Tilaṅg

Here the minor thirds Ni♭–Pa and Pa–Ga are balanced to some extent, while the flow of the descending line is disrupted at Ga, thus preventing an easy comparison of the complete tetrachords.

From the foregoing discussions it will be apparent that most pentatonic *rāg*s are based on balanced scales, but an unbalanced scale does not necessarily preclude the possibility of a pentatonic *rāg*, for symmetry may still be produced within it by means of temporary omissions, accidentals and oblique movements. Some of the recently introduced pentatonic *rāg*s do not reveal the same propensity for tetrachordal symmetry as the traditional *rāg*s, a situation comparable to that which also occurs in the recently introduced heptatonic *rāg*s.[2] The *rāg*s *Devrañjnī* and *Meghrañjnī* are obviously exceptional, containing gaps of a fourth and an augmented fourth respectively—virtually a denial of the two tetrachord scheme. The *rāg*s *Ābhogī* and *Kalāvtī* (the modal series from the Ma of *Ābhogī*) seem to indicate a new trend for they are largely unbalanced:[3]

Ex. 112. Ābhogī

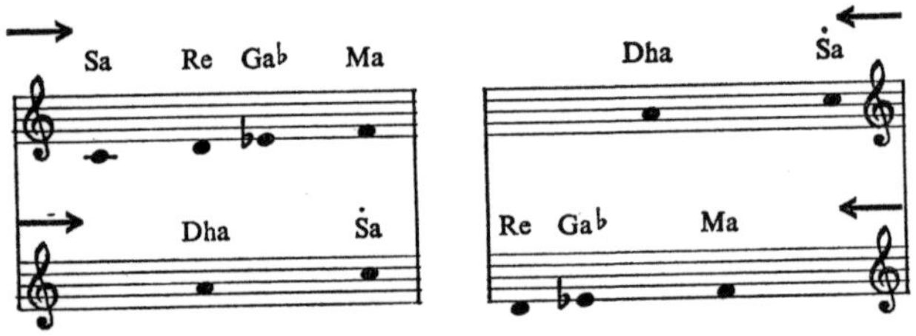

Ex. 113. Kalāvtī

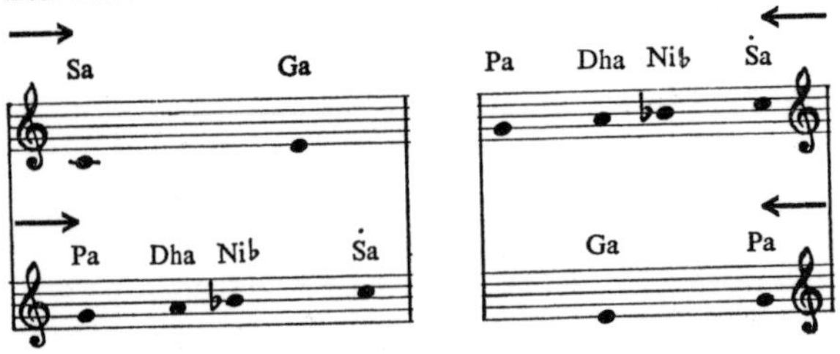

[1] *K.P.M.* V, p. 283.
[2] See p. 88.
[3] This also applies to the *rāg Haṃsdhvanī* which has been discussed on p. 89.

The successive intervals of *Kalāvtī* are interesting: major third, minor third, wholetone, semitone and wholetone, the intervals gradually decreasing by semitones to the Ni♭. The same of course applies to *Ābhogī* where the successive intervals decrease by semitones from its Ma. These two *rāg*s seem to be constructed on triads, *Ābhogī* on Ma–Dha–Ṡa and *Kalāvtī* on Sa–Ga–Pa. Nevertheless, there appears to be some sign of balance even within these *rāgs*. In *Ābhogī* a measure of symmetry is possible by making Ga♭ *vakr* in descent, a characteristic feature of the *Kānhṛā* family of *rāgs* to which *Ābhogī* belongs, and by occasionally omitting Ga♭ in ascent:

Ex. 114. rāg Ābhogī

In *Kalāvtī* the following two ascending phrases are quite characteristic:

Ex. 115. rāg Kalāvtī

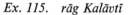

In the first the minor third Ga–Pa is balanced by Dha–Ṡa. In the second an extra minor third, Pa–Ni♭, is added. In both these *rāgs* the symmetry does not extend over a full tetrachord. The growing popularity of these and other similar *rāgs* suggests the possibility that full tetrachordal symmetry may no longer be an essential governing factor in the natural selection of *rāgs*.

In contrast to pentatonic *rāgs*, which naturally lend themselves to balance, hexatonic forms generally tend to disrupt the balance in a scale. For instance, the omission of the Ni in *Bilāval ṭhāṭ* will not only leave the Ma unbalanced (descending conjunct) but will also remove a support from the Ga (ascending disjunct). Thus it is inevitable that most hexatonic scales are inherently unbalanced and symmetry can occur only in the *rāgs*.

The most obvious examples of hexatonality occur in *Mārvā* and *Toṛī ṭhāṭs* in which the Pa is omitted in a number of *rāgs*. This, as we have mentioned earlier, is the usual device whereby balance is created. There is some justification, however, to think of some of these as pentatonic, for the Sa (second order balance note) is also omitted in many of the phrases in these *rāgs*, but, being the ground-note of the system, cannot be omitted entirely. In *Pūrvī ṭhāṭ*, where the Pa is also unbalanced, the omission of the Pa is not entirely necessary for balanced disjunct tetrachords already exist in the octave from Ṇi to Ni. The omission of the Pa may be considered functional when viewed in terms of conjunct tetrachords where the Pa is seen in relation to the Re♭, but this omission will disrupt the balance in the ascending disjunct tetrachords of

Pūrvī. In *Mārvā* and *Toṛī ṭhāṭ*s, however, the Pa must be omitted in order to produce any tetrachordal balance:

Ex. 116.

(a) *Mārvā ṭhāṭ* (b) *Pūrvī ṭhāṭ* (c) *Toṛī ṭhāṭ*

There are four hexatonic *rāg*s of *Mārvā ṭhāṭ* in which the Pa is omitted: *Mārvā*, *Sohnī*, *Pūriyā* and *Pūrbyā*. Of the three principal *rāg*s in *Toṛī ṭhāṭ*, one, *Gujrī Toṛī*, is also hexatonic, Pa being omitted. In addition, Pa and Sa are frequently omitted in the *rāg Toṛī* itself. In *Pūrvī ṭhāṭ*, on the other hand, there are no hexatonic *rāgs* omitting Pa, while there is one, *Triveṇī*, in which the Ma♯ is omitted, still preserving a measure of balance: Sa–Re♭–Ga, and Pa–Dha♭–Ni.

Apart from the hexatonic *rāg*s of these *ṭhāṭ*s, the majority of hexatonic *rāg*s given in Bhātkhaṇḍe's works are closely related to pentatonic forms. These occur principally in *Bilāval*, *Kāfī* and *Bhairav ṭhāṭ*s, which all have the common feature of balanced disjunct tetrachords. Nevertheless, the parallelism in their hexatonic *rāgs* may be either conjunct or disjunct.

In *Bilāval ṭhāṭ* Bhātkhaṇḍe gives only one hexatonic *rāg*, a version of the *rāg Hem Kalyāṇ*. Here the Ga is treated as an oblique note, thus maintaining a disjunct balance in the descending line:[1]

Ex. 117. rāg Hem Kalyāṇ

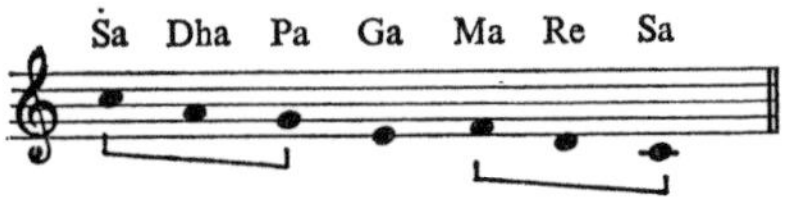

In *Kāfī ṭhāṭ* there are two main groups of *rāg*s which are hexatonic. Four of these belong to the *Sāraṅg* group of *rāg*s and three to the *Kānhṛā* group. In the pentatonic *Sāraṅg rāgs*, *Vrindāvnī* (or *Brindābnī*) and *Madhmād*, the symmetry lies in the descending conjunct tetrachords:

Ex. 118. rāg Vrindāvnī Sāraṅg

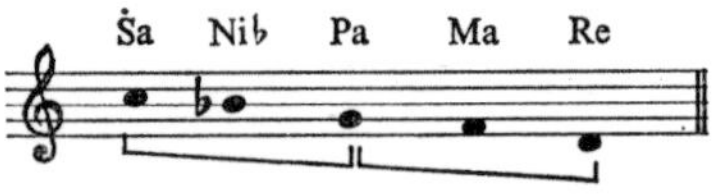

[1] *K.P.M.* V, pp. 99 and 100. The descent given is abstracted from the *calan* on p. 100.

In the hexatonic *rāg Śuddh Sāraṅg* this symmetry is maintained while the added note, Dha, is used around the pivot Pa, together with the accidental Ma♯, as in the following example:[1]

Ex. 119. rāg Śuddh Sāraṅg

In *Mīyā̃ kī Sāraṅg* the Dha is attached to the Ni♭, more or less as an ornament:[2]

Ex. 120. rāg Mīyā̃ kī Sāraṅg

In *Sāmant Sāraṅg* the Dha is used in an alternative descending line while the normal balanced pentatonic descent of *Sāraṅg* remains. In *Baṛhaṃs Sāraṅg* the Dha is only occasionally used as a passing note but only in ascent.

In all three hexatonic *rāg*s of the *Kānhṛā* group, *Nāykī*, *Sūhā*[3] and *Devsākh*, the descent maintains conjunct balance by the oblique use of Ga♭:

Ex 121. rāg Nāykī Kānhṛā

Bhātkhaṇḍe gives one hexatonic *rāg* in *Āsāvrī ṭhāṭ*, *Gopikā Vasant*, in which the Re is omitted so that it resembles *Mālkoś* but has a Pa. This *rāg* follows the *Mālkoś* parallel scheme of conjunct tetrachords by oblique use of the Pa as in the following descending line:[4]

Ex. 122. rāg Gopikā Vasant

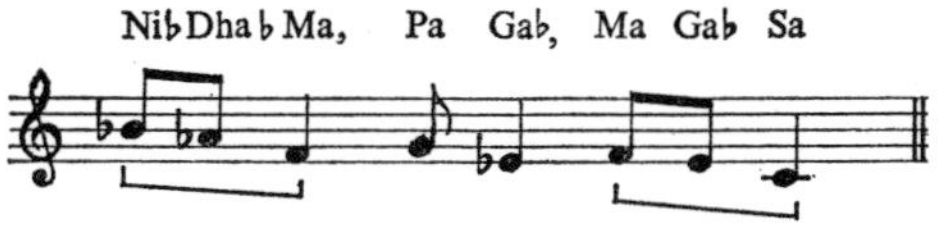

[1] Abstracted from *K.P.M.* VI, pp. 482–3.

[2] Abstracted from *K.P.M.* VI, pp. 189 and 489. Dha is often omitted leaving the pentatonic descent.

[3] See accompanying record and notation in Appendix B, pp. 200, 201.

[4] Abstracted from *K.P.M.* VI, p. 421. Here it is said to be a South Indian *rāg*.

In *Bhairav ṭhāṭ*, *Baṅgāl Bhairav* still maintains parallel descending disjunct tetrachords by the oblique use of Ga:[1]

Ex. 123. rāg Baṅgāl Bhairav

The *rāg Jogiyā* occurs in several different variants. In Bhātkhaṇḍe's system it is pentatonic in ascent and hexatonic in descent, the ascent having disjunct balance:

Ex. 124. rāg Jogiyā

The Ni, introduced in the descent, spoils this parallel movement. However, a measure of non-tetrachordal symmetry is maintained by making Pa oblique and the Ni–Dha♭ is balanced by Dha♭–Ma:[2]

Ex. 125. rāg Jogiyā

In two of the six songs in this *rāg* given by Bhātkhaṇḍe, however, the Ni does not occur at all and the *rāg* is completely pentatonic and has disjunct balance.[3] In another song the Ni occurs only in descent as a grace note and is balanced by the Ga which is used in the same way.[4] There is a very prominent tradition[5] in which the ascent remains pentatonic, but the descent is heptatonic and has disjunct balance:

Ex. 126. rāg Jogiyā

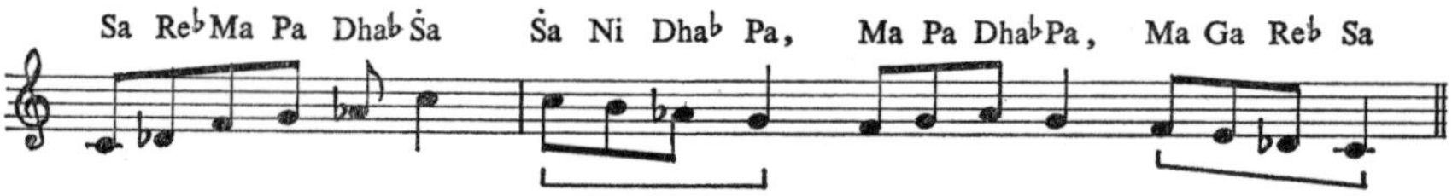

To summarise, the hexatonic *rāgs* of *Mārvā* and *Toṛī ṭhāṭs* appear to have been derived from heptatonic scales. However, the other hexatonic *rāgs* seem to have been

[1] *K.P.M.* V, p. 334.
[2] *Ibid.*, p. 378.
[3] *K.P.M.* V, songs on pp. 382 and 384.
[4] *Ibid.*, song on p. 380.
[5] The tradition followed by *Ustād* Bundu Khan and his son, *Ustād* Umrao Khan.

derived from pentatonic scales and the additional note generally appears in between the two parallel descending segments of the pentatonic series, often in an oblique melodic figure, as in Exx. 119, 121 and 123.

From the foregoing discussion it will be apparent that the *rāgs* of a balanced heptatonic *ṭhāṭ* do not always show this simple heptatonic balance. If the straight ascent is characteristic of one of these *rāgs*, then the ascent may be oblique or transilient in others. In fact, the straight ascent and descent of the *ṭhāṭ* can generally be considered too simple a scheme for an individual *rāg*. The *rāgs* of one *ṭhāṭ* are often distinguished by the different ways in which the symmetry of that *ṭhāṭ* is worked out in each. In many *rāgs* the *ṭhāṭ* symmetry is altered by the omission of two balanced notes in either ascent or descent. This can be called directional transilience. Directional transilience is not motivated by imbalance, as we have suggested complete transilience to be, and indeed the notes omitted in this way are usually perfectly balanced. This could be brought about by experimentation (probably at an unconscious level)—notes being omitted more or less at random, until a pleasing combination emerges. Here again, balance plays an important part in the result, for the omitted notes are generally a fourth or a fifth apart. The *rāg Jogiyā* (Ex. 126) is a typical example of directional transilience, being pentatonic in ascent and heptatonic in descent. The notes Ga (III) and Ni (VII) which are omitted in ascent are perfectly balanced.

The *rāg Khamāj* is particularly interesting since it is described as being hexatonic in ascent and heptatonic in descent.[1] In spite of the hexatonic ascent, a large measure of balance is maintained, as the hexatonic ascent is really an amalgamation of two alternative pentatonic ascents, one in which the Re (II) and Pa (V) are omitted, the other in which the Re (II) and Dha (VI) are omitted. Since the Re is omitted in both, it is described as hexatonic. The former leaves parallel conjunct tetrachords (Ex. 127a), the latter parallel disjunct (b), while the third alternative ascent is really a combination of the two (c):

Ex. 127. rāg Khamāj

This last is unbalanced, but since phrases in the *rāg* usually begin from Ga, the ascending imbalance is not easily apparent.[2]

The notes omitted in directional transilience are often 'weak' (*durbal*) notes in the *rāgs*.[3] The term 'weak' here does not refer to the inherent dynamic function of a note

[1] *K.P.M.* II, p. 122.
[2] A further discussion of this *rāg* is found in the next chapter.
[3] This is not always the case. In the *rāgs Śuddh Āsāvrī* and *Jaunpurī*, for example, Ga♭ which is given as the *saṃvādī* in these two *rāgs* by Bhātkhaṇḍe is omitted in ascent. Similarly, in *rāg Jhiñjhoṭī* the *vādī* Ga is one of two notes generally omitted in ascent.

due to consonance and dissonance, but rather to the dynamic function induced by its melodic context in the scheme of the *rāg*. Ga, for example, is a note with a high degree of consonance, but is nevertheless a weak note in many *rāg*s (as in *Jogiyā*, where it is usually omitted in ascent). The notes omitted in the ascent of a *rāg* are often weak in descent and may sometimes be omitted altogether, suggesting that directional transilience may tend to become complete transilience. In general, however, complete transilience is associated with scalar imbalance, while directional transilience is an unique characteristic of the individual *rāg*.

VIII

Symmetry, Movement and Intonation

In the preceding chapters we have examined certain facets of scale and tetrachord species which, we have suggested, lead naturally to the introduction of accidentals as well as to transilience in *rāgs*. A basic principle has emerged out of our discussions, that *rāgs* show a tendency to align themselves in symmetrical units, frequently, but not invariably, ranging over a tetrachord. These units are either conjunct, in which the parallel notes are a perfect fourth apart, or disjunct, in which they are a perfect fifth apart. Sometimes they are neither conjunct nor disjunct but express a 'false' symmetry. In view of the fact that *rāgs* are still evolving it is impossible to be certain whether this 'false' symmetry is just a temporary phase or a more permanent state on a par with conjunct and disjunct symmetry. While symmetry in a *ṭhāṭ* is a relatively simple and straightforward matter, the adaptation of this symmetry may become quite complex in different *rāgs*. This complexity is conditioned by melodic features which differentiate *rāg* from *ṭhāṭ*. One of these is oblique (*vakr*) movement.

OBLIQUE MOVEMENT

In the previous chapter we referred to oblique movement in connection with hexatonality, and suggested that this was a device whereby pentatonic symmetry could still be preserved in a hexatonic *rāg*. This is only one manifestation of oblique movement. There are many instances where it appears to be associated with the introduction of an accidental and may indeed have been motivated by it.

In Chapter V we suggested that an accidental is introduced initially as an inflexion of the nearest diatonic note which gradually gains recognition and develops into an oblique ascending or descending line. The Ma♯, for instance, occurring as an accidental would first be merely an inflexion of the Pa and gradually form an oblique ascending line:

Ex. 128.

Its chromatic counterpart, Ma♮, will, at first, continue in its own ascending line as a direct ascending note, and there may be two ascending lines, the oblique incorporating Ma♯, the direct incorporating Ma♮. If the former gains in prominence, the latter may fall into disuse and eventually become discontinuous—a vestige of the original. The discontinuous line may become progressively shortened until the Ma♮ is no longer an ascending note, as will be seen in the following series:

Ex. 129.

(a) (b) (c)

Ex. 129c provides an oblique descending parallel for the oblique ascent incorporating Ma♯ (Ex. 128, *x*). This kind of inverted non-tetrachordal parallel movement associated with the two alternatives of Ma is seen in a number of *rāg*s, either as in *Bihāg* (Ex. 130a) or as in *Hamīr* (b):

Ex. 130.

(a) *rāg Bihāg* (b) *rāg Hamīr*

The use of the two alternatives also makes possible directional non-tetrachordal parallelism, as in the following examples:

Ex. 131.

(a) *rāg Gauṛ Sāraṅg* (b) *rāg Kedār*

(c) *rāg Kāmod*

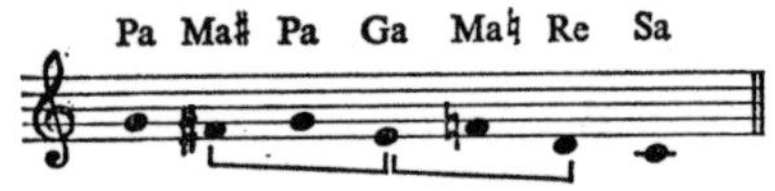

In general terms then, associated with each *ṭhāṭ* are characteristic oblique movements as well as typical accidentals and transilience. The oblique movements, too, often appear to be connected with imbalance in scale and tetrachord species. As with accidentals and transilience, we can speak of first and second order oblique movements. However, once the oblique motion is initiated there seems to be a tendency to continue it, the classic example being the *rāg Gauṛ Sāraṅg*, whose ascent and descent are given as follows:[1]

[1] *K.P.M.* IV, p. 142.

Ex. 132. rāg Gauṛ Sāraṅg

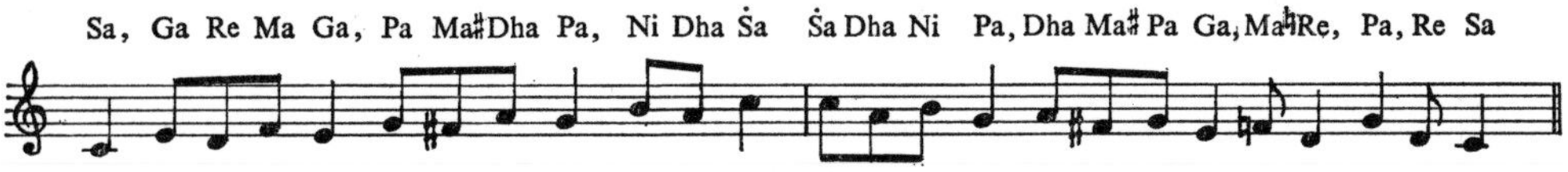

Before continuing this discussion of oblique movement, we should remind the reader of the different interpretations in the rendering of many *rāg*s. In most cases the differences are matters of detail, which do, nevertheless, preclude a definitive analysis. Bhātkhaṇḍe's own interpretations of many *rāg*s, as found in his *svarvistār*, are influenced to some extent by a theoretician's desire to differentiate clearly between one *rāg* and another. As a result his own interpretations do not always compare with the bulk of songs (*cīz*) notated in his works, most of which have been composed by traditional musicians. It is clear that certain melodic features are common to several *rāg*s in a *ṭhāṭ*. This is not always apparent in Bhātkhaṇḍe's interpretations; for instance, similar descending lines are found in many of the songs in the *rāg*s *Hamīr*, *Kedār*, *Kāmod*, *Chāyānaṭ*, *Śyām Kalyāṇ* and *Gauṛ Sāraṅg*:

Ex. 133. rāgs Hamīr, Kedār, Kāmod, etc.

In these songs the Ni♭ is quite unmistakable, yet in Bhātkhaṇḍe's *svarvistār* the Ni♭ occurs in only two of these *rāg*s, *Chāyānaṭ* and *Kedār*.[1] It would appear that where there are two or three alternative descents in these *rāg*s Bhātkhaṇḍe has chosen, wherever possible, the line which is unique, as representative of that *rāg*. It is, however, the similarities in *rāg*s which concern us in our study of the relationship between *rāg* and scale. Let us now consider the characteristic oblique movements which occur frequently in the *rāg*s of a few *ṭhāṭ*s.

In the *rāg*s of *Kalyāṇ ṭhāṭ*, as given by Bhātkhaṇḍe, the typical oblique movement is associated with the two Ma's (Ex. 134a) which commonly leads to the second order oblique movement involving the two Ni's (Ex. 134b):

Ex. 134. conjunct symmetry in *Kalyāṇ ṭhāṭ rāg*s

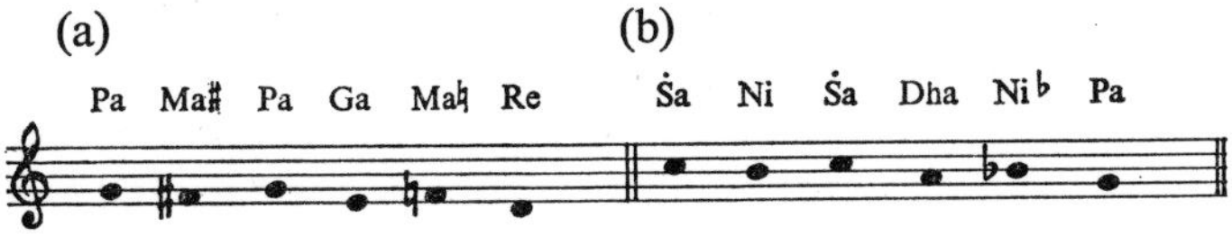

The second of these is not always accepted by Bhātkhaṇḍe, but occurs quite frequently in the songs. It is an important device for preserving symmetry in the *rāg*,

[1] Bhātkhaṇḍe acknowledges, however, that the Ni♭ may be used a little in those *rāg*s which have both the Ma♮ and Ma♯. *H.S.P.* I, p. 110.

a symmetry which is not always apparent in Bhātkhaṇḍe's *svarvistār*. In the *rāg Hamīr*, for instance, Bhātkhaṇḍe gives the descending line as follows:[1]

Ex. 135. rāg Hamīr

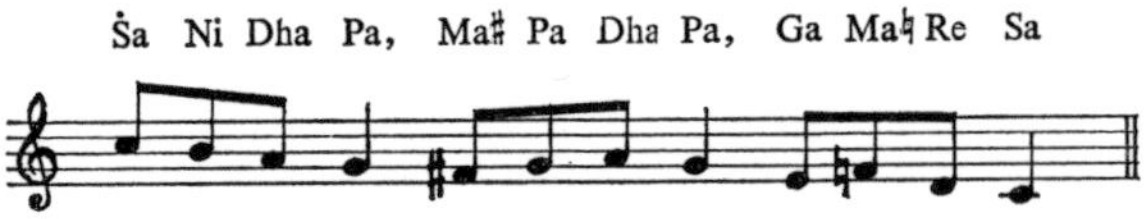

Here the two disjunct tetrachords are unbalanced. However, in nineteen of the thirty-two songs (most of them composed by traditional musicians) notated by Bhātkhaṇḍe in the *rāg*, the upper tetrachord has Ṡa–Dha–Ni♭–Pa, which is symmetrical with the lower tetrachord. In addition, there is a common tendency to omit the Ni in descent, producing pentatonic balance as follows:

Ex. 136. rāg Hamīr

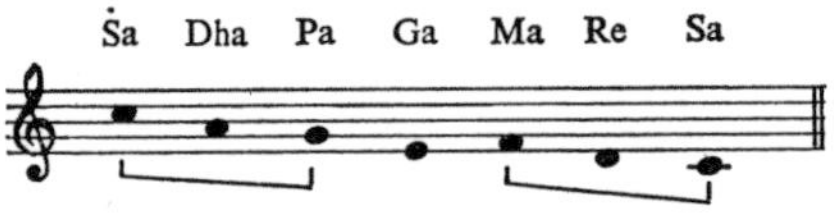

This tendency is also apparent in Bhātkhaṇḍe's *svarvistār*. Disjunct balance is, however, characteristic of *Bilāval* rather than *Kalyāṇ ṭhaṭ*, another argument in favour of the classification of *rāg*s such as *Kedār* and *Hamīr* in *Bilāval ṭhāṭ*.[2]

In the *rāg*s of *Bilāval ṭhāṭ* both Ma♯ and Ni♭ are first order accidentals, thus the oblique movements involving both these notes are also of the first order. Once the Ni♭ has been introduced and the associated oblique movement (Ex. 137a) established, this may lead to the second order conjunct parallel (b). Both of these are typical of *Bilāval ṭhāṭ rāg*s and also occur in *Hamīr*, *Kedār*, etc.

Ex. 137. conjunct symmetry in *Bilāval ṭhāṭ rāg*s

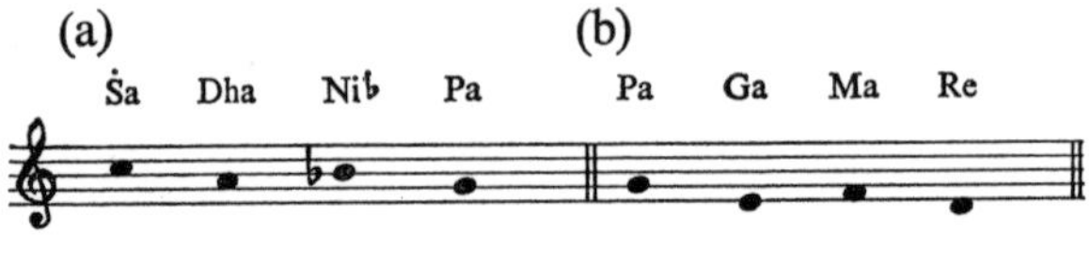

It will be apparent that oblique movement is not only associated with accidentals but also with directional transilience since it requires at least temporary omission of a note in ascent or descent. In *Bilāval ṭhāṭ rāg*s the omission of the Ni♮ in descent can be said to be a preparation of the ground for the introduction of the Ni♭. The Ni♭ can then easily be introduced as an ornament attached to the Dha and may gradually gain prominence. Similarly, the associated omission of the Ga♮ in the descent of

[1] *K.P.M.* III, p. 68.
[2] See p. 53.

*Bilāval ṭhāṭ rāg*s paves the way for the introduction of the Ga♭ as in the following example, a phrase which is characteristic of the *rāg*s *Jaijaivantī* and *Gāṛā* (*Gārā*) of *Khamāj ṭhāṭ*:

Ex. 138.

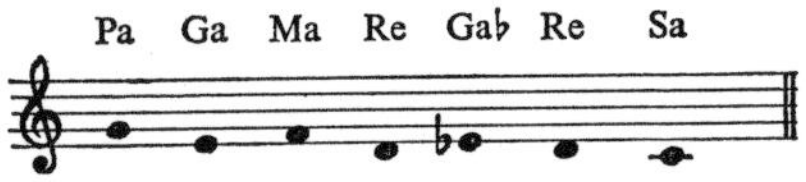

This is not, however, the most typical oblique movement found in the *rāg*s of *Khamāj ṭhāṭ*. In a number of *rāg*s, *Khamāj*, *Des*, *Jhiñjhoṭī*, *Tilak Kāmod* and *Khambāvtī*, there is a strong tendency to treat the Pa and the Re as oblique notes. In view of the fact that *Khamāj ṭhāṭ* has conjunct balance, Pa and Re should have considerable importance, being the bottom notes of descending conjunct tetrachords, Ṡa–Pa and Pa–Re. This oblique movement does not necessarily preclude the possibility of emphasising the Pa and the Re, and indeed, these are the two most important notes in the *rāg Des* (in addition to the Sa). Yet a characteristic descending line[1] prevents the direct comparison of the two parallel tetrachords Ṡa–Pa and Pa–Re since the Pa is omitted in the lower tetrachord *x*:

Ex. 139. rāg Des

However, the balance in *Khamāj ṭhāṭ* is also ascending conjunct, Sa–Ma and Ma–Ni♭ where the Re and Pa are the second degrees in the two tetrachords respectively. The parallel movements can thus be expressed as follows:

Ex. 140. rāg Des

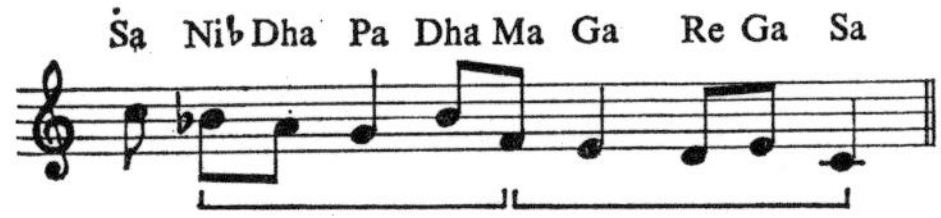

[1] *K.P.M.* III, p. 251. Bhātkhaṇḍe gives the descending line of *Des* as follows:

rāg Des

In his *svarvistār*, however, he frequently treats the Pa as oblique (*ibid.*, p. 760, variation 9):

rāg Des

While the justification for this oblique movement seems apparent, there does not appear to be any necessity for it as the tetrachords are initially balanced. It would seem, nevertheless, to be a functional element in view of the fact that this tendency is apparent in a number of *rāgs*. Perhaps the explanation may be as follows: at one stage in the evolution of these *rāgs* the straight parallel conjunct descent (Ṡa–Pa and Pa–Re), which is still used in *Des* and *Khamāj*, may have been characteristic. The movement Ga–Sa may have been introduced to emphasise the position of Re as the base of the tetrachords by providing a discontinuity in the movement and making Re oblique:

Ex. 141. rāg Des

This use of the oblique Re could then have been transferred to the Pa which is its conjunct parallel in the upper tetrachord:

Ex. 142. rāg Des

In *Des* these turns are often carried one step further, to the conjunct tetrachord above Pa, and the following descent is quite common:

Ex. 143. rāg Des

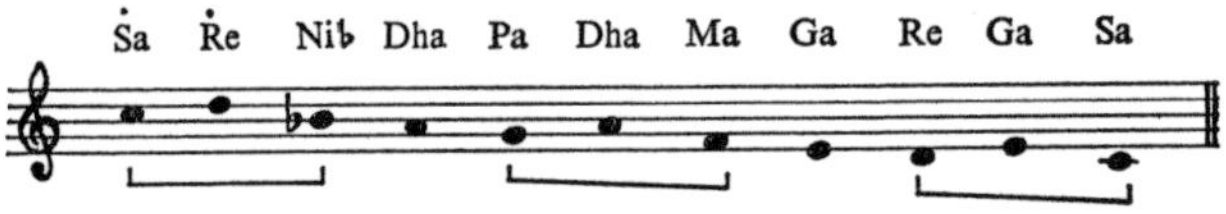

These descending major thirds, Ga–Sa and Dha–Ma, can be particularly satisfying in view of the ascending major thirds which occur in both *Khamāj* (Sa–Ga and Pa–Ni♮) and *Des* (Pa–Ni♮). The leading note, which is so prominent in this *ṭhāṭ*, however, prevents the completion of the octave in the ascending conjunct scheme. Thus, in the *rāg Khamāj*, the disjunct parallel ascending line (Ex. 144a) is more usual than the conjunct (b):

Ex. 144. rāg Khamāj

(a) (b)

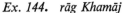

In *Jhiñjhoṭī* and *Khambāvtī* the symmetry is once again disjunct:[1]

Ex. 145. *rāgs Jhiñjhoṭī—Khambāvtī*

The *rāg Des* is, however, unbalanced in ascent because of the leading note (Re–Ma is a minor third, while Pa–Ni is a major third):

Ex. 146. *rāg Des*

This unbalanced ascent suggests the possibility that the Ni♭ may initially have been an ascending note in *Des*, but that it has gradually been drawn up to enhance the effect of the resolution in the Sa. Earlier we had mentioned that the Ni♭ is still used in discontinuous ascent in certain traditions, including Bhātkhaṇḍe's.[2] This may be a vestige of the original ascending line. The *rāg Tilak Kāmod* is very similar to *Des* but its upper tetrachord often tends to be completely transilient, as though the leading-note quality of the Ni♮ could not adequately compensate for the resulting imbalance and was then often omitted. This is an over-simplification, for in other melodic contexts, Ni♮ is a very important note in *Tilak Kāmod.* In descent the conjunct parallel scheme of this *rāg* requires the Ṇi at the end of the lower tetrachord, as in the following phrase:

Ex. 147. *rāg Tilak Kāmod*

The Ni is of course a very dissonant note and will finally resolve in Sa, so that the Ni does serve as a leading note in certain phrases.[3] Bhātkhaṇḍe gives the ascending and descending lines of this *rāg* as follows:[4]

[1] *Op. cit.* V, p. 261. Bhātkhaṇḍe gives the ascending line of *Jhiñjhoṭī* as follows:

However, he does not use the Ni♭ in ascent in his *svarvistār.* We are following the tradition represented by the songs on pp. 265, 267, 270, 271 and 272, where the ascent is pentatonic, with the occasional use of the Ga as a discontinuous ascending note.

[2] See p. 109.

[3] *Ustād* Vilayat Khan uses the Ni quite frequently as a leading note in his recording of *rāg Tilak Kāmod* on the accompanying record, and there is only one instance in which he makes the upper tetrachord transilient in ascent.

[4] *K.P.M.* III, p. 298.

Ex. 148. rāg Tilak Kamod

The ascending line can be seen as two symmetrical conjunct segments ending on Pa (*w*), the Ṡa being added above just to complete the octave. Bhātkhaṇḍe does not refer to symmetry in his works and it seems very likely from the phrasing (i.e. the placing of the commas in his notations) that he is quite unaware of this melodic symmetry. In descent the Pa initiates the symmetry (*x*) and the upper tetrachord is once again transilient. Bhātkhaṇḍe gives the characteristic phrase (*pakaṛ*) of this *rāg* as follows:[1]

Ex. 149. rāg Tilak Kāmod, characteristic phrase

Here the Ni of the lower register is clearly used in ascent and the phrase begins from P̣a thus stressing the octave register from P̣a to Pa. The ascending Ni in this phrase can be justified in terms of inverted symmetry since the figure P̣a–Ṇi–Sa, a rising major third followed by a semitone with which the *rāg* is usually introduced, is balanced by the cadence Ga–Sa–Ṇi, a falling major third followed by a semitone (*z*). A further indication of symmetry is the tendency to make the lower tetrachord transilient in keeping with the upper tetrachord (*y*).

One of the characteristic oblique movements in several *rāg*s of this *ṭhāṭ* is the oblique use of Pa in descent as we have mentioned earlier in connection with the *rāg Des*. In *Tilak Kāmod,* too, this is a central feature and is also found in other *rāg*s, for instance, *rāg Jhiñjhoṭī*. Consequently there is a certain measure of ambiguity among these *rāg*s. The characteristic symmetry of *rāg Des* (*x*), *Tilak Kāmod* (*y*) and *Jhiñjhoṭī* (*z*) can be seen in the following example:

Ex. 150. rāgs Des, Tilak Kāmod, Jhiñjhoṭī

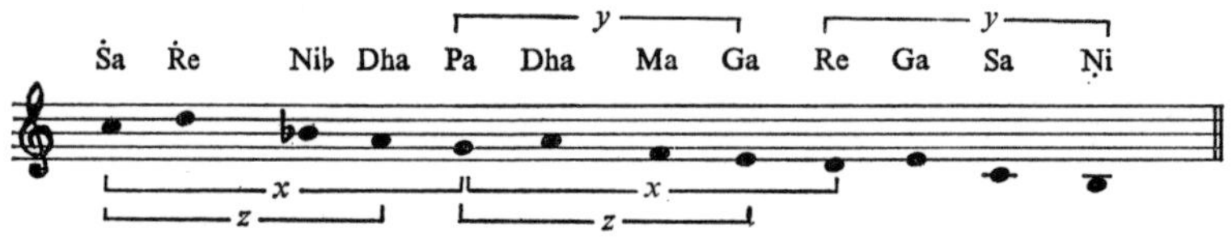

It will be seen that the central figure involving the oblique use of Pa is, in *Des*, balanced in the tetrachord above, while in *Tilak Kāmod* and *Jhiñjhoṭī* it is balanced in the tetrachord below. *Des* and *Jhiñjhoṭī* require the Ni♭ to produce symmetry, while

[1] *K.P.M.* III, p. 298.

Tilak Kāmod needs Ni♮. In many respects *Des* and *Tilak Kāmod* complement each other and there is a tendency to merge the two. Thus it is not surprising that some musicians use Ni♭ in *Tilak Kāmod*[1] producing a symmetry in the upper tetrachord very much as in *Des.*[2] In spite of the prominence of the Ni♮ and the absence of Ni♭ in his version, Bhātkhaṇḍe has no hesitation in ascribing *Tilak Kāmod* to *Khamāj ṭhāṭ*, a fact which lends support to the argument that it has evolved from a *rāg* in *Khamāj ṭhāṭ*.

The *rāgs* in *Kāfī ṭhāṭ* have their own characteristic oblique movement. Let us consider a simple *rāg* in this *ṭhāṭ*, *rāg Bhīmplāsī*. Bhātkhaṇḍe gives its ascent and descent as follows:[3]

Ex. 151. rāg Bhīmplāsī

This is one of the *rāgs* in *Kāfī ṭhāṭ* in which some musicians use the leading note Ni♮, while others, like Bhātkhaṇḍe, do not. However, Bhātkhaṇḍe's simple ascent and descent does not really do justice to the *rāg* for musicians frequently tend to increase the tension of the Ni♭ in two ways: by sharpening the note slightly in ascent, the raised note being referred to as *caṛhī* or *sākārī*, and by introducing a very subtle oblique movement involving a slide (portamento) from Ṡa to Ni♭. In view of this, the upper tetrachord in ascent could be given more accurately:

Ex. 152. rāg Bhīmplāsī

An extreme example of the way Ni♭ is used to create tension is found in the following fragment of a song from Bhātkhaṇḍe's works:[4]

Ex. 153. rāg Bhīmplāsī—tritāl

[1] According to Bhātkhaṇḍe the musicians of Maharashtra use both Ni's in this *rāg*, and this does occur in a few of the songs notated by him.

[2] Both the *rāgs Des* and *Tilak Kāmod* are played by *Ustād* Vilayat Khan in the accompanying record and are discussed further in Appendix B, pp. 193, 195. In Vilayat Khan's rendering of *Tilak Kāmod* Ni♭ occurs as a grace note, an ornament of Dha.

[3] *K.P.M.* III, p. 562.

[4] *K.P.M.* III, p. 565, *Antrā.*

By means of this slide the Ni♭ is used as a substitute for the leading note Ni♮. The slide from Ṡa to Ni♭ passes through the Ni♮ and must create a momentary impression of it. This slide is characteristic not only of the *rāgs* in this *ṭhāṭ* but, in general, of those *rāgs* in which the Ni♭ is used in ascent. In *Bhīmplāsī*, as in many other *rāgs* of *Kāfī ṭhāṭ*, a similar movement also occurs in the lower of the two parallel disjunct tetrachords in the slide from Ma to Ga♭. In Bhātkhaṇḍe's system these are not essential features of the *rāg Bhīmplāsī*; nevertheless, they occur very frequently in the songs found in his works, as will be seen in the following example:[1]

Ex. 154. rāg Bhīmplāsī—tritāl

The Ga♮ is a first order accidental in this *ṭhāṭ* and, presumably, there must be a measure of expectation associated with this note in *Kāfī ṭhāṭ rāgs*. The slide from Ma to Ga♭ exploits this feeling, suggesting the Ga♮ and supplying it for a brief instant in passing. It parallels the slide from Ṡa to Ni♭ in the upper disjunct tetrachord. Thus the complete ascending line of *Bhīmplāsī* could be given as follows:

[1] *K.P.M.* III, p. 582, *sthāyī.*

Ex. 155. rāg Bhīmplāsī

In descent, as may be expected, the Ni♮ is not particularly significant since its importance lies in its function as a leading note in ascent. Consequently, the descending movement from Ṡa to Ni♭ is not usually accomplished in a slide. However, the Ga♮, being a balance note rather than a leading note, remains a force and often leads to an oblique movement in the descending line as well, the disjunct symmetry being, nevertheless, maintained:

Ex. 156. rāg Bhīmplāsī

Although this slide from Ma to Ga♭ is not considered by Bhātkhaṇḍe to be an essential feature of *Bhīmplāsī*, it is generally thought to be an essential characteristic in a number of other *rāg*s in both *Kāfī* and *Āsāvrī ṭhāṭ*s. These include all the *rāg*s in the *Kānhṛā* (*Kānṛā*) group and many in the *Malhār* (*Mallār*) group. As we have already indicated, these groups contain *rāg*s which share certain melodic features, but do not necessarily have the same scale. For instance, the *Kānhṛā rāg*s generally have the following descending cadence:

Ex. 157. Kānhṛā cadence

They differ from each other either in the ascending line, or in the upper tetrachord of the descending line, or both. The upper tetrachord is generally treated in one of three ways: first by omitting the Dha, thus preserving a pentatonic symmetry, as in the *rāg*s *Sūhā*[1] and *Nāykī Kānhṛā* (Ex. 158a); secondly by making the Dha oblique, as in *Sughrāī* (Ex. 158b) or as in *Śahānā* (Ex. 158c), both of which show essentially the same pentatonic symmetry; and thirdly by using Dha♭ as an oblique note in a slide from Ni♭, thus producing two perfectly symmetrical conjunct segments as in

[1] This *rāg* can be heard on the accompanying record and is discussed in Appendix B, p. 200.

Darbārī (*Darbārī Kānhṛā*) (Ex. 158d). It is not surprising that this last *rāg*, belonging to *Āsāvrī ṭhāṭ*, is the most popular of the *Kānhṛā rāgs*.[1]

Ex. 158.[2]

(a) *rāgs Sūhā* and *Nāykī Kanhṛā*

(b) *rāg Sughrāī*

(c) *rāg Śahānā*

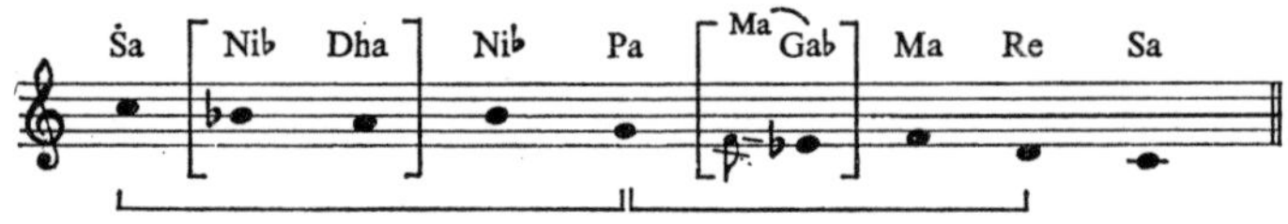

(d) *rāg Darbārī*

In *Darbārī* particularly, the method of increasing tension by a slide between two notes is carried much further, resulting in an oscillation around Dha♭, Ga♭ and, frequently in ascent, Ni♭. The Dha♮ and the Ga♮ are, in *Āsāvrī ṭhāṭ*, the first order and second order accidentals respectively, while the Ni♮ is the leading note. Although these are not used as such, the oscillations clearly seem to imply the accidentals, as will be seen in the following graphic notation of a fragment from a record of the

[1] According to Bhātkhaṇḍe (*H.S.P.* IV, p. 555), *Kānhṛā* is a corruption of *Karṇāṭa* which was in Locana's *Rāgataraṅginī*, and still is in Karnatic music, the equivalent of modern *Khamāj ṭhāṭ*. Thus it appears that the *Kānhṛā rāgs* have evolved around the Circle from *Khamāj* to *Kāfī* and some to *Āsāvrī*. The *rāg Darbārī* can be heard on the accompanying record and is discussed further in Appendix B, pp. 197, 198.

[2] In these examples the lower of the two notes placed in brackets is a kind of appoggiatura, an ornamental note connected with its upper neighbour. It appears that, from the standpoint of symmetry, such notes may be ignored.

Dagar Brothers singing the *rāg Darbārī*.[1] The illustration begins approximately forty seconds from the beginning of the record.[2]

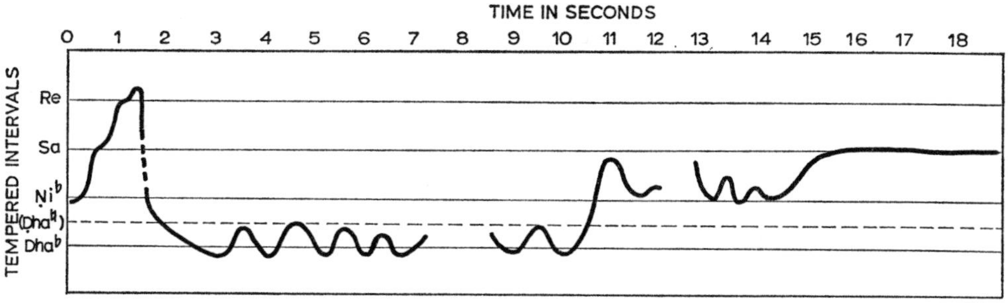

Here we see the voice rising from the Ṇi♭ to the Sa and Re, then dropping to the Ḍha♭ and oscillating approximately between the Ḍha♭ and the Ḍha♮. After a short break for breath, the voice resumes this oscillation, then rises to the Sa and drops to a slightly sharp Ṇi♭. After another short break, the voice oscillates between the Ṇi♭ and the Ṇi♮ before rising to the Sa which is then sustained.

From this recording it seems quite clear that the range of the oscillations is approximately a semitone and does not extend to the next diatonic note, but to the vicinity of its own chromatic counterpart. Thus the tension created by this oscillation is through the alternation of the scalar note, either Dha♭ or Ni♭, with its accidental, Dha♮ or Ni♮. In the lower tetrachord of *rāg Darbārī* there is a similar suggestion of the accidental Ga♮ (second order balance). As in the *rāg Bhīmplāsī*, there is seldom a slide between Ṡa and Ni♭ in descent, while the other two slides between Ni♭ and Dha♭ and between Ma and Ga♭ remain, and the notes Dha♭ and Ga♭ are made oblique (Ex. 158d). In *Darbārī* there is also a tendency to omit these oblique notes producing a pentatonic descending conjunct balance, but the *Kānhṛā* cadence (Ex. 157) invariably concludes these phrases.

[1] H.M.V. EALP 1291. See also Appendix B, p. 198.

[2] The graph was constructed without the aid of electronic instruments, and as such is bound to be inaccurate. The only instruments used were a stop watch and a dodecachord tuned in semitones. To estimate the extent of the oscillation, the record was slowed to half speed and the extremes of each oscillation were compared against the semitones on the dodecachord. From this graph it will be seen that the voice is a fluid instrument and that the notes of a scale should not always be thought of as exact points in the spectrum of sound. Notation systems are inevitably deceptive as they reduce the fluidity of sound into precise units, as will be seen from the following example in which we have attempted to translate the graph into approximate musical notation:

It is interesting that in *Darbārī* there is no suggestion of Re♭ which is one of the two first order balance accidentals in *Āsāvrī ṭhāṭ*—Re♮ being held as steady as Sa and Pa. Pa and Re are the bases of the conjunct parallel tetrachords of *Āsāvrī ṭhāṭ*, a scheme which is very important in the *rāg Darbārī*, and Re♮ is here treated virtually as an immovable note in parallel with Pa. The very satisfactory conjunct parallel scheme of this *rāg*, to some extent, diverts attention from the diminished fifth Re♮–Dha♭.

From the preceding discussion it will be apparent that oblique movement is, in most instances, a functional melodic feature of *rāg*s, and as such is intimately connected with accidentals, transilience and the internal symmetry of a *rāg*.

INTONATION

In Chapter II we mentioned the opinion of a leading musician, according to whom *śruti*s can only be heard in oscillations of the kind which occur in the *rāg Darbārī*.[1] We have also referred to other traditions in which certain notes in a few *rāg*s are consciously recognised to be slightly flatter or sharper than is considered to be normal. A coherent discussion of intonation is extremely difficult, for there is no common accepted performing standard against which these divergent intervals can be compared. In theory, of course, there are a number of standards available, but these are absolutes, which do not take into consideration the context in which the sound occurs. It is certain that unconscious variations in intonation—as between ascent and descent, one performer and another, the beginning of a performance and the end, slow passages and fast, to mention but a few—may be as sizeable as the conscious deviation, and until such time as we can separate one from the other, no conclusive word can be brought to bear on the subject. Therefore, we do not intend to discuss this matter in terms of absolute values, but to attempt to explore on the basis of a few examples the motivating factors which might lead to intentional changes in intonation.

In all of these traditions, so far as it is known, the Ma and Pa have a constant relationship with the Sa. Not only are these notes the most perfect consonances, but they are commonly the base notes of the second tetrachord and are in this respect secondary ground-notes. In the conjunct tetrachord scheme, however, the intonation of the Ni♭ (upper note of the ascending conjunct scheme) and the Re (lowest note of the descending conjunct scheme) will be equally positive. This last is clearly apparent in the *rāg Darbārī* as we have shown. The remaining notes are not so positively positioned, although they all tend to be self-regulating, i.e. the intonation of one note will tend to influence the intonation of its counterpart in the second tetrachord, both conjunct and disjunct. This, in turn, will influence its second counterpart in the first tetrachord. For example, the intonation of the Ga♭ (III♭) will tend to influence the intonation of the Dha♭ (VI♭) (conjunct) and the Ni♭ (VII♭) (disjunct). The Dha♭ will, in turn, tend to influence the Re♭ (II♭) (disjunct), while the Ni♭ will tend to be heard in relationship with the Ma♮ (IV♮) (conjunct) and be regulated by it since its position

[1] See p. 35.

is fixed (see tetrachord scheme of *Bhairvī ṭhāṭ*, p. 81). This self-regulating scheme[1] can be applied perfectly to scales which are abstract entities. In particular *rāg*s, however, the attention is focused on specific relationships and symmetries, and the imperfect relationship between two notes, for instance the Re♮ and the Dha♭ in *Darbārī*, may not in fact be realised.

There are occasions in certain *rāg*s when unbalanced intervals are sometimes brought into focus, and it is on these occasions that we can expect divergent intonation. In the *rāg Śuddh Āsāvrī* of Bhātkhaṇḍe's system, for instance, the Ga♭ and Ni♭ are omitted in ascent, leaving two unbalanced conjunct or disjunct tetrachords:

Ex. 159. rāg Śuddh Āsāvrī

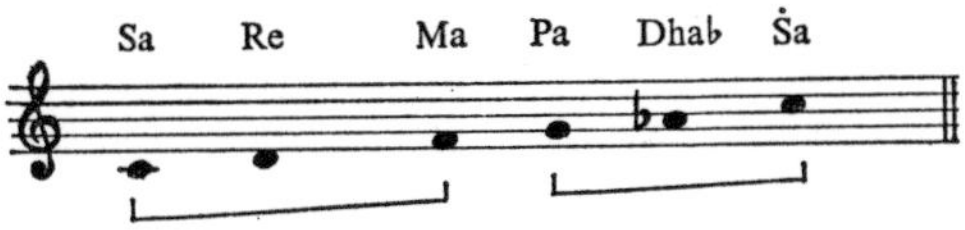

The imbalance between Re♮ and Dha♭ is particularly noticeable in the ascending line of this *rāg*, the lower tetrachord comprising a wholetone and minor third, and the upper a semitone and major third. It would not be unreasonable to expect some feature which will ease the effect of this imbalance. In most of the songs notated by Bhātkhaṇḍe this is accomplished by means of a slide (portamento) from Ni♭ to Dha♭. In ascent the suggestion of Ni♭ used as an oblique grace note hints at the completion of a parallel conjunct tetrachord scheme:

Ex. 160. rāg Śuddh Āsāvrī

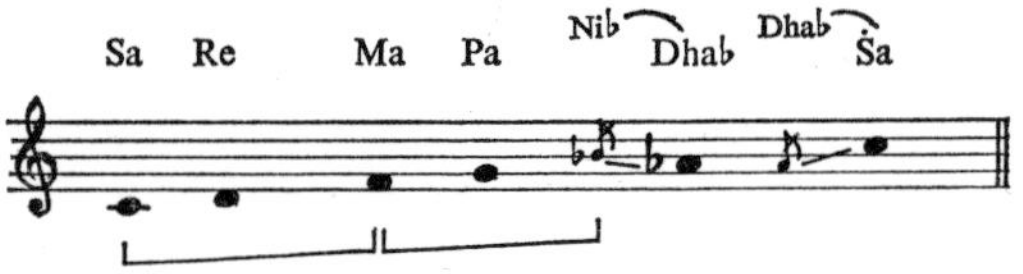

In descent this slide is even more prominent, as will be seen in the following example:[2]

Ex. 161. rāg Śuddh Āsāvrī—cautāl[3]

[1] This is, in fact, the cyclic application of perfect fourths and fifths, which is sometimes also called the up and down principle, i.e. the alternation of upper fifths with lower fourths, or vice versa.

[2] *K.P.M.* II, p. 357, *Sañcārī*.

[3] *Cautāl* is a time measure of twelve units (*mātrā*) similar to *Ektāl*.

Since Re is the bottom note of the parallel conjunct tetrachord scheme (Ṡa–Pa and Pa–Re) its position is fixed and the slide from Ni♭ to Dha♭ is parallelled in the lower conjunct tetrachord by a slide from Ma to Ga♭, thus producing two symmetrical conjunct segments:[1]

Ex. 162. rāg Śuddh Āsāvrī

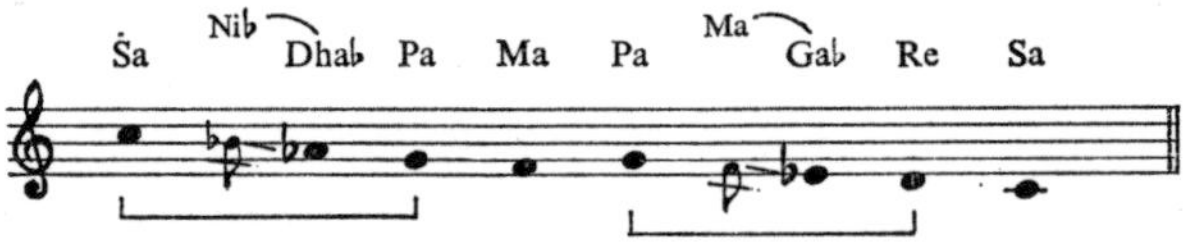

According to Bhātkhaṇḍe there is a tradition in which the Dha♭ of *Āsāvrī* is made consciously flatter than the same note in the *rāg Bhairvī*.[2] In this latter *rāg*, however, the Dha♭ is balanced in the conjunct tetrachords by the Ga♭ and in disjunct tetrachords by the Re♭. Here the intonation of the Dha♭ is much more stable than in the *rāg Āsāvrī*, where in the essentially unbalanced ascending line Dha♭ is often seen in relation to Re♮. As a result Dha♭ is not held as a steady note but oscillates, suggesting Dha♮, somewhat as in the *rāg Darbārī*. This oscillation is then transferred to its conjunct counterpart, Ga♭. However, if we interpret Bhātkhaṇḍe's statement correctly, in the tradition referred to, Dha is considerably flattened not merely in the process of oscillation, but is sustained in this position as a steady note. This can be interpreted in two ways: on the one hand it may be an attempt to accentuate or draw attention to the imbalance (which is unstable from the evolutionary point of view) so that it becomes a prominent and characteristic feature in the *rāg*; on the other hand it may be seen as an attempt to camouflage the discrepancy by flattening the note Dha beyond the chromatic limit so that it is not easily compared with its counterpart Re♮. (Raising the Dha♭ slightly would serve to accentuate the imbalance by making its relationship with Re even more dissonant.) In any case, this obvious imbalance appears to

[1] *K.P.M.* II, p. 355. Bhātkhaṇḍe gives the straight descent:

But, in fact, he only uses this once in his *svarvistār*, where he generally has an oblique descent, e.g., *ibid.*, p. 490, variation 2:

Unfortunately, he does not indicate slides in his *svarvistār*. He does, however, show this slide quite clearly in *H.S.P.* IV, p. 430:

[2] *H.S.P.* IV, p. 428.

have been a spur to evolution, for a second tradition of the *rāg Āsāvrī*—often called *Komal Āsāvrī* because it has Re♭ in place of the Re♮ of *Śuddh Āsāvrī*—has ascending disjunct balance:

Ex. 163. rāg Komal Āsāvrī

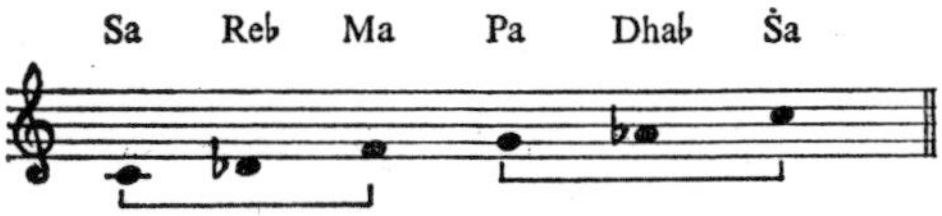

Komal Āsāvrī, which has probably evolved from the other, still retains the slide from Ni♭ to Dha♭ which is now no longer a functional element. This slide is balanced in the disjunct tetrachord by a slide between Ga♭ and Re♭ (whereas in *Śuddh Āsāvrī* it was balanced by a conjunct parallel slide from Ma to Ga♭), as will be seen in the following example:[1]

Ex. 164. rāg Komal Āsāvrī—rūpak tāl (7 units)

A second frequently quoted example of divergent intonation is the Ga♭ in *rāg Toṛī*, which is generally said to be very flat.[2] *Toṛī* has parallel conjunct tetrachords, Re♭ to Ma♯ and Ma♯ to Ni, provided that Pa is omitted as it frequently is.[3] This omission is usually accomplished by a slide from Dha♭ to Ma♯ in most of the songs given by Bhātkhaṇḍe, as in the following example:[4]

[1] *K.P.M.* II, p. 366, *sthāyī.*

[2] The various traditions do not always agree; for instance, in the January issue of the Indian musical journal, *Saṅgīt* (1960), G. N. Goswāmī, on p. 11, gives the intervals of the *rāg Toṛī* in which the minor third, Sa–Ga♭, is 315 cents (slightly larger than the tempered minor third). In the same issue, Urmilā Sūrī, on p. 19, says that the Ga♭ in *Toṛī* is *ati-komal* (very flat), which should indicate something flatter than the tempered minor third. This view is also expressed by Danielou in *Northern Indian Music*, London, 1954, II, p. 49, when he gives a value equivalent to 275 cents for this same interval.

[3] The parallel movement of *rāg Toṛī* can also be expressed as Ḍha♭–Ṇi–Re♭ and Ga♭–Ma♯–Dha♭.

[4] *K.P.M.* II, p. 436, *sthāyī.*

Ex. 165. rāg Toṛī—tritāl

However, the Pa is not completely omitted in *rāg Toṛī* and its presence disturbs the parallel movement. As Re♭ and Ma♯ are the initiators of the parallel tetrachords, Ga♭ and Dha♭ are the balanced second degrees in the two tetrachords where the Pa is omitted. When the Pa is used, however, it becomes the second degree in the upper tetrachord and is unbalanced with the Ga♭. This could well influence the intonation of the Ga♭, especially as it has no disjunct balance in *Toṛī* (Ga♭ to Ni♮ being an augmented fifth) which would help to stabilise it. It is not surprising that the intonation of Ga♭ is affected, but here, as in *Āsāvrī*, it would be meaningless to give any exact values to the deviations.

As a final illustration, we consider the *rāg Śrī*, where the Re♭ and Dha♭ are said by some to be very flat.[1] In this *rāg* these notes are closely tied to each other, being in perfect disjunct relationship, but neither is in a perfect relationship with any other notes in the *rāg*. The Dha♭ has no conjunct balance, Ga to Dha♭ being a diminished fourth, while the Re♭ has only conjunct enharmonic balance, Re♭ to Ma♯ being an augmented third rather than a perfect fourth, and is not significant in this *rāg* where disjunct balance is characteristic. This in itself would not necessarily affect the intonation of these two notes. According to Bhātkhaṇḍe, however, the *rāg Śrī* has a pentatonic ascent and a heptatonic descent:[2]

Ex. 166. rāg Śrī

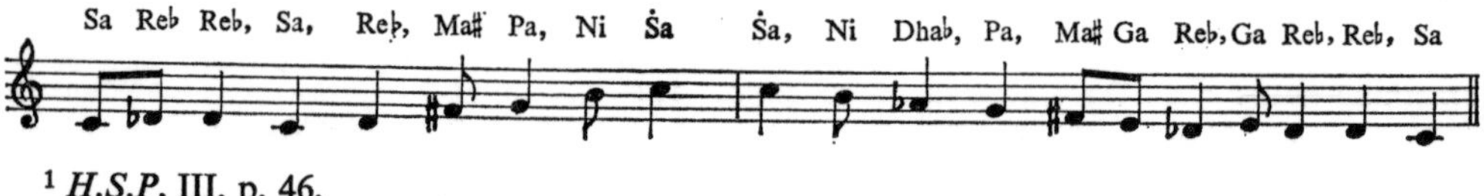

[1] *H.S.P.* III, p. 46.
[2] *K.P.M.* III, p. 361.

The ascent is unbalanced, but in descent symmetry is achieved by the temporary omission of Sa, as in the following phrase:[1]

Ex. 167. rāg Śrī

The ascent draws attention to the imbalance between Re♭–Ma♯ (augmented third) and Pa–Ni (major third) and it is probably this which is responsible for the deviant intonation of the Re♭.[2] Once this deviant intonation is established it is transferred to Re♭'s disjunct counterpart, Dha♭.

It appears that it is a combination of two factors which leads to the relatively rare instances where divergent intonation is consciously used. These are: (1) that under certain circumstances the scalar imbalance in a *rāg* becomes a focal point of that *rāg*, and (2) that at least one of the two notes concerned in the imbalance is not precisely and firmly fixed in the *rāg*. There is no indication, however, that this divergent intonation itself has influenced, or will in the future influence the course of evolution. It is a counter to the imbalance in a *rāg*, but not a complete solution, and as such may, at best, delay the evolutionary process a little.

FUNCTION OF NOTES

In Chapter II we discussed the terms *vādī* and *saṃvādī* and indicated that the choice and application of these in Bhātkhaṇḍe's system was not entirely based on objective principles. The usual definition of *vādī* as the most important note in a *rāg* is meaningless unless it is preceded by a clarification of the various functions of notes and the establishing of a principle whereby the function of *vādī* can be determined. To take a simple example, the leading note, Ni♮, demands resolution in the Sa. This is an expression of inherent function, but which of these is the more important, the tension created by the leading note, or the relaxation of this tension in the ground-note? Surely one is meaningless without the other.

In the *rāg Jaunpurī*, for instance, Bhātkhaṇḍe gives Dha♭ and Ga♭ as the *vādī* and

[1] *K.P.M.* III, p. 768, variation 15.

[2] There are indications that this unbalanced ascent is not very satisfactory as most of the songs given by Bhātkhaṇḍe begin in the upper tetrachord, proceed to the upper Ṡa then gradually descend to the middle Sa. The infrequent ascents are generally as follows:

rāg Śrī

The straight pentatonic ascent only occurs in one or two of the songs given in this *rāg*.

saṃvādī. These notes are treated as parallel in the descending conjunct tetrachords, Ṡa–Pa and Pa–Re, as follows:

Ex. 168. rāg Jaunpurī

Dha♭ is an extremely dissonant note and has, in addition, a very high dynamic function since it is the penultimate note in the descending tetrachord Ṡa–Pa. It therefore acts as a powerful 'leading note' to the Pa. The longer Dha♭ is sustained, the more urgently it needs to resolve on Pa and, correspondingly, the more satisfying is the resolution. To call Dha♭ *vādī* is to say that in *rāg Jaunpurī* suspense is more important than resolution. In our opinion this is an oversimplification. In the following two songs,[1] for example, it will be seen that the emphasis can be placed on either Dha♭ (Ex. 169a) or Pa (b) without violating the *rāg*:

Ex. 169. rāg Jaunpurī—tritāl

(a)

(b)

[1] *K.P.M.* III, songs on pp. 649 and 665. The simplest method for determining the note which is emphasised in these songs is to see which note is on the main beat (*sam*) just after the double bar and marked with X in our notations. However, this does not necessarily apply in all instances.

In the *rāg Darbārī* we have a similar situation since the descending line, using the same notes, also consists of the same two parallel conjunct tetrachords (see Ex. 158d, p. 162). Here it will be seen that Dha♭ is denied the role of leading note to Pa and the symmetry is basically pentatonic, Ṡa–Ni♭–Pa and Pa–Ma–Re. Thus the high inherent dynamic function of Dha♭ is, to some extent, counterbalanced by the memory of the parallel movement characteristic in this *rāg*, where Dha♭ rises to Ni♭ before resolving on Pa. In this *rāg* too, Dha♭ and Ga♭ are extremely important notes and can be emphasised (in spite of the fact that the balance is basically pentatonic and both these notes are often omitted) as in the following example:[1]

Ex. 170. rāg Darbārī—tritāl

However, Bhātkhaṇḍe gives the Re and Pa as the *vādī* and *saṃvādī* in *rāg Darbārī*, thereby stressing their significance as the base notes of the parallel tetrachords.

The above examples show how arbitrary is the attempt to determine the most important note in a particular *rāg*. There is obviously a certain measure of latitude in the treatment of the notes, so that a musician might, on one occasion, place greater emphasis on the aspect of suspense, withholding the resolution for quite long periods, while on another he may resolve his phrases relatively easily and sustain the consonant notes. Thus it will be seen that the terms *vādī* and *saṃvādī*, if they are to be meaningful, must be purely descriptive and relate to the dynamic structure of the notes in a *rāg*.

The inherent dynamic function of notes based on consonance and dissonance, which falls into two main patterns founded on the most frequently heard drone combinations, Sa–Pa and Sa–Ma, describes the dynamic function of notes in the abstract,

[1] *K.P.M.* IV, p. 663.

without reference to particular *rāg*s and context of occurrence. Superimposed on this inherent structure of the scalar notes are the dynamic functions which are induced by the characteristic melodic movements in particular *rāg*s. In the *rāg Tilak Kāmod*, for instance, Ni♮ is the base note of the two parallel descending conjunct tetrachords, Dha–Ga and Ga–Ṇi♮, as seen in the following characteristic phrase:

Ex. 171. rāg Tilak Kāmod

As such, the Ṇi♮ is the base of the system and has something of the quality of permanence and repose associated with the ground-note. It has, in this instance, acquired a much lower dynamic level and is commonly used as a terminal note of phrases in this *rāg*. At the same time, the dynamic level of the Sa has been raised considerably, for there is now a sense of incompleteness upon arriving at it, the tension caused by the need for symmetry overriding the very low inherent dynamic level of the ground-note. Here we have a complete reversal of the inherent dynamic functions of the two notes. Sa is now the 'leading note' to the Ṇi.

In the *rāg Mārvā* the natural function of the Sa is affected even further by the melodic context of the *rāg*. Here the parallelism in the two tetrachords can only be maintained if the Sa is omitted, Ṇi–Re♭–Ga and Ga–Ma♯–Dha, and the inclusion of the Sa in either ascent or descent is superfluous. As a consequence, the Sa is omitted for a great deal of the time and when it is used it is generally in an oblique movement, as is exemplified by the ascending and descending lines of *Mārvā* given by Rām Nārāyaṇ:[1]

Ex. 172. rāg Mārvā

Here we can say that the Sa has so high an induced dynamic intensity when used in direct ascent or descent that it is altogether omitted in these contexts.

In these two examples we have considered the dynamic functions of the two notes Sa and Ni because they are dynamic extremes as far as their inherent function is concerned. The melodic context may also impose its own dynamic considerations on the other notes of the scale. Re, for instance, can become an important terminal note as in the *rāg*s *Des* (see pp. 155, 156) and *Darbārī* (see p. 171) because of their parallel descending conjunct tetrachords where Re is the base note. While there are many

[1] On the record *Inde du Nord*, B.A.M. LD 094.

instances where the dynamic function induced by the melodic context reinforces the inherent dynamic function of the notes, there are indications that it is the interplay between the inherent and the induced functions, especially when they differ widely, which may be an important subconscious factor in determining the melodic features of *rāg*s. Thus the natural scalar symmetry which tends to emphasise Sa, Ma and Pa, the notes with low inherent dynamic function, is often replaced by a more complex symmetry which places the emphasis on more dissonant notes. This may explain, for example, why nearly all the *rāg*s in *Bilāval ṭhāṭ* (which has disjunct balance and would naturally tend to emphasise Sa and Pa) have either the accidental Ni♭ or Ma♯ (or both), notes which make conjunct balance and so alter the inherent dynamics of the notes in the *rāg*s of *Bilāval ṭhāṭ*.

In any melodic context the induced dynamic function is caused by a sequence of notes[1] and the dynamic function of each note depends on the memory of the previous notes and, to some extent, on the anticipation of the notes to follow. It cannot be measured on an objective level. Its existence is transitory, while the inherent dynamic function is a more permanent state which can be measured, at least in theory (see Ch. IV). The interaction of these two, the inherent and the induced, results in a constantly changing dynamic pattern of the notes in a melody line. If, for instance, a note, whose low dynamic function is induced by its occurrence at the base of two parallel tetrachords, is sustained, its inherent dynamic function will gradually reassert itself as the memory of the melodic context in which it has occurred slowly fades. Thus the Ṇi♮ in the *rāg Tilak Kāmod* which is the base of the tetrachord scheme will gradually appear to become more dissonant when sustained, until finally the full inherent dynamic function of the note will return.

We have mentioned earlier that the *vādī* and *saṃvādī* of Bhātkhaṇḍe's system frequently give an indication of the parallel movements in a *rāg*, but that there are also instances where they do not appear to do so. This would seem to be, at least in part, caused by Bhātkhaṇḍe's attempt to reconcile the position of the *vādī* with his time theory of *rāg*s, as for instance in the *rāg Tilak Kāmod*, in which he acknowledges the importance of the Ni, but gives the *vādī* as either Re or Sa, which would suit his theory better.[2] In other instances, however, it may be that the obvious parallel tetrachord scheme of the scale is not so significant in the *rāg* as a complex non-tetrachordal scheme, and that the given *vādī* may relate to the latter. For instance, in the *rāg Khamāj* there are two obviously balanced alternative ascending lines, the

[1] The induced dynamic function of notes is undoubtedly influenced by factors other than the symmetry manifest in a *rāg*. The associations often expressed (for example in *The Harvard Dictionary of Music* under Melody) of predominantly 'rising' melodies with tension and energy and of 'falling' melodies with the relaxation of this tension; of melodies moving in consecutive steps ('conjunct motion') with emotion and expressiveness and melodies with wide steps ('disjunct motion') with stability and reservation, etc., suggest that ascent, descent, transilience, oblique movement and use of accidentals may all influence the dynamic functions of the notes. Similarly, time measure (*tāl*) and the rhythm of each individual phrase will also be significant factors. The precise influence of these factors has not yet been investigated.

[2] See Chapter II, p. 43.

disjunct (Ex. 173a) and the conjunct (b). Nevertheless, perhaps the most common ascent in the *rāg* has no tetrachordal balance (c):

Ex. 173. rāg Khamāj

This last ascent has a complex inverted symmetry, Ga–Ma–Pa (semitone and a wholetone) and Dha–Ni–Ṡa (wholetone and a semitone). The main tessitura of *Khamāj* is from Ga to Ṡa and these two notes are often treated as parallel, for example, in the characteristic terminal figures, Ga–Ma–Ga and Ṡa–Ni–Ṡa. This is well illustrated in the following song in the figures marked *x*:[1]

Ex. 174. rāg Khamāj—Dīpcandī[2]

This suggests that complex symmetry may sometimes be preferred to the more obvious balanced movement. Bhātkhaṇḍe gives the *vādī* of *Khamāj* as Ga which is the base of the non-tetrachordal inverted symmetry rather than the obvious tetrachordal symmetry. For the *saṃvādī* he gives Ni but does not specify whether he is

[1] *K.P.M.* II, p. 159.

[2] *Dīpcandī* is a time measure (*tāl*) of fourteen beats (*mātrā*). The rhythmic cycle is subdivided into four groups, 3 + 4 + 3 + 4.

referring to Ni♮, the leading-note accidental, or to Ni♭, the scalar note.[1] In fact, in the ascending inverted symmetry (Ex. 173c) neither of these is treated as the parallel of Ga and it is, instead, the upper Ṡa whose induced function compares with that of Ga. If the terms *vādī* and *saṃvādī* are to express parallel function, as they generally do in most *rāg*s where tetrachordal symmetry exists, Ga and Ṡa should be designated as *vādī* and *saṃvādī* in *rāg Khamāj* where this inverted symmetry is characteristic in a particular performance. However, in the descending line of *Khamāj* other symmetries are sometimes brought to the fore. Of these, the two most prominent are the scalar conjunct symmetry, Ni♭–Ma and Ma–Sa[2] (Ex. 175a), and a pentatonic conjunct symmetry which is found in the 'catch' phrase (*pakaṛ*) of this *rāg*[3] (b):

Ex. 175. rāg Khamāj

The second of these is particularly interesting: Re, being omitted in descent, influencing its conjunct counterpart, Pa, which then occurs in a turn between the two parallel segments. In both of these the bases of the two parallel tetrachords, Ma and Sa, are also entitled to be referred to as *vādī* and *saṃvādī*. In the disjunct pentatonic ascent Sa and Pa are emphasised: in the non-tetrachordal ascent, Ga and Ṡa; in the conjunct descent, Ma and Sa. So, in the course of a normal performance of *Khamāj*, the '*vādī*' will change from one moment to the next as the musician explores the different facets of the *rāg*.[4] While the *rāg Khamāj* is particularly noted for its variety, it is by no means an exception in this respect. In many other *rāg*s, too, different notes may be emphasised during the course of a performance and the indication of a single *vādī* is often quite inadequate.

In a *rāg* which has tetrachordal symmetry the *vādī* will generally be a terminal note of melodic phrases as it is usually at the base of one of the two symmetrical tetrachords. When the terminal note is sustained its inherent dynamic function

[1] Danielou, *Northern Indian Music*, II, p. 168, gives Ni♮ but many other writers, following Bhātkhaṇḍe, do not specify which Ni is *saṃvādī*.

[2] In *Khamāj* the parallel tetrachords are necessarily ascending conjunct as Re, the base of the descending conjunct tetrachords, is a weak note in the *rāg* and is often omitted.

[3] *K.P.M.* II, p. 122. The given *pakaṛ* actually begins on Ni♭ and ends on Ga. We have added the Sa on each end to complete the octave. There are indications that the Ga is treated as the base, and we may once again have an instance of inverted non-tetrachordal symmetry, Ni♭–Dha–Ma (a semitone followed by a major third) being balanced by Dha–Ma–Ga (a major third followed by a semitone).

[4] Bhātkhaṇḍe is aware of the importance of other notes, for he says that the individuality of *Khamāj* lies in the notes Ga, Ma, Pa and Ni and that these are commonly used as terminal notes of *tān*s (melodic figures comparable to the 17th and 18th-century method of divisions) (*ibid.*). According to Sanyal, *Raga and Ragini*, p. 58, only 8% of songs in *Khamāj* considered by him show Ga as the dominant note. He concludes that Sa, Ga, Ma and Dha may each be emphasised. While agreeing with him in principle, we question the inclusion of Dha in this category and can quote several instances where Pa is the dominant note.

gradually returns, so that it is largely with these terminal notes that consonance and dissonance are significant factors. In the flow of melody, however, it is primarily the induced functions which are significant. This explains why consonant and dissonant notes can both be used in passing without any distinction between the two. It also explains why, in the course of melodic movement, the tonic and its fifth—the most consonant notes—may both be omitted without creating a sense of loss and the fifth may be omitted entirely in certain *rāg*s even though the drone will be sounding it as a prominent harmonic of the tonic.[1]

On the other hand, with terminal notes, consonance and dissonance are of some importance—not in the choice of the terminal note, but in the psychological effect of the note when its inherent dynamic function returns. Here we can distinguish two basic categories of terminal notes. The first is exemplified by the Sa, whose natural state is one of repose and occurs as a terminal note in all *rāg*s, even if its induced function is highly dynamic. This applies, in a diminishing degree, to Pa and Ga when the drones are Sa and Pa, and to Ma and Dha when the drones are Sa and Ma. The second category is exemplified by the Ni♮, Dha♭, Ma♯ or Re♭ whose natural function is so highly dynamic that they only occur as temporary terminal notes when in the melodic context they have a very low dynamic function. The other notes fall somewhere in between these two extremes.

There is a difference in principle between these two categories. The natural terminals, Sa, Pa, etc., make no demands on the future; a phrase terminating on the Sa is complete and the following phrase may either be an elaboration of the same phrase, or a completely new melodic idea. The dissonant induced terminals do, however, influence the future, for although the melodic idea may be complete on the Ni♮, the feeling of completeness rapidly vanishes as it is sustained. Consequently, the following phrase either extends this suspense, or resolves finally on the Sa. In practice, there are exceptions, as for instance when certain musicians, following a convention, habitually leave phrases incomplete, the mind of the listener, guided by the drone and the memory of the cadence of the *rāg*, supplying the final note or notes.

We have attempted to show that the concept of *vādī* must be related to the induced dynamic structure in a *rāg* and that the *vādī* need not be consonant to the ground-note. This induced dynamic structure is composed of two symmetrical sections and it is generally the base of one of these two sections which is given as the *vādī* of the *rāg* by Bhātkhaṇḍe. The *saṃvādī* will then naturally be the base of the second section and will be either a perfect fourth (conjunct) or a perfect fifth (disjunct) from the *vādī*, except when non-tetrachordal symmetry is characteristic in a *rāg*.

Ascribing the *vādī* to one of the two symmetrical segments naturally places emphasis on a particular tetrachord. Bhātkhaṇḍe often decides which of the two tetrachords is more important in a *rāg* on the basis of his time theory.[2] The relative importance of

[1] Musicians often perform *rāg*s such as *Mārvā*, where Pa is omitted, with the conventional Sa–Pa drone tuning.

[2] We have suggested earlier (p. 43) that, in some instances, Bhātkhaṇḍe's choice is quite arbitrary.

one tetrachord over the other has an influence on the ambitus of a *rāg* which, in a few instances, is an important distinguishing feature between two otherwise similar *rāgs*. The pentatonic *rāgs Bhūpālī* and *Deśkār*, for instance, are distinguished by their ambitus and their *vādī* and *saṃvādī*, which in *Bhūpālī* are Ga and Dha and in *Deśkār* Dha and Ga. While their scalar symmetry is descending conjunct where Pa and Re are the base notes, the predominant symmetry in these two *rāgs* is in the two parallel segments Ṙe–Ṡa–Dha (or Re–Sa–Ḍha) and Dha–Pa–Ga, with Dha and Ga as the base notes. This does not completely exclude the scalar symmetry and both Pa and Re are occasionally used as terminal notes.[1] In *Bhūpālī* with Ga as the *vādī*, Bhātkhaṇḍe states that the lower tetrachord is more prominent, and in *Deśkār* with Dha *vādī*, the upper. This is apparent in many phrases of the two *rāgs*, where in *Bhūpālī* the tessitura is largely from Ḍha to Dha with Ga as the focal point, while the emphasis in *Deśkār* is on Dha with a predominantly higher tessitura extending to Ṙe in the upper octave. Thus in *Bhūpālī* the parallel phrases tend to be disjunct, and in *Deśkār* to be conjunct. This can be seen in schematic form as follows:

Ex. 176.

(*a*) *rāg Bhūpālī*

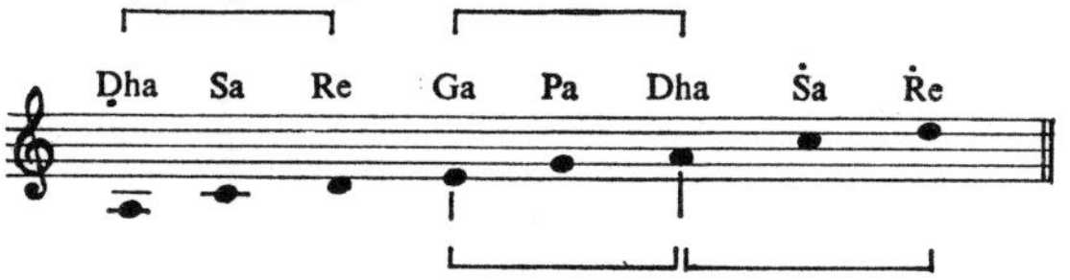

(*b*) *rāg Deśkār*

In both instances the *vādī* is the base note of the upper tetrachord and the distinction between the two *rāgs* manifests itself on the conscious level by a regulation of the ambitus in the two *rāgs*. In *Bhūpālī* it is not only the lower tetrachord which is prominent, but also most of the upper tetrachord in the lower register, while in *Deśkār* it is the upper tetrachord of the middle register and part of the lower tetrachord of the upper register.[2]

Similarly, ambitus is an important distinguishing feature between the *rāgs Darbārī* and *Aḍānā* of *Āsāvrī ṭhāṭ*. In the former the emphasis is on the lower tetrachord where the *vādī*, Re, is located, while in the latter, where the *vādī* is Ṡa, the upper tetrachord is more prominent. Thus the characteristic ambitus of the two *rāgs* can be shown in the following schematic form:

Ex. 177.

(*a*) *rāg Darbārī*

(*b*) *rāg Aḍānā*

[1] For instance, in *rāg Bhūpālī* the Pa occurs as a terminal note in *K.P.M.* III, p. 750, variations 5 and 10, the Re in variation 12.

[2] Not all musicians observe the indications of ambitus and there are many instances among Bhātkhaṇḍe's songs where the distinction between the two *rāgs* is not clearly maintained.

The differentiation of two *rāg*s primarily on the basis of ambitus and the related *vādī* and *saṃvādī* occurs in only one or two instances in North Indian classical music. It does, however, draw attention to the relationship between the tetrachord species and the octave registers, where conjunct parallelism becomes disjunct when the symmetrical segments are extended above or below the middle register, and vice versa. Thus even the simplest *rāg* will have an element of both conjunct and disjunct symmetry.

Summary

In this work our primary purpose has been to discuss some of the underlying principles which have helped to shape the *rāg*s of the modern period. It has been our contention that *rāg*s have been conditioned largely by musical factors, the main exceptions being those which have been introduced recently into North Indian music and have not yet had sufficient time to develop a clearly defined shape.

Contrary to commonly accepted opinion, we feel that *rāg*s are unstable and that change is one of their most prominent characteristics. Yet the rate of change is controlled to a large extent by the force of tradition as well as the need to keep *rāg*s distinct from each other.

The primary motivating force in the evolutionary process of *rāg*s is the inherent imperfection of all diatonic scales, based as they are on the principles of consonance. At least one imperfect consonance must exist in all these scales. In Indian music, however, this imperfection is not appreciated directly except perhaps when it occurs in immediate relationship to the ground-note, and even in this context it is not necessarily undesirable, as is evident from the prominence of the Ma♯ in Indian music. The drones tend to divide the octave into two tetrachords plus a wholetone which may occur between the two tetrachords (disjunct species), at either end (conjunct species), or be divided and placed at both ends. The significance of a tetrachord as a unit is comparable to that which underlies the octave as a unit where any note can be identified with its octave. In the same way a note can be identified, to a lesser degree, with its consonant fourth and fifth. Consequently, there is an urge to repeat the intervals of one tetrachord in the other, just as the intervals are repeated in different octave registers. While this repetition is possible in the two tetrachords of one species, either conjunct or disjunct, it is not possible in both the species of any one scale. It is the unbalanced tetrachord species of a scale which provides the stimulus for evolution.

We have applied this principle at different levels. In connection with scales, we have indicated that the successive correction of this imbalance led from one serial *ṭhāṭ* to another. The progress beyond these could only be accomplished by enharmonic compromise leading finally to a circle of ten *ṭhāṭ*s, of which one is not used at the present time. Although *Bhairav ṭhāṭ* does not belong to this circle we attempted to show its connection with the circle and suggested that its unstable nature could easily lead to the introduction of many new scales. The historical evidence suggests, however, that *Bhairav ṭhāṭ* was introduced before the Circle of *Ṭhāṭ*s was completed.

Summary

In connection with *rāgs*, the use of accidentals and alternative notes also appears to be associated with scalar imbalance, except in the case of those accidentals which appear as leading notes. Alternative notes have the effect of producing temporary balance in the *rāgs*. They can be seen as evidence for the evolution of scales, and we have attempted to show the gradual process by which the scale of a *rāg* might change over a period of time without the conscious realisation of the process.

Similarly, we have explained transilience as an attempt to correct the scalar imbalance by the omission of the unbalanced notes, and were able to derive a number of pentatonic scales from the Circle of *Ṭhāṭs* and from *Bhairav*, most of which are prominent in North Indian classical music today. Since symmetry is an important feature, pentatonic scales fit quite naturally into the system, whereas hexatonic scales, which are unbalanced, have to be modified by an oblique movement if balance is to be created. Thus oblique movement is associated with transilience, but, we have suggested, it may also be induced by the introduction of an accidental. It is often parallelled in the second tetrachord, either conjunct or disjunct, and sometimes in both. Once initiated, oblique movement tends to become extended.

The accidental need not occur as a steady note, but may instead be suggested by a slide (portamento) between the adjacent scalar notes. This is an essential characteristic of certain *rāgs*. An extension of this idea in some *rāgs* results in a slow oscillation about the scalar counterpart of the accidental which extends approximately a semitone towards the accidental. The oscillation is a response to the imbalance in a scale, which once again tends to transfer itself to the second parallel tetrachord. In some *rāgs* the imbalance still remains very prominent and it is in these that divergent intonation appears to be used. This, we have suggested, is probably an attempt to camouflage the imbalance, and is a temporary stage in the evolutionary process.

It will be seen that the scalar imbalance may be resolved in the *rāgs*, to some extent at least, by the introduction of accidentals, omission of notes, oblique movement, slides, etc., each *rāg* providing its own temporary solution in which symmetry appears to be a vital factor. Memory and anticipation, which are involved in the perception of symmetry, impose new sets of dynamic values on the notes during the flow of melody giving emphasis to the notes either at the base or at the top of the symmetrical segments. In some *rāgs* more than one symmetrical scheme may be characteristic and several notes may be emphasised. The induced dynamic function is often in striking contrast to the inherent dynamic functions of the notes, and there are indications that this contrast may be an important factor in determining the melodic features of *rāgs*.

APPENDIX A

The System of Thirty-two Ṭhāṭs

In presenting this system our primary concern is to show relationships between the thirty-two *ṭhāṭ*s, rather than to list them in groups based, for instance, on the number of altered notes (*vikr̲it svar*), or on tetrachord species (*aṅg*). The underlying principle in our system is that scales which differ in only one note are directly related to each other, and it is this relationship which the system shows.

For this purpose the gamut of twelve semitones can be represented by an icosahedron, a regular three-dimensional form with twenty sides meeting at twelve points, each of which would then correspond to a semitone of the gamut. Any two opposite points may be selected as the Sa and Pa which then become the immovable axis of each scale. The direction of the axes of all the thirty-two scales are made consistent within the system. The icosahedron can now be thought of as being in two parts: one with the Sa and the five points surrounding it, the other with the Pa and the five points surrounding it. The two sets of five alternative notes can then be distributed, one around the Sa and the other around the Pa. These alternative notes may be arranged in a number of different ways. In the following scheme we have placed the Re Ga Ma♯ Dha♭ and Ni♭ around the Sa, and the Re♭ Ga♭ Ma Dha and Ni around the Pa in such a manner that each note is directly opposite its alternative (see Fig. 2, p. 182). Although, at first sight, this might seem arbitrary, there is justification for this arrangement. Each of these series is made up of six wholetones, and thus the two groups balance each other. Further, there are no perfect fourths or fifths in either of these groups, and, as the two series of notes interlock to form the icosahedron, the interlocking notes are largely perfect fifths.[1] This can be seen in Fig. 1, p. 182.

As a result of this arrangement the more consonant musical scales can be shown by the interlocking notes from the two groups, the Sa and Pa being implicit in the system.

On paper this icosahedron can be represented in a view looking down the Sa–Pa axis. In this view, eleven of the twelve points can be seen. The only point not visible is the other pole representing the Pa, which lies directly below the Sa. In Fig. 2 the notes connected to the Sa by a solid line belong to the Sa series, while those

[1] There are two exceptions: Ma♯ to Re♭ which is really a diminished minor sixth, and Ma to Re (the last of the Pa series and the first of the Sa series) which is a major sixth. Both these are discussed in Chapter III.

Fig. 1

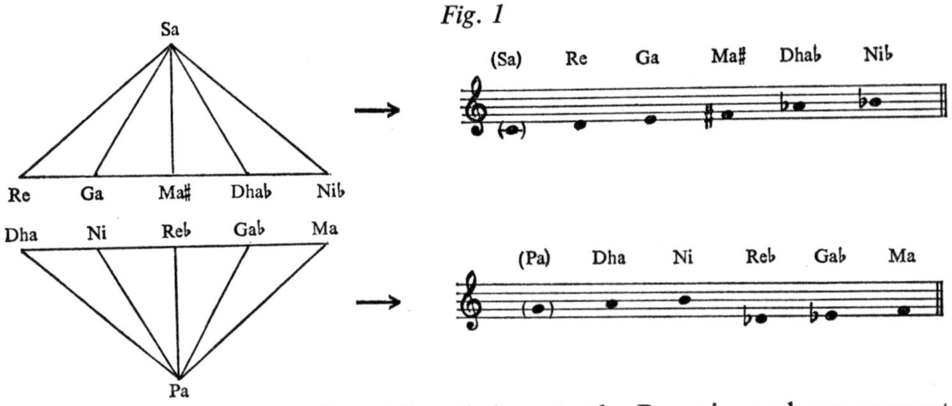

connected to the centre by dotted lines belong to the Pa series and are connected to the Pa at the other pole:

Fig. 2

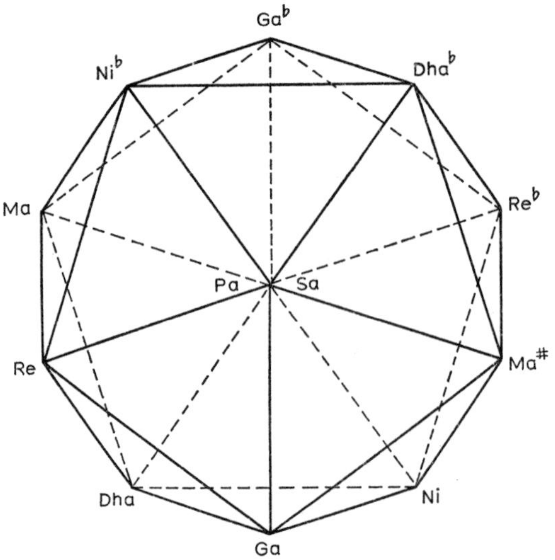

With this icosahedron as a basis we can now show each of the thirty-two scales. Of the ten alternative notes shown on the perimeter of the diagram above, only five are used in any of these scales. These can be represented by lines extending outwards from the five appropriate points. A scale with all the alternative notes in their higher position, Sa Re Ga Ma♯ Pa Dha Ni Ṡa, is shown by lines extending from the five points in the lower half of Fig. 2, while a scale with the alternative notes in their lower position, Sa Re♭ Ga♭ Ma Pa Dha♭ Ni♭ Ṡa, is shown by lines extending from the five points in the upper half. In this way, the thirty-two scales are represented, each with its own combination of arms extending from the icosahedron.

The icosahedron can readily be represented on paper as a decagon (a ten-sided figure), with the understanding that the Sa and Pa are taken for granted in these scales. Now we can connect the scales which differ from each other in only one note by linking the appropriate arms. This will become apparent from the following illustration in which five scales are shown in their relationship to Kalyāṇ, the scale with the alternatives in their higher positions:

Fig. 3

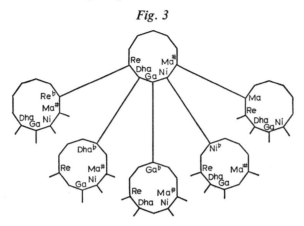

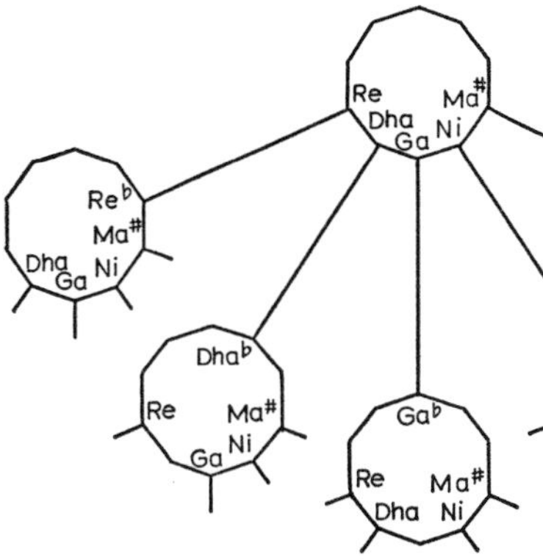

Each of these five scales is connected to four others, the process continuing until all the thirty-two scales are tied together forming a complete closed system. This system, as we have indicated earlier, is three-dimensional, so that the scales are not all on the same plane, although we are obliged to show them thus on paper. It therefore appears that the connecting arms of two scales frequently go through a third, whereas, in fact, the third scale is in a different plane, either above or below the line of the other two. To obviate this difficulty, we have drawn these connecting arms to circumvent the intervening scale in Fig. 4 on the next page which shows the complete system.

In this figure all the decagons have a constant alignment and each pair of alternative notes is placed opposite each other, as in Fig. 2, retaining the same positions for all of the scales; thus the Ga♭ and Ga♮ will always be found at the top and bottom respectively of each scale, even when they are not specifically indicated. In the centre of the diagram there are two scales, one at the top of the system (No. D1) Sa Re Ga Ma♯ Pa Dha♭ Ni♭ Sa, the other at the bottom (No. D2) Sa Re♭ Ga♭ Ma Pa Dha Ni Sa. The arms of the latter are shown in dotted lines. These two scales being furthest removed from the outer ring of consonant scales are, of course, the most dissonant in the system.

The photograph facing p. 184 shows a model of this system. For practical reasons scales are represented here not on icosahedrons as discussed above, but on dodecahedrons which are closely related to the former. While the icosahedron has twenty sides meeting at twelve points, the dodecahedron has twelve sides meeting at twenty points. Thus in the model the semitones are represented not by the points, but by the sides, each of which is painted a different colour, and the notes of each scale are shown by arms extending from the centre of the appropriate sides. In all essentials, however, the model corresponds to the diagram.

The scales in this system have been given numbers for easy reference. The method

The System of Thirty-two Ṭhāṭs

Fig. 4

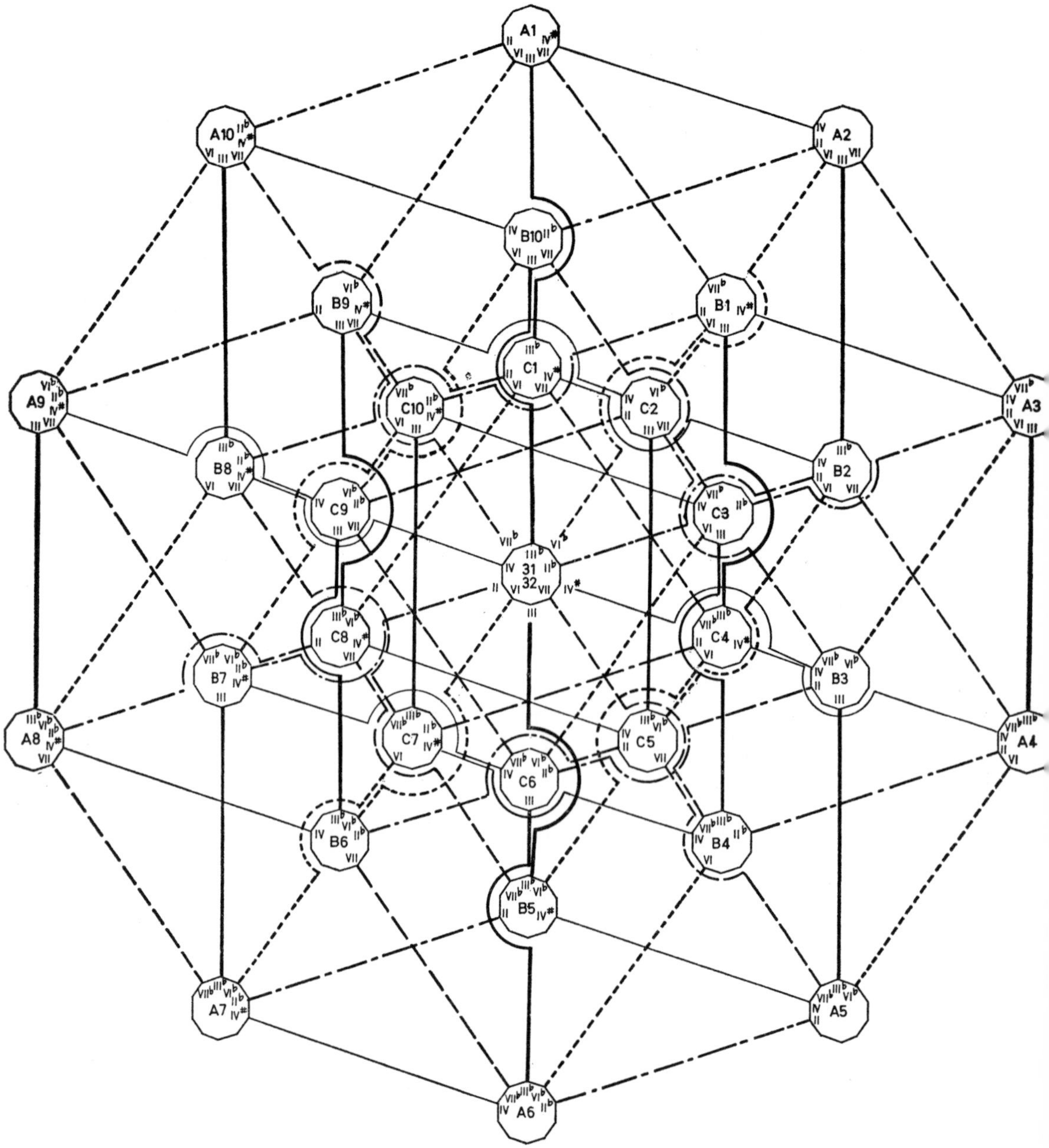

finally adopted is designed not only to facilitate the location of these scales, but to show certain relationships, particularly those associated with the outer circle (here designated as the 'A' group) which contain the most consonant scales and are extremely important in North Indian music. The five scales related to an 'A' group

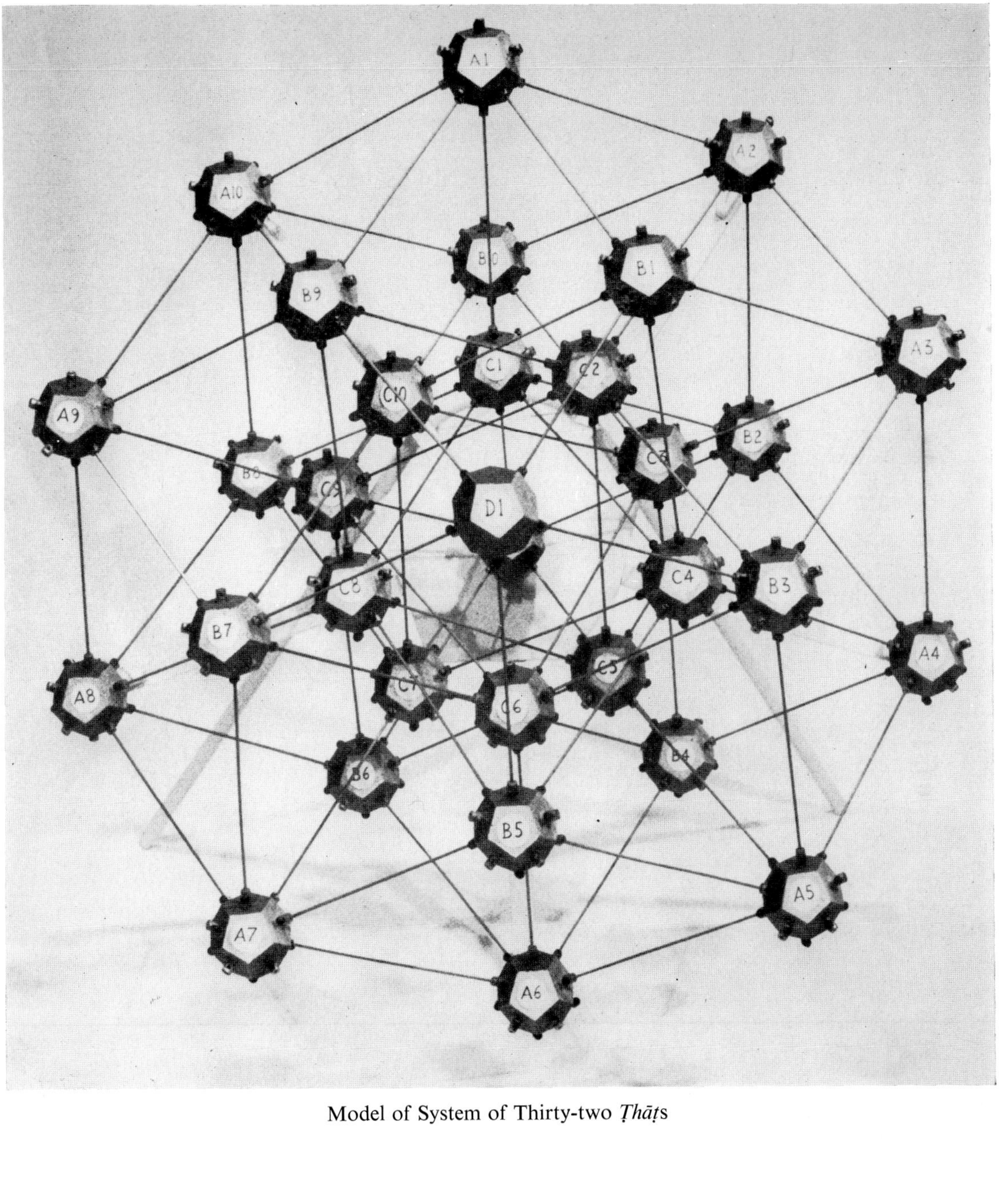

Model of System of Thirty-two *Ṭhāṭ*s

scale are the two adjacent 'A' group scales, the corresponding 'B' and 'C' group scales, and a second 'B' group scale two integers below. These relationships can be expressed in symbols as follows, where *n* stands for the number of the scale under consideration:[1]

A*n* is related to: $An + 1$
$An - 1$
Bn
Cn
$Bn - 2$.

Similarly the relationships of the 'B' group and the 'C' group scales can also be expressed in symbols as follows:

B*n* is related to: An
$An + 2$
$Cn - 1$
$Cn + 3$
if *n* is odd, with D1
if *n* is even, with D2

C*n* is related to: An
$Bn + 1$
$Bn - 3$
$Cn \pm 3$

[1] If the resultant number in the following examples exceeds ten, the related scale is obtained by subtracting ten. If, however, the resultant number is less than one, the related scale is obtained by adding ten.

APPENDIX B

Description and Notation of Recorded Music Examples

There is always a considerable gap between musical theory and musical practice which can perhaps never be completely bridged. It is with a view to reducing this gap that we felt it imperative to include a sound recording in this book. The record contains short illustrations showing the characteristic melodic features of eight of the *rāg*s which have been discussed in the main body of the text. These are not reproductions of the melodic phrases quoted in the text, but are in the form of *ālāp* as one might hear in a real performance. The reader will immediately see the enormous gulf between the bare skeleton notations in the text and the highly elaborated melody line as it occurs in practice.

The performer has not seen the text of this book, nor was he required to conform to any theories therein. As a result it was inevitable that there would be some divergence from the notations of *rāg*s in the text which were based largely on Bhātkhaṇḍe's works. These divergences will give the reader some idea of the deviations in the precise interpretation of *rāg*s to be found among musicians. The recordings have provided new source material to which some of the theories expressed in the book could be applied and provide an independent check on their validity.

Three factors influenced the choice of musician for these illustrations: (1) that he should have had a traditional musical training in the *gharānā* system; (2) that he should not be influenced by Bhātkhaṇḍe's theories; (3) that he should be one of the leading musicians of India.

Ustād Vilayat Khan fulfilled these conditions perfectly. Recognised as one of the foremost musicians of India, he is descended from a family of musicians who trace their ancestry back about three hundred years to the fabulous Tānsen, the leading court musician of the Moghul Emperor Akbar. Vilayat Khan's grandfather, Imdad Khan, and his father, Enayet Khan, were both brilliant musicians and pre-eminent in their generations. Vilayat Khan was brought up to be a professional musician and began his concert career before he had reached his teens. He has had a traditional musical education and has been trained in singing as well as in *sitār* technique. His repertoire includes songs which are said to have been composed by Amīr K͟husraw at the beginning of the 14th century. Nevertheless, his creativity refuses to be circumscribed by conservative orthodoxy. This is in the best Indian musical tradition where pride of place has always been given to those great musicians who have left their mark on Indian music through their innovations. In this respect Vilayat Khan is very much like his father and grandfather who also played a very prominent part in the reshaping of instrumental music.

Vilayat Khan's most outstanding innovation is the introduction of the *gāykī* (vocal) style on the *sitār* in which the phrasing and ornamentation are based on voice technique. This has only been possible because Vilayat Khan is also an accomplished singer. The voice is regarded in India as the most versatile of instruments and virtually without limitations, while all other instruments are restrictive. With plucked stringed instruments, such as the *sitār*, the sharp sound of attack and the subsequent decay of the sound are unavoidable and legato passages are extremely difficult to produce. In this Vilayat Khan has succeeded to a remarkable extent. This has necessitated a modification of the *sitār* as well as an adjustment in playing technique. The *gāykī* style depends to a great extent on the increased use of *portamento* effects which are achieved by the sideways deflection of the melody strings, as will be apparent from the accompanying record in which there is extensive use of ornaments and grace notes produced in this manner. This style has now gained wide acceptance and has influenced many Indian musicians.

Among Vilayat Khan's other innovations one is of particular importance in connection with this record. He has evolved a new method of tuning the playing strings of the *sitār*, which necessitates the removal of the bass, third and fourth strings, usually of copper or bronze, and the replacement of these by a single steel string. Given overleaf are Vilayat Khan's new tuning of his six-stringed *sitār*[1] and two traditional *sitār* tunings.

In Vilayat Khan's method the important notes of the *rāg* being played often determine the tuning of strings 3 and 4. The traditional method of tuning is based on the Sa–Pa or Sa–Ma drones. Vilayat Khan generally keeps this basis, but adds to it. If the *rāg* has a prominent Ga, he will often tune string 3 to this note. This, as we have suggested earlier (p. 72), is merely an extension of a natural occurrence as Ga is a prominent part of the sound spectrum produced by the Sa–Pa drones. Vilayat Khan uses this tuning in the *rāg*s *Yaman* and *Śaṅkrā* on the accompanying record. It should be mentioned that the third string is only occasionally sounded in the drone and the listener may not hear it every time the drone strings are plucked. There are also some occasions when Vilayat Khan tunes this third string to the Ga♭, for instance in the *rāg Miyā̃ kī Toṛī* where Dha♭ and Ga♭ are the two important notes. In the *rāg*

[1] Not including the sympathetic strings, usually 11 or 13, which remain more or less as in the traditional method of tuning.

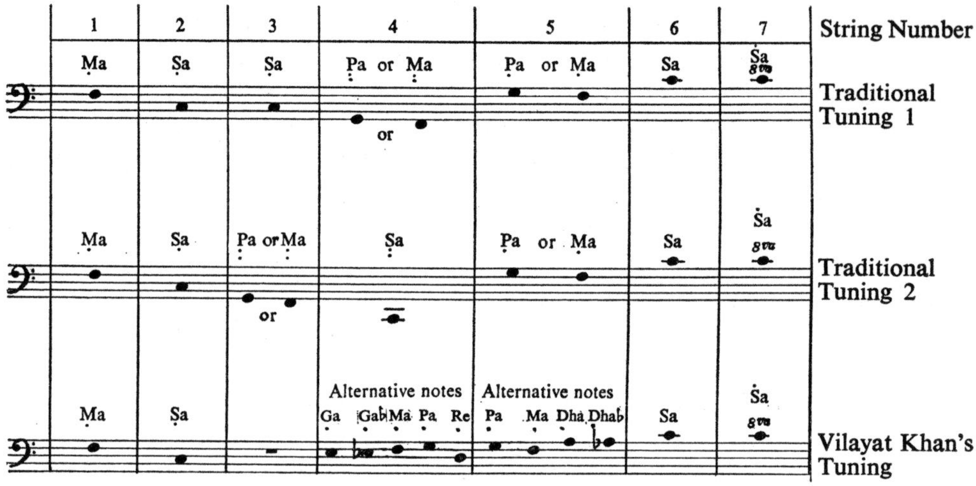

Gujrī Toṛī there are great problems with conventional *sitār* tunings since the *rāg* has neither Pa nor Ma♮. Here Vilayat Khan tunes his third string to Ga♭ and the fourth string to Dha♭, the two important notes of the *rāg*.[1] In the traditional tunings, one is obliged to tune the secondary drone to Pa, a note which is omitted from the *rāg*, and whenever the Dha♭, which is the *vādī* in this *rāg*, is sustained, its extreme dissonance against the Pa drone demands resolution on it, and of course this is forbidden in the *rāg Gujrī Toṛī*. The same applies to the hexatonic *rāg*s in *Mārvā ṭhāṭ*, *Mārvā*, *Pūriyā* and *Sohnī*, which have Ma♯ and no Pa. In *rāg Mārvā*, which can be heard on the accompanying record, Vilayat Khan tunes his third string to Ga and his fourth to Dha, this in spite of the fact that Ga is not an important note in this *rāg* (Dha is the *vādī* of this *rāg*). The justification for this is that Ga is not only a prominent harmonic of Sa but also of Dha, and would be heard in the drone in any case. This does not, however, influence Vilayat Khan's rendering of the *rāg* and he gives due importance to Re♭ which is the other important note in *rāg Mārvā* (*vādī* in Bhātkhaṇḍe's system).

The result of these additional drones is that greater emphasis is placed on the important notes of a *rāg* in Vilayat Khan's rendering than is usual. This is exemplified in the musical examples on the record where Vilayat Khan generally ends his illustrations, not on the ground-note, but on one of the important notes of the *rāg*. This is primarily for purposes of demonstration and in a normal concert, which is usually accompanied by a *tambūrā* drone, the drone notes, in which Sa would be predominant, would continue to sound after the melody line had been concluded.

Perhaps the greatest virtue of this kind of tuning is that the added drones provide a richer texture against which the musician can improvise. It also enhances the multiple modality of the *rāg* and gives greater emphasis to the important notes

[1] This tuning can be heard on the record of *Gujrī Toṛī* performed in duet by Vilayat Khan and Bismillah Khan, E.M.I. ALP 2295.

which may then tend to sound even more like the ground-note. A case in point is the *rāg Mārvā* on the accompanying record where the Sa–Ga–Dha drone may suggest to the Western listener the first inversion of the minor chord with Dha as the root and thus the tonic of *rāg Mārvā*. But to one who is familiar with *Mārvā*, the Dha drone seems to intensify the feeling of the *rāg* and does not in fact suggest that Dha has replaced Sa as the tonic. This tends to corroborate our earlier suggestion that all the notes evoke, to a greater or lesser degree in relation to their importance, their own modal series (p. 73). Dha being a prominent note in *Mārvā* evokes its modal series even when it is not supported in the drone, and when it is, this merely accentuates this series which is already an inherent feature of *rāg Mārvā*.

These experiments with added drones are, by and large, to be expected and are developments within the musical system. Vilayat Khan's tunings have been adopted by a number of other *sitār* players and it is now even possible to purchase six-stringed *sitār*s designed specially for this tuning. While the extra drone notes on *sitār*s is a relatively modern innovation, this type of tuning of *tambūrā*s appears to be somewhat older. In recent times five-stringed *tambūrā*s which allow greater variety in tuning have become increasingly popular. It remains to be seen whether this will have a lasting effect and will change or modify some of the fundamental elements of the musical system.

NOTATION

The notation of the musical extracts on the record is intended to help the listener to follow the music, but is not intended as a score for a performer. The extreme subtlety of the ornamentation virtually defies accurate notation, even when the recording is studied at half its original speed. This is inevitable since a characteristic feature of the music is the manipulation of the dying sound, often suggesting notes which in a cold analytical light are not actually present. In notating this kind of music, one is faced with a dilemma; whether to attempt to notate it absolutely objectively as a machine would (assuming a sufficiently precise machine were available) or to take into account human factors, such as the occasional discrepancy between the musician's conception and its realisation. We are concerned, in this work, primarily with the musician's conception of *rāg*s, but since this conception is not on a verbal level and can only be conveyed through the medium of musical sound, we have endeavoured to notate the music as accurately as possible. Nevertheless, the careful listener will find one or two instances where we have made allowance for the human factor.

Following the practice in the text, the musical examples are notated in both Western staff and in Indian *sargam* which, for convenience, has been abbreviated further to the initial consonant of the Indian note-names. It must be remembered that the use of C for Sa does not indicate its actual pitch in the recording, which is somewhere between C♯ and D, but is again a matter of convenience. Since the shape of the melodic line is our main concern, only very approximate duration values are indicated. *Ālāp* is of course in free time and there is no fixed pulse against which durations can be measured. Thus we distinguish only three duration levels: quick notes, which are indicated by quaver tails (whether as grace notes or as full quavers), medium notes, which are indicated as blackened circles without tails, and sustained notes, which are shown as white circles, i.e. as semibreves.

One of the greatest difficulties we have faced with this notation concerns the concept of grace note as a non-essential embellishment of a melody. From the standpoint of a work of art one could argue that there is no such thing as a non-essential embellishment; each nuance is essential in the production of such a work. From the standpoint of a particular *rāg*, however, it would be reasonable to say that some of the nuances were obligatory in a particular context of a *rāg*, while others could be thought of as ornaments because they were non-essential in their context of occurrence, as for instance, in the following phrase in the *rāg Kedār*, where the main notes seem to suggest the straight descent Ga Re Sa:

But in the descending line of *Kedār* Ga is an oblique note and the descent Ga Ma Re is a characteristic feature. In the phrase above the notes shown as grace notes may be of the same duration; nevertheless, one of the Ma's between Ga and Re is obligatory, the others we could classify as ornaments. Of course, it has sometimes to be an arbitrary decision as to which one of these is obligatory, but without such an indication the reader could well be misled into the notion that in *Kedār* Ga may be used as a direct descending note. Thus it would seem more reasonable to show one of the Ma's (perhaps the last one) as a full note, while keeping the quaver tail to show that it has the same duration as the grace notes:

A particular advantage of this kind of notation is that it provides a bridge between the notations that are found in theory books and in the main body of this work, which are concerned primarily with the main (obligatory) notes, and the actual music with all its elaboration.

In the Indian notation the quick notes are written in slightly smaller letters and placed slightly above the main notes. Sustained notes are indicated by commas after the notes, following traditional Indian practice. The duration of the quick obligatory notes is not shown in the Indian *sargam*, but the Indian reader can easily recognise these in the Western staff by their tails.

An important aspect of *sitār* technique is the sideways deflection of the melody string producing *portamento* effects or slides (*mīṇḍ, mīṛ*). It is possible for a musician to play, in this manner, a number of notes over a range of about a fifth with just one plectrum stroke. All the notes produced in this manner with one stroke are linked by a slur sign:

All notes produced by deflection are naturally slides, although some are less noticeable as such than others. The more obvious slides are shown by a line joining the two notes:

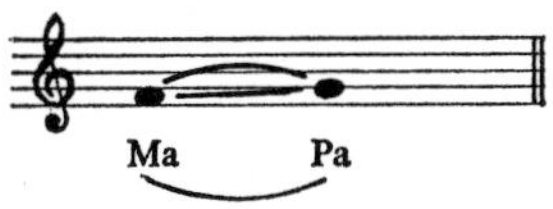

Various other devices are used on the *sitār*, partly to prolong the duration of a plucked note, partly to extend the apparent range of the slide, or just as a device to produce ornaments. These are produced by manipulations of the left hand—sliding from one fret to another, plucking with the second finger while stopping with the first, or hammering with the second finger to the next higher fret. These are also linked by a slur, but have in addition accents below the appropriate notes to show that the attack on these notes is more acute than that produced by the deflection of the string:

The periodically struck drone strings are shown:

A sustained note slightly shaken in pitch, but not rising or falling as far as its neighbouring note (either chromatic or diatonic) is shown:

Indeterminate rise or fall, before or after a note, is notated:

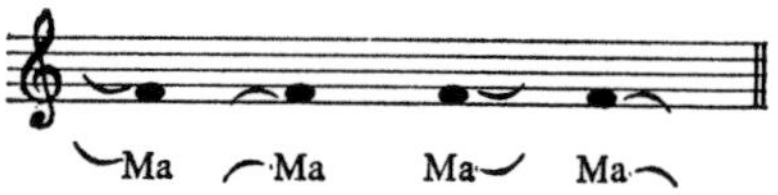

MUSICAL EXAMPLES

The musical examples on the accompanying record were recorded in London in 1968. The original recordings also included the ascending and descending lines (*āroh-avroh*) of the *rāg*s. These have, however, been omitted from the record, but can be seen in the notations.

The *ālāp*s played by Vilayat Khan on the record each have two sections, *sthāyī* and *antrā*. These sections are usually separated by a melodic figure called *mohrā*, which signifies the conclusion of any section of the *ālāp*.[1] The two parts, *sthāyī* and *antrā*, are generally associated with tessitura and vary from *rāg* to *rāg*, *sthāyī* usually being limited to the low (*mandr*) and middle (*madhy*) octave registers, while the *antrā* begins about half-way in the middle register and extends into the upper (*tār*). It will be seen from the notation of *rāg Des* that the *sthāyī* extends to the Re in the upper register, presumably because the characteristic descending symmetry of the *rāg* begins at this point (see p. 158). In *rāg Tilak Kāmod* the *sthāyī* extends only to Dha, the uppermost note of its characteristic symmetry (see p. 158). In *rāg Darbārī* the range of the *sthāyī* is from Ṗa to Ma. This includes the characteristic *Kānhṛā* cadence (see p. 161) and its parallel below. In *rāg Sūhā* the characteristic symmetry (p. 162) extends to the upper Sa, and this is, in fact, the extent of the *sthāyī* in the recording (see p. 200). This also applies to *rāg Śaṅkrā*, where the characteristic overlapping symmetry also extends to the upper Sa (see p. 139). In *rāg Yaman* the range is from Ṗa to Pa which provides for the two symmetrical disjunct tetrachords Pa Ma Ga Re and Sa Ṇi Ḍha Ṗa. In the other two *rāg*s, *Mārvā* and *Kedār*, the correlation is not nearly so clear;[2] nevertheless, the evidence seems to suggest that there may be a connection between the *sthāyī* of a *rāg* and the range of its characteristic symmetry. If this is so, then the *antrā* would, in general, begin at the second half of the *sthāyī* and carry the symmetry a tetrachord higher as, for instance, in the following example:

[1] Two of the other well-known sections are *joṛ* and *jhālā*. In the notations the *mohrā* is followed by a single bar and is specifically shown in the notation of *rāg Darbārī*.

[2] In *rāg Mārvā* the range of the *sthāyī* is from Ṃa♯ to Re♭, only an enharmonic fifth (actually a diminished minor sixth). This naturally precludes any symmetry. In *rāg Kedār* the tessitura of the *sthāyī* is mainly from Sa to Pa, whereas one would have expected a range from Ṗa to Ma to include the symmetry Ma Re Sa and Sa Ḍha Ṗa. In the beginning of the *antrā* section Vilayat Khan quite unexpectedly starts with this descent into the lower register. This suggests that he may have felt the need to complete the characteristic symmetry.

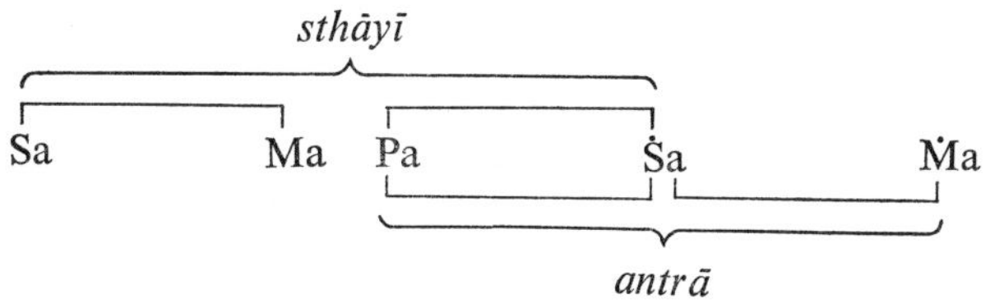

Thus the *sthāyī* and *antrā* show both the disjunct and conjunct aspects of the characteristic symmetry of a *rāg*. While this might be the basis underlying the concept of *sthāyī* and *antrā*, musicians, in fact, do not limit themselves to just these three tetrachords. It remains, however, that anything beyond these three tetrachords is a duplication since both aspects of symmetry are contained in just three tetrachords.

We will now briefly consider each of the eight *rāgs* as they have been played by *Ustād* Vilayat Khan.

RĀG DES[1]

In the *āroh-avroh* of this *rāg* Vilayat Khan gave one ascending line and two, alternative, descending lines. His ascending line is unbalanced due to the occurrence of Ni♮ as leading note (see p. 157). His first descending line shows the simple descending conjunct symmetry of the *ṭhāṭ* which concludes on Re (*a*). This descent is not usually heard in *ālāp* (perhaps because it is too simple), but is quite common in faster passages. The second descending line shows the characteristic turn, Pa Dha Ma, but does not show its upper conjunct parallel, Ṡa Ṙe Ni♭. Nevertheless, this descending line also has two symmetrical conjunct tetrachords Ni♭–Ma and Ma–Sa (*b*). In the *ālāp*, however, one can clearly see the upper conjunct parallel, with its turn around Ṡa, for instance on line 2 (*b*) which is then balanced on line 3 (*b*), with the turn around Pa, and is finally echoed on line 4 (*b*) with the turn around Re—the parallelism being particularly striking in the last two. But behind this one can also see the larger symmetry, Ṡa Ṙe Ni♭ Dha Pa and Pa Dha Ma Ga Re, by extending the first two of these (adding *b′*). Here Pa and Re are seen as the base notes of the symmetrical segments and these are the two most important notes of the *rāg*.

Another characteristic symmetry used by Vilayat Khan is the conjunct parallel Pa–Ni♭ for the ascending minor third Re–Ma. This is clearly seen on lines 9 and 10 (*c*). The figure Re Ṇi♮ Sa, a descending minor third followed by a rising semitone (on lines 5 and 7), may be interpreted as an inverted echo of this minor third in the figure Re Ma Ga . . . (a rising minor third followed by a descending semitone). In the recording one can also find the use of Dha and Ga as discontinuous direct ascending notes,[2] the former on line 3, the latter on line 7 (*d*).

[1] *Rāg Des* is discussed on pp. 38ff, 155ff.
[2] Discontinuous direct ascending notes are discussed on p. 41.

Āroh-Avroh

Alternative *Avroh*

Ālāp

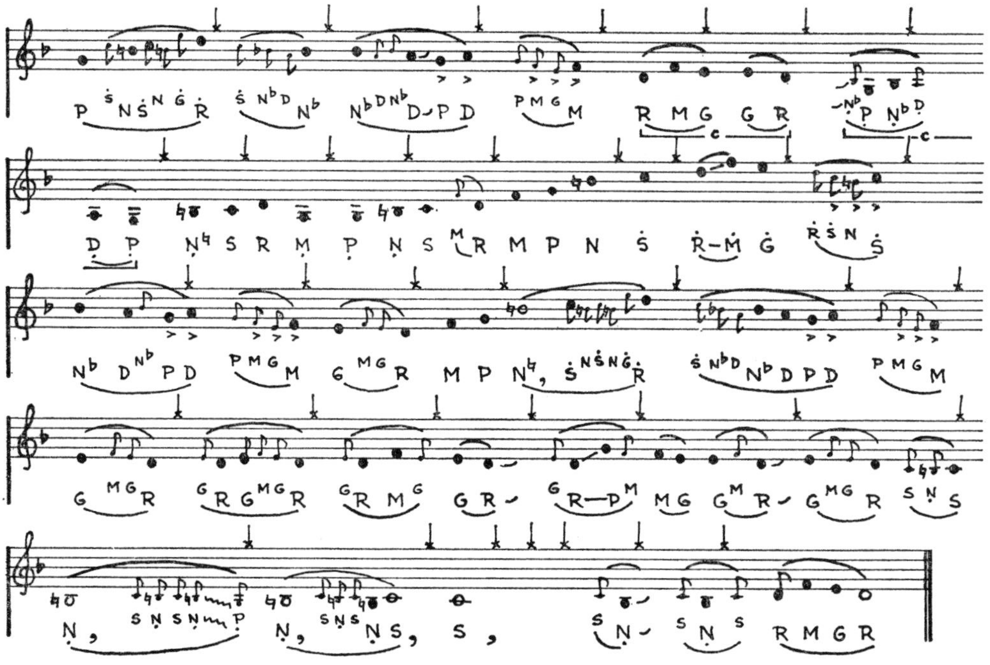

RĀG TILAK KĀMOD[1]

In the *āroh-avroh* of this *rāg* Vilayat Khan gave one ascending line and three, alternative, descending lines. In the ascent Vilayat Khan clearly used Ni♮ as a leading note, with the result that the ascent is asymmetrical as in *rāg Des*. Nevertheless, the tendency to omit the Ni in ascent and to make the upper tetrachord transilient is quite apparent in the *ālāp*, for instance on line 6 (*a*). Of the three descending lines, the second is perfectly symmetrical (*b*) and is virtually the same as that discussed on p. 158. It would seem that Vilayat Khan is conscious of this symmetry, for in the first descent he stops on Sa, a note short of the complete tetrachordal symmetry. In the second he completes the symmetry which takes him to Ṇi. In the third he adds an extra note, resolving the phrase on the Sa. A particularly interesting feature of these three descending lines is that the upper segment is identical and, although the lower segments vary, the number of plectrum strokes remains constant at four, providing a kind of rhythmic parallel to the upper segment. This suggests the possibility that rhythmic symmetry may, on occasion, be a temporary substitute for melodic symmetry. In the *ālāp*, line 2 (*c*), he shows yet another melodic variant of this segment which also maintains the rhythmic unity of four plectrum strokes.

All these descending lines draw attention to the transilient upper tetrachord and

[1] *Rāg Tilak Kāmod* is discussed on pp. 157, 158, 172.

to the characteristic symmetry (*b*), which places Ga and Ni, the two most important notes of the *rāg*, at the base of the two segments. In Vilayat Khan's tradition, as in Bhātkhaṇḍe's, Ni♭ is not a scalar note in *Tilak Kāmod*, presumably because extensive use of this note will eventually lead to the characteristic symmetry of *rāg Des*. Yet Vilayat Khan does use Ni♭ as a grace note, for instance, on line 4 (*d*) which is more or less parallel to (*e*) on the following line, suggesting that there is an inclination towards ascending conjunct symmetry. The slight hint of Ni♭ obviously adds something to the *rāg* as it satisfies the needs of symmetry. This could be given as an example of the modern concept of *vivādī*,[1] that is, a note which is generally not permitted in a *rāg*, except when played or sung by a great musician where it seems to enhance the melodic features of the *rāg*, rather than to add a new feature.

Āroh-Avroh

Avroh Alternatives

Ālāp

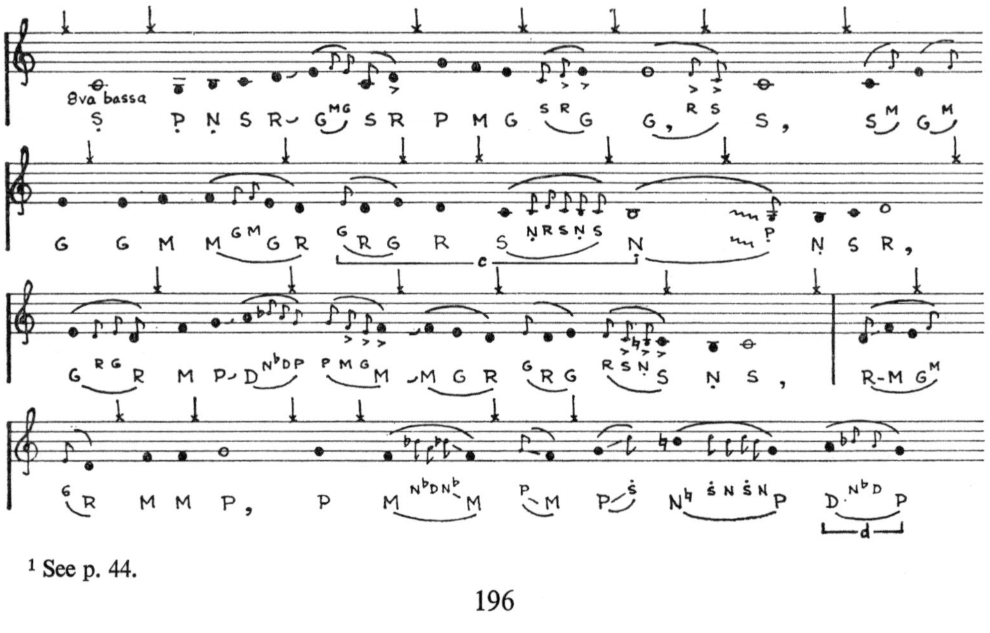

[1] See p. 44.

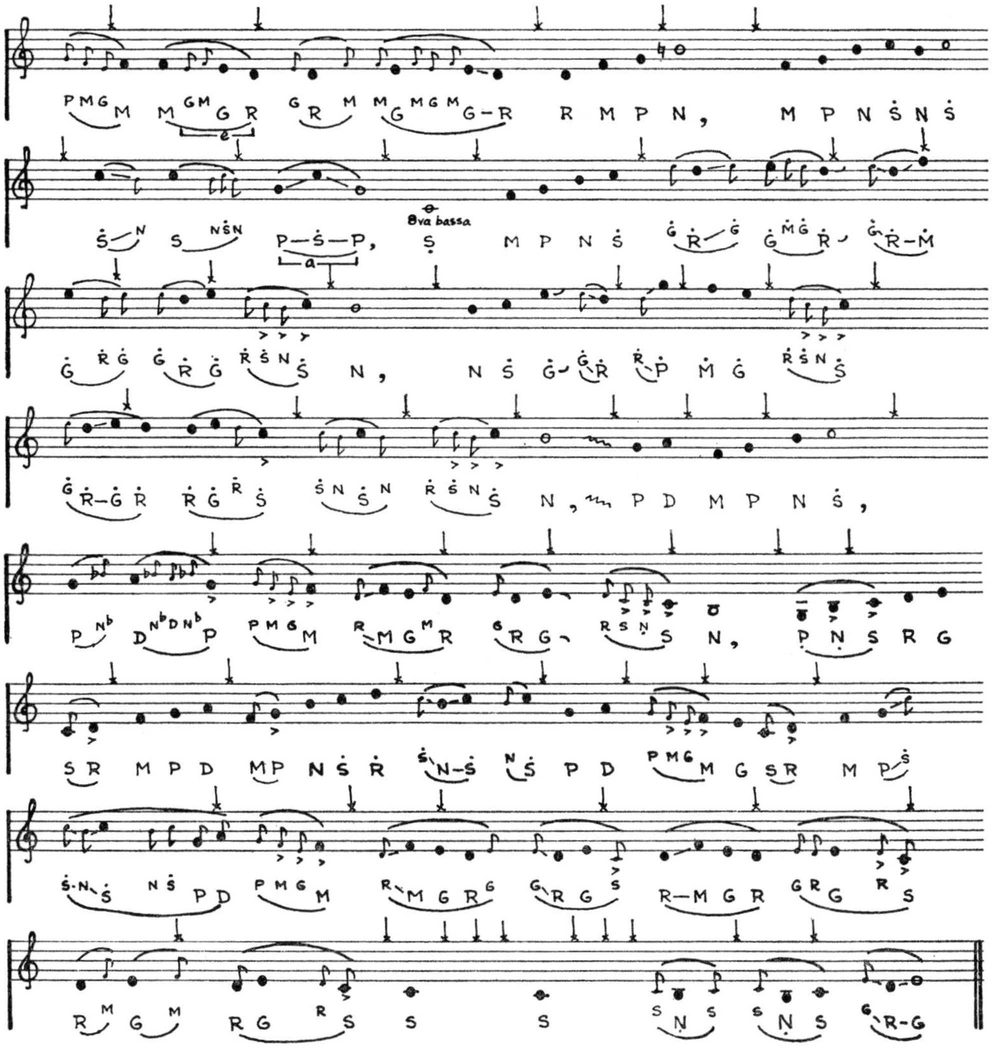

RĀG DARBĀRĪ[1]

From the standpoint of symmetry, *Darbārī* is perhaps the most obvious example. Yet the ascending line given by Vilayat Khan does not show the ascending conjunct symmetry, Sa Re ^{Ma}Ga♭ Ma and Ma Pa $^{\text{Ni♭}}$Dha♭ Ni♭, which is sometimes quite explicit. His ascending line is composed of two asymmetrical parts. However, descend-

[1] This *rāg* is discussed on pp. 162ff, 171, 177.

ing conjunct symmetry is clearly apparent in his descending line (*a*). What is perhaps not so obvious is that elements of this symmetry appear to be carried a stage further. The basic symmetrical segments are Ṡa Dha♭ Ni♭ Pa and Pa Ga♭ Ma Re, where Pa and Re, the important notes of the *rāg*, are at the base of the two tetrachords. The first three notes of these segments appear to have a further conjunct balance Re Ṇi♭ Sa (line 1, *b*), and there appears to be a tendency to repeat the descending minor third, Ni♭ Pa, a further conjunct tetrachord above, Ġa♭ Ṡa (line 10, *c*).

The most remarkable feature of this *rāg* is the extended oscillation (*āndolan*) of Dha♭ and Ga♭. These, we have suggested earlier, extend not to the adjacent diatonic notes, as is shown, for instance, in Bhātkhaṇḍe's notations, but to their chromatic counterparts. Vilayat Khan's rendering of the *rāg* substantiates this thesis. The oscillation of the Ni♭ is basically melodic since it occurs in ascent and is associated with a slightly sharpened (*sākārī*) Ni♭, which increases the dissonance of the note so that the effect of resolution in Sa is enhanced. This occurs on lines 7 and 8 and is marked with a + above the note. While the oscillation of the Ni♭ is basically melodic, it must be remembered that there will be some tendency to transfer the oscillation from the Ga♭ to its disjunct counterpart, Ni♭, which may account for the extensive oscillation of this note. But the Ni♭ does not always lead directly to Sa, Ṇi♭ Re Sa (as in the *āroh-avroh*) being equally characteristic. This could be interpreted in melodic terms as a withholding of the Sa. It could also be interpreted as the inverted parallel of Re Ṇi♭ Sa.

There is a fairly strong pentatonic tendency in *Darbārī*. It may seem curious that the Dha♭ and Ga♭, the oscillation of which is such a characteristic feature of the *rāg*, are the very notes which tend to be omitted, for instance on line 6 (*d*) and line 10 (*e*). In *Darbārī* Dha♭ is out of balance with Re, one of the important notes of the *rāg*. The oscillation of Dha♭, we have suggested earlier, results from this imbalance and is then transferred to Ga♭ to produce conjunct symmetry. We have also suggested earlier that the unbalanced notes are often omitted (pp. 125, 126), thus the Dha♭ tends to be omitted. This feature is also transferred to Ga♭ which is then a second order omission.

Āroh-Avroh

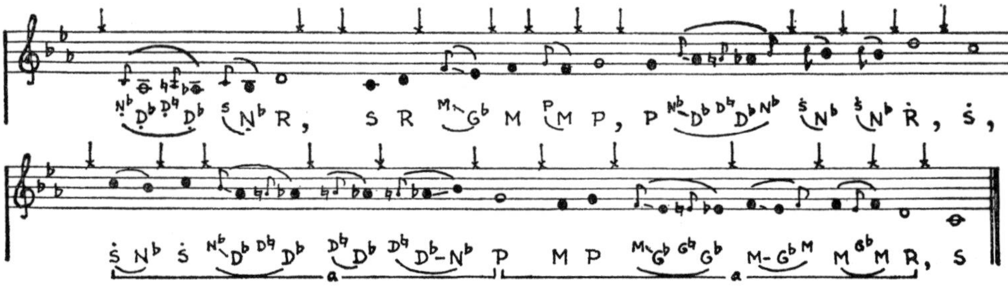

Ālāp

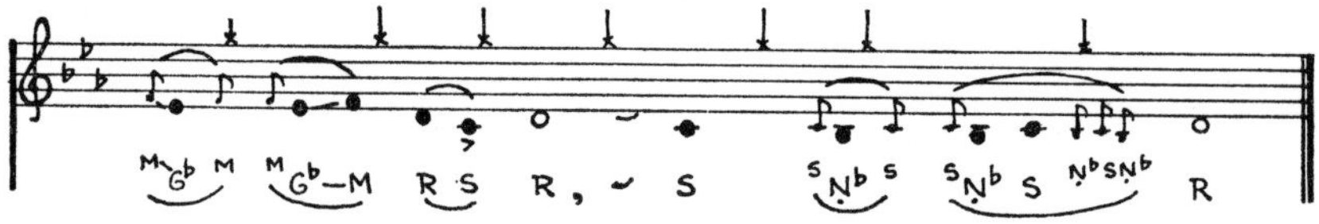

RĀG SŪHĀ[1]

This is a hexatonic *rāg* (Dha being omitted) which is ascribed to *Kāfī ṭhāṭ* in Bhātkhaṇḍe's system. It is one of the *Kānhṛā* group of *rāg*s, as is *Darbārī*, whose characteristic feature is the oblique Ga♭ in the lower descending tetrachord, Ma Ga♭ Ma Re Sa. In ascent the *rāg* is pentatonic and has disjunct symmetry (*āroh-avroh, a*). Since Ga♭ is an oblique note, the descending line is also pentatonic. Here the conjunct symmetry can only be appreciated if the turn around Ga♭ is ignored (*āroh-avroh, b*). Thus this *rāg* has elements of both conjunct and disjunct symmetry. There is an indication that there is a tendency towards disjunct symmetry, which is characteristic of *Kāfī ṭhāṭ*, in the descending line as well, since Dha♮ occurs occasionally as a grace note attached to its nearest diatonic neighbour, Ni♭. This results in a kind of turn, for instance on line 1 of the *ālāp* (*c*), which is paralleled in the lower disjunct tetrachord, as on line 4 (*c*). The emphasis, in this *rāg*, is in the upper tetrachord, and therefore on the ascending line,[2] so that Ma and Ṡa, the final notes of the ascending disjunct symmetrical tetrachords, are the two important notes in the *rāg*. As in *rāg Darbārī*, the Ni♭ is slightly sharpened when leading to the Ṡa, and is shown by a + sign above the Ni♭, for example, at the beginning of line 4.

Āroh-Avroh

Ālāp

[1] This *rāg* is discussed on pp. 161, 162.
[2] Vilayat Khan concludes his *ālāp* with an ascent to the upper Ṡa.

RĀG MĀRVĀ[1]

We have suggested earlier that the scale of this *rāg* is asymmetrical unless Sa is omitted. This tendency is clearly evident in Vilayat Khan's *āroh-avroh* of *Mārvā* (*a*). This leaves two conjunct symmetrical segments which can be seen either as Ṇi Re♭ Ga and Ga Ma♯ Dha or as Re♭ Ga Ma♯ and Ma♯ Dha Ni. The former is the basis of the *rāg Pūriyā* which is, in scale, identical to *Mārvā*. In *Pūriyā* Ga and Ni, which are the base notes of the two symmetrical segments, are its two important notes. The latter scheme appears to be the basis of *Mārvā*. We should then expect Re♭ and Ma♯, the base notes of the two symmetrical segments, to be the important notes of the *rāg*. In fact, Re♭ is an important note, but Ma♯ is not. This is not surprising in view of the fact that if Ma♯ were sustained as a terminal note, its extreme dissonance would require resolution in Pa, the note which is omitted in the *rāg*. In Vilayat Khan's rendering of the *rāg*, the octave register Re♭–Ṙe♭ is clearly emphasised and Re♭ sustained as a base note, for instance on line 10 (*b*), but the Ma♯, which is often the initial note of a phrase, for instance on line 4 (*c*), is never used as a terminal note.

Going across this scheme is a second scheme based on the tessitura Ḍha–Dha, for instance on lines 3 and 4 (*d*). Here Dha is not the base note of any symmetry within the *rāg* and appears to function as an independent ground-note, on a par with Sa, which of course need not be justified in terms of symmetry. The successive intervals of *Mārvā* (without Sa) from Ḍha give the common pentatonic scale of *rāg Bhūpālī* (see p. 130). Similarly, if we consider the successive intervals from Re♭ (again omitting Sa), we get the pentatonic scale of the *rāg Mālkoś* (see p. 130). The evocation of these two well-known pentatonic *rāgs* is a basic feature of *Mārvā*, but this is not appreciated on a conscious level.

It will be clear from the recording that Re♭ and Dha are the two most important notes in *Mārvā* and these are recognised as such by Bhātkhaṇḍe, in spite of being an augmented fifth apart. Some musicologists, confusing the modern and ancient concepts of *vādī* and *saṃvādī*, are disturbed by the fact that the important notes of a *rāg* (modern concept of these terms) are not a perfect fourth or a perfect fifth (ancient concept), and give Dha and Ga as the *vādī* and *saṃvādī* of this *rāg*.[2]

[1] See pp. 83, 114, 115, 188 for a discussion of this *rāg*.
[2] See f.n. 2, p. 44.

Āroh-Avroh

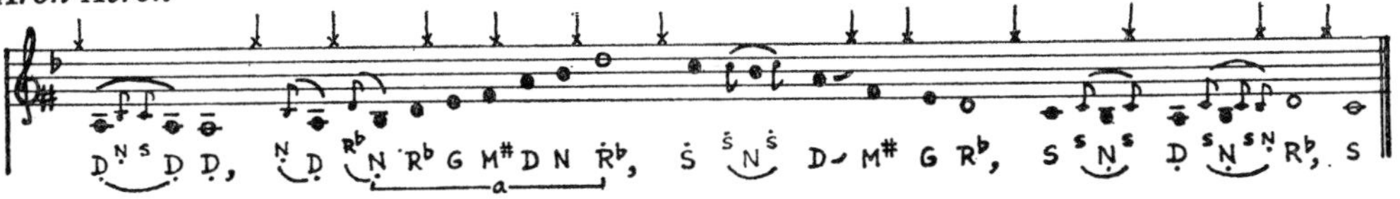

Ālāp

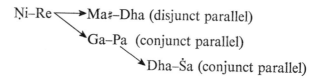

RĀG YAMAN[1]

The scalar symmetry of *rāg Yaman* is descending conjunct, Ṡa–Pa and Pa–Re. When Sa and Pa are omitted, which is often the case particularly in ascent, the symmetry becomes disjunct, Ṇi Re Ga and Ma♯ Dha Ni. This disjunct symmetry is quite obvious in Vilayat Khan's *āroh-avroh* of this *rāg* (*a*). In descent, however, one would expect to see the conjunct symmetry emphasised. This is not so readily apparent; in fact, in the descending line played by Vilayat Khan, there is still evidence of disjunct symmetry, although it only extends over a major third (*b*). In the course of his *ālāp*, however, there is a perfect example of this descending conjunct symmetry (line 8, *c*) where the Re functions as the base note of the lower of two symmetrical segments. This symmetry would appear to be quite unconscious, since Vilayat Khan gives no indication of it in his *āroh-avroh*.

In Vilayat Khan's present rendering of *Yaman*, Sa and Pa are not omitted to any great extent,[2] although the tendency is clearly there. Equal emphasis appears to be given to the omission of Ma♯ and Ni. We have pointed out earlier that there is a tendency to omit the unbalanced notes, in *Yaman* Sa and Ma♯. Each of these may lead to a second order omission, Sa to the Pa, and Ma♯ to the Ni. This leaves four pairs of notes which are all related in terms of symmetry, as follows:

Ṇi–Re → Ma♯–Dha (disjunct parallel)
↘ Ga–Pa (conjunct parallel)
↘ Dha–Ṡa (conjunct parallel)

By combining these in pairs, Vilayat Khan also achieves an oblique symmetry, Ḍha Sa Ṇi Re and Ga Pa Ma♯ Dha, for instance, on line 2 (*d*).

[1] This *rāg* is discussed on pp. 82, 126, 187.

[2] On Vilayat Khan's record of the *rāg Yaman*, E.M.I. ASD 2425, the omission of Sa and Pa is more evident.

It is also interesting to note the slight suggestion of Ma♮ which occurs on several occasions as an inflexion of the Ga. This is, of course, the conjunct parallel of Sa, and can be regarded as another instance of *vivādī*.[1]

In a *rāg* such as *Yaman* the *vādī* and *saṃvādī* would naturally fluctuate, depending on whether the ascending disjunct segments were being emphasised or the descending conjunct. In the former, Ga and Ni would qualify as the two most important notes (Ṇi Re Ga and Ma♯ Dha Ni); in the latter, Pa and Re (Ṡa Ni Dha Pa and Pa Ma Ga Re). It is not surprising that there are a number of divergent opinions, and Banarji mentions just these four notes which qualify as *vādī* in the different traditions he has encountered.[2]

Āroh-Avroh

Ālāp

[1] See p. 44.
[2] See p. 42, f.n. 5.

RĀG ŚAṄKRĀ[1]

We have discussed earlier (p. 131) the pentatonic version of this *rāg* which has the notes Sa Ga Pa Dha Ni Ṡa. In the hexatonic version Re is added and provides the disjunct balance to Dha. Thus the ascending line has a measure of disjunct symmetry (*a*). We had suggested, largely on the basis of Bhātkhaṇḍe's notations, that the characteristic symmetry involved a turn whereby Sa–Ga–Pa was balanced by Pa–Ni (disjunct) and Dha–Ṡa (conjunct). This symmetry is also apparent in Vilayat Khan's rendering of *Śaṅkrā*, for instance on line 3 of the *ālāp* (*b*). Equally prominent seems to be a tendency to produce a mixed conjunct–disjunct symmetry in the descending line, where Dha Ṡa Ni Dha Pa are balanced by Ga Pa (conjunct) Ga Re Sa (disjunct), as at (*c*). The invariable use of Re between these conjunct and disjunct elements can be interpreted as a device to disguise the discontinuity and perhaps to provide a rhythmic substitute for the Ma♯ which would have been necessary to complete the conjunct symmetry.

In Vilayat Khan's rendering of *rāg Śaṅkrā*, Ni is a very prominent leading note, so that when Ṡa is approached from Dha, as in the characteristic turn, Pa Ni Dha Ṡa, it is invariably followed by a descent (for example on line 3, following *b*), as it is not felt to be resolved. The extensive use of Ṇi in turns (mordents) around Sa is paralleled

[1] This *rāg* is discussed on pp. 131, 139.

by a similar treatment of its disjunct Ma♯ (which remains basically a grace note) in turns around Pa, as will be seen on lines 1 and 2 (*d*). The hint of Ma♮, largely as an inflexion of Ga (line 3, *e*), suggests that Sa also has some influence on its conjunct counterpart.

Āroh-Avroh

Ālāp

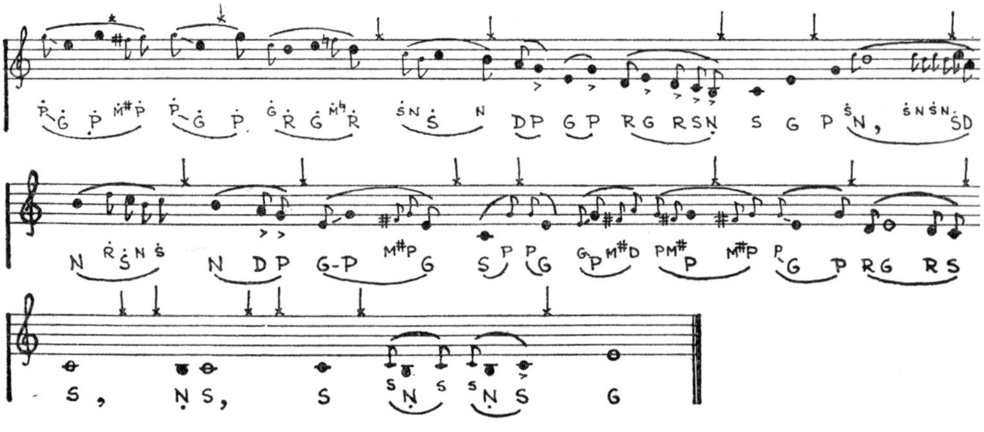

RĀG KEDĀR[1]

The ascending line of *rāg Kedār* is quite extraordinary and consists basically of two transilient tetrachords bridged by a disjunction, Sa Ma, Ma Pa, Pa Ṡa. This is, of course, an over-simplification as all three notes, Sa, Ma and Pa, act as tonal centres around which turns (mordents) are based. These are perfectly symmetrical, as in the ascending line given by Vilayat Khan (*a*). Thus *Kedār* has elements of both conjunct and disjunct symmetry, so that the melodic figure Sa Ṇi Re is echoed a fourth above, Ma Ga Pa, as well as a fifth above, Pa Ma♯ Dha, the last necessitating the use of the accidental, Ma♯, for reasons of symmetry.[2] In descent, however, the symmetry is basically disjunct and pentatonic, Ṡa Dha Pa and Ma Re Sa, as in Vilayat Khan's descending line (*b*), although an element of conjunct symmetry is found in the occurrence of the Ni♭—sometimes just as an inflexion of Dha—suggesting the figure Dha Ni♭ Pa, as on line 6 (*c*), which provides symmetry for Ga Ma Re in the lower tetrachord (e.g. on line 5, *c*).[2]

With the exception of this conjunct symmetry, which is not yet well defined, all the other symmetries in the *rāg* place emphasis on the three most consonant notes, Sa, Ma and Pa, which are important terminal notes. However, only two can be given as *vādī* and *saṃvādī*, and it is usual for Ma and Sa to be recognised as such. This gives importance to the ascending line in which Ma and Ṡa are the final notes of the

[1] This *rāg* is discussed on pp. 103, 104, 152ff.

[2] Bhātkhaṇḍe's own version of this *rāg* shows virtually no symmetry, *K.P.M.* III, p. 118:

However, the majority of songs he has notated show more or less the same elements of symmetry as are found in Vilayat Khan's rendering.

disjunct tetrachords and a performance of this *rāg* usually opens with the characteristic jump Sa–Ma, as in Vilayat Khan's recording.

Āroh-Avroh

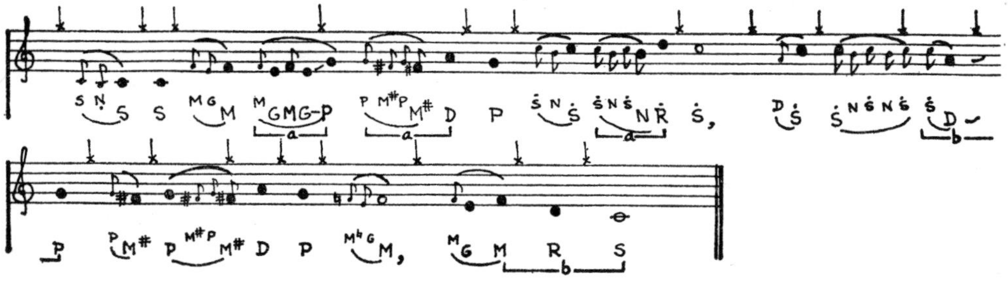

Ālāp

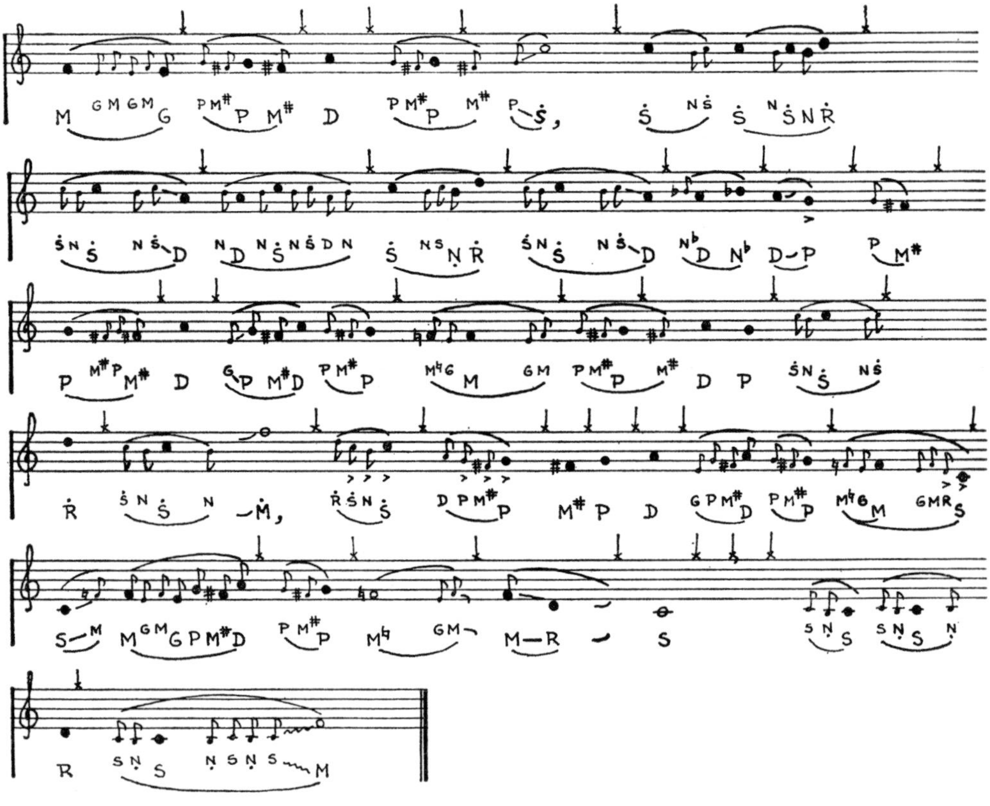

Select Bibliography

1 European Languages

Ahmad, Nazir, 'Lahjat-i Sikandar Shahi' in *Islamic Culture*, Vol. 28, 1954.
Aḥmad-ul-Umri, *The Lady of the Lotus*, tr. L. M. Crump, London, 1926.
'Allāmī, Abu'l-Fazl, *Ā'īn-i-Akbarī*, tr. H. Blochmann, Calcutta, 1873.
Bake, A. A., 'The Music of India' in *The New Oxford History of Music*, London, 1957.
Bake, A. A., 'Indische Musik' in *Die Musik in Geschichte und Gegenwart*, Allgemeine Enzyclopädie der Musik, Bd. 6, Kassel, 1957.
Bhātkhaṇḍe, V. N., *A short historical survey of the music of Upper India*, Bombay, 1934.
Bhātkhaṇḍe, V. N., *A comparative study of some of the leading music systems of the* 15*th*, 16*th*, 17*th*, *and* 18*th centuries*,—A series of articles published in *Saṅgīta*, Lucknow, 1930–1.
Daniélou, A., *Northern Indian Music*, Vol. II, London, 1954.
Dunk, J. L., *The Structure of the Musical Scale*, London, 1940.
Farmer, H. G., *A History of Arabian Music*, London, 1929.
Fox Strangways, A. H., *Music of Hindostan*, Oxford, 1914.
Gangoly, O. C., *Rāgas and Rāginīs*, Bombay, 1958.
Grosset, J., 'Inde: Histoire de la musique ...' in A. Lavignac, *Encyclopédie de la Musique*, *I*, Paris, 1921.
Halim, Abdul, *Essays of History of Indo-Pak Music*, Dacca, 1962.
Helmholtz, H. von, *Sensations of tone*, trans. A. J. Ellis, London, 1875.
Jairazbhoy, N. A., 'Svaraprastāra in North Indian Classical Music', *Bulletin of the School of Oriental and African Studies*, Vol. XXIV part, 2, 1961, pp. 307–25.
Jairazbhoy, N. A., 'Bharata's concept of Sādhāraṇa', *Bulletin of the School of Oriental and African Studies*, Vol. XXI, part 1, 1958, pp. 54–60.
Jairazbhoy, N. A., with Stone, A. W. 'Intonation in present-day North Indian classical music', *Bulletin of the School of Oriental and African Studies*, Vol. XXVI, Part 1, 1963, pp. 119–32.
Jeans, James, *Science and Music*, Cambridge, 1937.
Kaufmann, W., *Musical notations of the Orient*, Bloomington, 1967.
Mangahas, R., *The Development of Rāgalakṣaṇa*, A thesis submitted to the University of London for the degree of Doctor of Philosophy (Music), June, 1967.
Mirza, M. W., *Life and Works of Amir Khusraw*, Calcutta, 1935.
Popley, H. A., *The Music of India*, Calcutta, 1950.
Powers, H. S., 'Indian music and the English language; A Review Essay', *Ethnomusicology*, ix, January, 1965.
Ranade, G. H., *Hindustāni Music*, Poona, 1951.
Roy, H. L., *Problems of Hindustani Music*, Calcutta, 1937.
Roychoudhury, M. L., 'Music in Islam', *Journal of Asiatic Society*, Letters, Vol. XXIII, No. 2, 1957.
Sanyal, A. N., *Ragas and Raginis*, Calcutta, 1959.
Smith, V., *Oxford History of India*, Oxford, 1958.
Sprenger, A., *El Mas'udi's historical encyclopaedia*, '*Meadows of Gold ...*', London, 1841.
Willard, N. A., *Music of India*, Calcutta, 1962.
Zuckerkandl, V., *Sound and Symbol*, *Music in the External World*, New York, 1956.

2 Sanskrit and other Indian Languages

Ahobala, *Saṅgītapārijāta*, Hathras, 1956.
Banarjī, K., *Gīta Sūtra Sāra*, Calcutta, 1934 (Bengali).
Bharata, *Nāṭyaśāstra*, Kashi Sanskrit Series, No. 60.
Bhātkhaṇḍe, V. N., *Hindusthānī Saṅgīt Paddhatī*, Vols. I–IV, Hathras, 1951–57 (Hindi edition).
Bhātkhaṇḍe, V. N., *Kramik Pustak Mālikā*, Vols. I–VI, Hathras, 1954–9 (Hindi edition).
Bhātkhaṇḍe, V. N., (under pseudonym, Catura Paṇḍita Viṣṇu Śarmā), *Śrimal-lakṣyasaṅgītam*, Poona, 1934.
Dāmodara, *Saṅgītadarpaṇa*, Hathras, 1962.
Kaṇṭha, *Rasakaumudī*, Gaekwad's Oriental Series, 1963.
Locana, *Rāgataraṅgiṇī*, Bihar, 1934.
Mataṅga, *Bṛihaddeśī*, Trivandrum, 1928.
Nārada, *Saṅgītamakaranda*, Baroda, 1920.
Nārāyaṇa, Hṛidaya, *Hṛidayakautaka*, Bombay, 1920.
Nārāyaṇa, Hṛidaya, *Hṛidayaprakāśa*, Bombay, 1920.
Pāṭvardhan, V. N., *Rāg Vijñān*, Vols. I–VII, Poona, 1962 (Hindi).
Rāmāmātya, *Svaramelakalānidhi*, Annamalai, 1932.
Śārṅgadeva, *Saṅgītaratnākara*, Adyar Library Series, 1943.
S̲h̲āh, Ibrāhīm 'Ādil, *Kitāb-i-Nauras*, Poona, 1956 (Dakhani).
Siṃh, Pratāp, *Saṅgītsār*, unpublished manuscript, quoted by Bhātkhaṇḍe (Hindi).
Śivan, Mahā-vaidya-nātha, *Mela-rāga-mālikā*, Adyar, 1937.
Somanātha, *Rāgavibodha*, Adyar Library Series, 1945.
Toṃwar, Mān Siṅgh, *Mān Kautūhal*, unpublished manuscript, quoted by Bhātkhaṇḍe (Hindi).
Tulaja, *Saṅgītasārāmṛita*, Madras, 1942.
Vasant, *Rāg Koś*, Hathras, 1962 (Hindi).
Veṅkaṭamakhī, *Caturdaṇḍīprakāśikā*, Madras, 1934.
Viṭṭhala, Puṇḍarīka, *Rāgamāla*, Bombay, 1914.
Viṭṭhala, Puṇḍarīka, *Rāgamañjarī*, Bombay, n.d.
Viṭṭhala, Puṇḍarīka, *Sadrāgacandrodaya*, Bombay, 1912.

Index

Index

Index

Index

Index